MEXICO'S
COPPER CANYON COUNTRY

D0180276

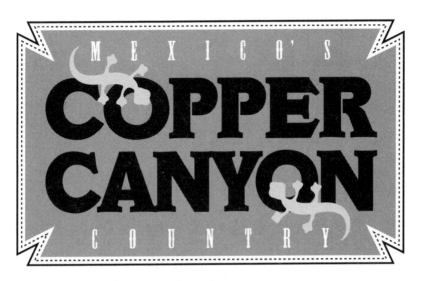

MEXICO'S COPPER CANYON COUNTRY

A Hiking & Backpacking Guide

M. JOHN FAYHEE

REVISED EDITION

A Cordillera Press Guide
Johnson Books: Boulder

© 1989, 1994 by M. John Fayhee
All rights reserved. First edition 1989
Revised edition 1994

9 8 7 6 5 4 3 2 1

Cover design by Bob Schram/Bookends
All cover photographs by Gay Gangel-Fayhee
Interior photographs by Gay Gangel-Fayhee

Library of Congress Cataloging-in-Publication Data
Fayhee, M. John
    Mexico's Copper Canyon country : a hiking and backpacking
guide / M. John Fayhee. —Rev. ed.
       p.   cm
    Includes bibliographical references (p.   ) and index.
    ISBN 1-55566-124-6
    1. Hiking—Mexico—Copper Canyon Region—Guidebooks.
2. Backpacking—Mexico—Copper Canyon Region—Guidebooks.
3. Copper Canyon (Mexico)—Guidebooks.   I. Title.
GV199.44.M62C664   1994
796.5'1'097216—dc20   94-17399
                                                          CIP

NOTE: Parts of Chapters 5 and 6 first appeared in the November 1987
issue of *Backpacker* magazine in an article titled "Bottoming Out in
Mexico." Other parts of Chapter 6 first appeared in the September
1987 issue of *Rocky Mountain Sports and Fitness* in an article titled
"Beating Feet and Pounding Brews with the Tarahumaras." Parts of
several chapters appeared in the May-June 1989 issue of *Summit*.

**WARNING: Backcountry travel is a dangerous activity. Users of this
guide participate in backpacking and hiking activities solely at their
own risk.**

Printed in the United States of America by
Johnson Printing Company
1880 South 57th Court
Boulder, CO 80301

Contents

To Chuck and Marian Gangel,
of Cañon City, Colorado,
parents-in-law extraordinaire—
for their support,
their interest, and,
most of all,
their eldest daughter.

And to Jay Scott,
of Silver City, New Mexico,
who kept me focused,
and thus alive,
during those six crazy days
in Tararecua Canyon.

And in memory of Chu.

Preface to the
Revised Edition

It's mighty strange to come back to a project that's been sitting on the shelf, for better or for worse, for five years. Kind of like running into an old lover; there's both a desire to run over and hug her with the notion of reliving old times and a desire to run away in the exact opposite at a full gallop, screaming. Either way, here I am back again butt-deep in this book, bringing it up to date, adding some new stuff, and taking some old stuff out. And, as I got butt-deeper into this second edition, whatever trepidation I once harbored at the notion of re-establishing a relationship with this old "lover" has pretty much faded away.

I should point out that, in the five years between the first and second editions of this book (1989 and 1994), I never stopped traveling in and around Copper Canyon Country. It was just this book in which I stopped traveling in and around. Between 1989 and 1994, I hiked well over 500 miles in Copper Canyon Country, spread out over eight or ten trips. I guided paying customers on some of those trips, and took others just because Copper Canyon Country is a place I like to check out as often as possible. It recharges my batteries like no other place I have ever visited, and I have visited a lot of places.

There have been some pretty significant changes in Copper Canyon Country in the last five years. First of all, like most of Mexico, this place is economically booming. The tourist industry has, as I predicted in the first edition, become the backbone of the economy of Tarahumara-land. Though I understand full well that tourism-based economies certainly have their negative sides (I live in the biggest ski county in North America, so I have a grip on this subject), as I say over and over in this book, tourism, seemingly ironically, continues to provide the last remaining hope of the Tarahumara Indians maintaining their cultural integrity. I'll delve into my reasoning for that observation a lot more in the following chapters.

Tourism is flourishing throughout Mexico. In Copper Canyon Country, there have been at least five brand-new hotels built in the past few years, as well as several new restaurants.

More and more tour services have started. All in all, the place is certainly becoming more civilized, though little in the way of increased civilization has made its way into the backcountry, which is usually the way it works.

I have tried to leave well enough alone as much as I could in this second edition. All in all, I liked the first edition. It has done well by me, leading to several other book contracts, so I wanted to make certain I did well by it, by trying to keep the flavor of the original work. I updated a lot of material, added a few new chapters, and took out some stuff that I either no longer believe or that I learned was wrong.

Because I did not want to tamper too much with the material that did not need to be updated or changed, some of the flow might seem awkward. In one of the last chapters, Panalachi to Tehuerichi, for instance, I talk about finally getting the chance to visit a Tarahumara tesguinada—a corn beer party. Yet, in a couple of preceding chapters—new, second edition additions—I mention having consumed corn beer with Tarahumaras. Also, the first chapter, as well as the epilogue, probably could have been updated. But, hell, I liked those chapters the way they were, so I pretty much left them alone. What can I say except, maybe, that you should look at each chapter as a narrative world unto itself. Also, in the course of five years, any full-time writer worth his weight in salt will have changed as a person and as a writer. This makes for difficult decisions when you're plugging new material into already written chapters. So, please forgive me if, in the middle of a ten-thousand-word chapter, it seems like someone new jumps in and adds a few paragraphs. It's only me, and I have a right to be there.

The Moose Jaw Bar, Frisco, Colorado
January 17, 1994

Acknowledgments

The "job"—hey, someone's gotta do it—of researching this book would have been much more difficult were it not for the help provided me by Skip McWilliams and Suzanne Rossi, owners of Las Cabañas del Cobre in Cusarare, Chihuahua, Mexico, as well as by my many friends in Creel, Chihuahua, especially Oscar Loya, Rafael Morquecho, and the "Mexican Gandalf," Jesus Manuel Olivas. I would also like to tip my hat to the staff of Margarita's Casa de Huespedes in Creel. These people have given me a place to call home in Tarahumara-land, and I thank them.

I would also like to thank: Mark Fox and Russell Ray for use of the photos, as well as Dr. Robert Gedekoh, of Elizabeth, Pennsylvania, for providing the text on the Humira Bridge-Urique Narrows hike.

*Here nature chose
to think like a man.*

—Antonin Artaud
The Peyote Dance

1
What This Book Is, and What It Is Not

I'm sitting here in My Brother's Place, a little drinking establishment in the town where I live that has an antique Harley-Davidson hanging on the wall above my shoulder. Maps of the Copper Canyon region—Tarahumara-land I call it because this is the home turf of the Tarahumara Indians—are spread from one end of this beer-stained table to the other, and I'm staring down at them, feeling a little stunned.

As far as I can tell from the maps at hand, there are at least seventy-five potential multi-day backpacking trips to be had thereabouts—to say nothing of the potential for one-nighters and dayhikes. In this guide, I describe a mere dozen or so routes I have personally hiked, as well as several more that I have reliable information about. All told, less than twenty trips out of those seventy-five-plus.

In my own defense, I have put in a *lot* of backpacking and done a *lot* of hiking in Copper Canyon Country. But, the place is so immense that, after four separate trips covering many months, I realize that I have only scratched the surface. Which isn't necessarily bad.

Most of us are familiar with areas that have been guidebooked to death. The Appalachian Trail corridor comes to mind. There exists a series of A.T. guidebooks that are so detailed you literally know your route in tenth-of-a-mile increments before you even hoist your pack.

In my forays into Copper Canyon Country, I have found that one of the things that attracts people most about this place is the fact that it has not been guidebooked into a catatonic stupor. At the same time, just about every person armed with backpacks and boots I have met in Tarahumara-land has lamented the fact that—until now—there has been zilch in the way of informational resources targeted towards backpackers and day-hikers. These people were simply looking for a place to start—a couple of generalized recommendations, a few bewares, and a little insight into the culture of their Tarahumara hosts—written by and for backcountry users.

I've tried to meet that need without destroying the ambience of the unknown that is one of Copper Canyon Country's most tantalizing attributes. So, that's what this book is—something in between an agonizingly detailed guidebook and nothing. An introduction to hiking in Copper Canyon Country. A primer, as it were, to a special land and its special people.

I try to point you in the right direction with the kinds of hints—regarding gear, weather, trail conditions, local culture, particularly nice or not-so-nice areas—that you would lay on a fellow adventurer if you commenced swapping backpacking tales over a cold beer. And, while I'm at it, I'll toss in a few of the yarns I've been known to spin.

But, understand this. Most of the Copper Canyon region is very rough territory. It is generally well mapped, but not perfectly. It is very isolated. There are no search and rescue teams. Medical facilities are few, far between, and primitive.

This is an area where you must have a firm understanding of your personal limitations as a backcountry user, both physically and mentally.

If you know what you can and cannot handle—whether you are a world-class wilderness jock with the dust of Patagonia and Borneo on your boots or a relative neophyte whose big trip was a weekend in the Catskills—then this book will hook you up with the type of hike you will enjoy, whether you are looking to stretch your limits or not.

What I will not do, is lead you by the hand and tell you to take a left at the big tree with the knot in it, walk 17.23 meters and there, under the third-shortest bush, is a seep spring. If you *need* this kind of information, perhaps it would be better to chalk up a little more backcountry experience before you cruise down to Tarahumara-land.

And, if you just *want* that kind of information, know up front that the very nature of Copper Canyon Country makes giving specific trail and distance statistics tough. I talk about average hours required to knock off a given stretch of trail. Most of these times are based on the time it took my wife and I to hike that particular stretch. (We are not particularly fast walkers, we are not in particularly great shape, and we usually carry too much weight.) I have no choice about this. The trails in Tarahumara-land are not marked, let alone measured, and topographical variations and switchbacks make it frequently difficult to even guesstimate distances.

If you feel more comfortable with detailed, comprehensive information and you still want to visit the area, just hire a guide. I list several in the next chapter and note those instances where they might be helpful. For those of you who feel you can handle Copper Canyon Country without a guide, I make a number of assumptions—and they are a good way to gauge whether or not you have enough experience to be trekking around these parts in the first place. I assume you will:

- purchase maps of the area you intend to traverse—listed at the end of each chapter—and become as familiar as possible with the local topography;
- know how to use both the compass you will bring and those maps;
- arrive in fairly good shape with fairly reliable gear;
- inform a responsible party of your itinerary;
- have a good understanding of first aid;
- respect and prepare for the potential harshness of the climate—both hot and cold;
- learn as much Spanish as possible before arriving in Mexico;
- be willing to share your cigars if you meet me on the trail; and
- respect the Tarahumara and Mexican cultures at least as much as you pretend to respect you own.

I will give you enough information to get you started on your trip into Tarahumara-land—your personal exploration of one of the most beautiful and least-explored areas in North America. Remember though, in order for your trip to be successful—however you define that—you need to rely not on me, but on *you*. I will feel much better about my efforts if I know that you've spent less time with your eyes focused on these pages and more time with them focused on the trail.

In these pages, I will introduce you to my attractive and provocative friend. If you want to get to know my friend better, you will need to come up with your own seduction lines.

It's better that way.

My Brother's Place
Cañon City, Colorado
March 5, 1989

2
Nuts and Bolts

I read one time that Copper Canyon Country was not such a hot place for backpacking due to a lack of clearly marked and defined trails. Seriously, I laughed so hard I spilled a Carta Blanca all over my lap. The statement proves that you should always be somewhat skeptical of subjective viewpoints, mine included.

First of all, lots of folks I know prefer to hike in places with a conspicuous lack of clearly marked trails. But, more importantly, the statement is patently false. Copper Canyon Country is crisscrossed by a network of paths that, while not marked in the sense that we consider paths "marked" in Yosemite, are as obvious as sock stink in a small tent. I mean, this place is populated fifty thousand Tarahumara Indians who walk or run just about everywhere they go. They have been following the same routes from one ranchito or village to the next and back again and again for something on the order of five hundred years. These footpaths have always served, and continue to serve, as the Tarahumara highway system, and, consequently, in many areas, the trails are so ancient and well used that they are worn several feet into the ground.

This endless supply and array of trails very often connects places a backpacker or dayhiker might have an inkling to visit, such as between Panalachi and Tehuirichi (Chapter 18) or between Batopilas and Munerachi (Chapter 15), or, when you get right down to it, between a whole slew of provocative walking destinations—which is what this book is mostly about.

This is not to say that there aren't plenty of areas in Tarahumara-land void of trails. Some parts of Tararecua Canyon, spring to mind. (Please see the harrowing misadventures and "Oh, God, I'm gonna die!!!!!" parts of Chapter 5.)

Like most "highway systems," there are quality gradations of Tarahumara trails. At the top of the heap are the burro trails, which generally connect villages with villages, villages with roads, or villages with ranchitos. If someone tells you that there is a burro trail between wherever it is you are and wherever it is you want to go, that's as good as it gets in the backcountry of Tarahumara-land. Usually, this means that you will be able to follow one obvious trail all the way, unless, of course, you loose it and find yourself wandering aimlessly for a day or two through the cactuses alongside some nameless arroyo, like I have done on occasions too numerous to outline here.

Then, there are the foot trails, which generally connect ranchitos with ranchitos, ranchitos with things such as close-at-hand cornfields, or ranchitos with favorite tree-cutting or goat-grazing areas. These types of trails, which are often the most pleasant to walk on because they haven't had five hundred years of use and are not eroding away, are, at other times, the most frustrating. You can find yourself walking down a pronounced and passable path, only to find, once you've arrived at the cornfield or the other ranchito, that suddenly you are S.O.L. trail-wise. This might be okay if you're content with the place you are, but it means you will still need to find another trail to whatever your destination is.

Though it is my observation that Tarahumaras generally enjoy walking through the beauteous region they inhabit (how could they not?), they don't often take strolls solely for the sake of sightseeing. If you find yourself in an area that is not between two points that the Tarahumaras have reason to walk back and forth between, then the best you can hope for are meandering goat paths, which occupy the lowest rung on the Tarahumara trail ladder. Goat trails, by and large, are a serious drag to walk on unless you are a goat or a U.S. Grade-A masochist.

This is not to say that many of the more frequently used Tarahumara footpaths don't have their "captivating" sections. I have followed goat and foot trails for hours that would do the

Great Smokies proud, only to find myself suddenly facing an advanced rock-climbing move, 300 feet up on some crumbly cliff in order to proceed one millimeter further.

But all these "this is a heavy-duty place" messages I've been intertwining so far apply to the more rugged parts of Copper Canyon Country. Much of the area we'll be dealing with in this book is rolling, high-valley terrain around the deepest canyons—territory no more fearsome than the Berkshires, and twice, maybe nine times, as beautiful.

Which is just about as good a time as any to segue our way into nomenclature. When we talk about "Copper Canyon Country"—*Las Barrancas del Cobre* in local parlance—we are not being very specific. There are no signs welcoming you, and, if there were, the argument would rage for decades as to where they should be erected. You may see some references to "Copper Canyon National Park." This is an example of a "paper park," an entity that exists administratively, but not in reality. For all intents and purposes, there is no such thing.

While there is such a specific beast as "Copper Canyon," cartographers and others who spend time pondering this sort of thing are not totally in agreement as to what it is, or where it begins and ends. There is a certain amount of confusion because of the pluralization of the Spanish name one frequently hears for the area: *Las Barrancas del Cobre*, giving the impression, at least in translation, that there are several canyons in the vicinity sharing a common appellation, along with common degrees of renown and grandeur. (*Barranca* is Spanish for "canyon," though geologists generally consider it a specific type of canyon—one in which the walls descend in a series of benches rather than in one gigantic vertical plunge. *Cobre* is Spanish for copper.)

The English translation is almost always, simply, the singular, "Copper Canyon," giving the impression that there is one canyon that surpasses all others nearby in splendor, depth, and importance. This perspective is further reinforced by the fact that the only canyon most visitors see (from the railroad stop at El Divisadero) is that which is most often called simply "Copper Canyon"—the huge canyon of the Rio Urique (OO-ree-kay).

The 1:250,000-scale topographic map of the area, printed by the Instituto Nacional de Estadistica Geografia e Informatica (INEGI), designates the canyon formed by the Urique, *"Barranca del Cobre,"* from the Humira (sometimes spelled "Umira") Bridge downstream to where the Urique is joined by Arroyo Hondo. From that point on, it is called *"Barranca Urique."*

The 1:50,000-scale topos, which are also published by INEGI, call the canyon *"Barranca del Cobre"* from Humira Bridge to the junction of the Urique and Arroyo Hondo, where this essentially continuous canyon suddenly becomes *"Barranca del Urique."*

I have heard from people who have lived their whole lives in this area that there is no one "Copper Canyon," that all the canyons in Tarahumara-land, a canyon area of about 10,000 square miles, are part of a system of canyons known as *"Las Barrancas del Cobre."*

Other locals have said that Copper Canyon is that part of the canyon of the Urique from the Humira Bridge downstream to the "great bend" of the Urique—where Tararecua Canyon of the Rio San Ignacio enters the Urique.

Dr. Robert Schmidt of the University of Texas at El Paso, who has prepared a popular map of the area for sale at the Tarahumara Mission Store in Creel, as well as several local stores and hotels, says that, historically, Copper Canyon is that part of the canyon formed by the Urique near El Tejabán, which is between Humira Bridge and the great bend. A lot of copper mining went on around El Tejabán back in colonial days at a site on the Rio Urique called, *"Barranca del Cobre,"* which is still a village that's alive and kicking, in a limping, geriatric sort of way.

In this book, I refer to the entire area as the Copper Canyon system, because that is what people know this area as and, like they say where I grew up in eastern Virginia, "if that's what you call it, that's what its name is."

Then, to avoid confusion, or at least to ignore confusion, I call the canyon of the Urique River between its source up past Norogachi downriver to the great bend, "Copper Canyon." From that point downriver all the way to where it joins with

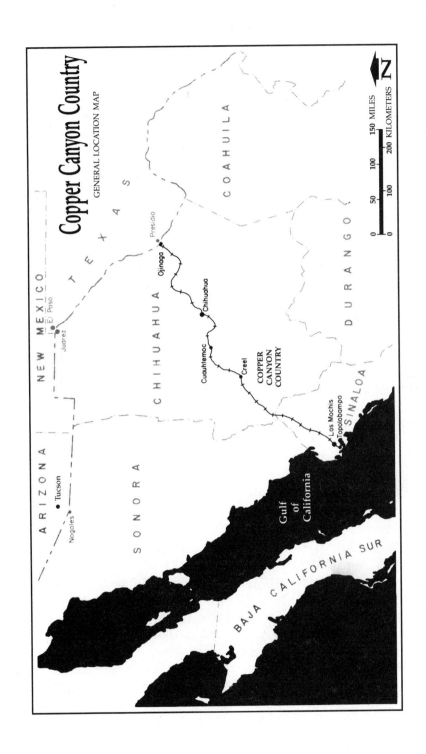

Copper Canyon Country

GENERAL LOCATION MAP

N

150 MILES

200 KILOMETERS

0   50   100

0   100

ARIZONA

NEW MEXICO

TEXAS

Nogales

Tucson

El Paso

Juárez

Presidio

Ojinaga

Chihuahua

Cuauhtemoc

Creel

COPPER
CANYON
COUNTRY

Los Mochis

Topolobampo

SONORA

CHIHUAHUA

COAHUILA

DURANGO

SINALOA

Gulf
of
California

BAJA CALIFORNIA SUR

the Rio San Miguel to become the Rio Fuerte, I go with "Urique Canyon."

Anyway, we're talking about a system of canyons that rivals any in the world in total square mileage, overall depth of individual canyons, displacement, beauty, ruggedness, the whole nine yards. The system, depending on where you want to draw the line, consists of at least seven significant canyons: Urique, Copper, Batopilas, Sinforosa Canyon of the Rio Verde, Tararecua, Cusarare, and the Conchos. All of these are deep, with the exception of the Conchos, which is the only major river in Tarahumara-land on the eastern side of the Continental Divide. Urique Canyon at the village of Urique is about 1,800 meters (5,900 feet) deep, as is Sinforosa Canyon near Guachochi. Batopilas Canyon at the town of Batopilas is about 2,100 meters (6,900 feet) deep, depending on where you measure it from.

I should point out here that there is no set system for measuring the depth of canyons or gorges. Do you measure them from the closest mountaintop to river level? From the highest rim to river level? From the lowest rim? How about averaging the distance from each rim to the river? I have researched this in some depth and, according to everyone I have talked with, including employees of the United States Geological Survey, the Guinness Book of World Records, and the National Geographic Society, no one or no entity has ever settled this question one way or the other.

The most persuasive arguments I have heard on this came from a couple of "uncredentialed" folks, who just happen to be the foremost canyoneers in the world. They are the ones who conquered Peru's Colca Canyon, perhaps the world's deepest. They argue that we should use the rim-averaging method. I personally think, when attempting to compare canyons, we should measure their displacement—that is: how much dirt would it take to fill the bugger back up, from start to finish, top to bottom? This takes care of comparison of width, depth, and length in one fell swoop. But, what the hell do I know?

The canyons of the Rio Urique, the Rio Verde, and the Rio Batopilas are, as far as I can tell, respectively the second, third and fourth-deepest in North America—the deepest being Hell's

Canyon on the border of Idaho and Oregon, with a depth of about 7,900 feet.

Copper Canyon Country is located roughly halfway between Chihuahua City, Chihuahua, which is about 250 miles south of El Paso, Texas, and Los Mochis, Sinaloa, which is about 300 miles south of Nogales, Arizona. Almost all of Copper Canyon Country is located in the Mexican state of Chihuahua.

Traveling in Mexico

It amazes me that there are still people who are scared to travel south of the border. Visions of the "we don't need no stinking badges" scene in *Treasure of the Sierra Madre* still affect many otherwise intelligent gringos—the universal and by no means derogatory term (well, sometimes it's a derogatory term) by which all Anglos are known.

Mexico, my friends, is a very easy place to be. Gone are the days of freaks in VW vans getting stomped by the *federales*. At least for the most part. I have only heard of gringos having bad experiences in Mexico a couple of times, which, when you cut the nut, is remarkable, being as how different our cultures are and how brazen and overbearing gringos sometimes justifiably seem to Mexicans.

This is not to say that there aren't dangers in our sister country, especially in the drug cultivation regions of Culiacan, Guerrero, Colima, Michoacan, Jalisco, and Sinaloa. As well, like urban centers everywhere, Mexico's largest cities have their bad parts and their bad people. Nightmares to be had in Mexico include various types of assault by private citizens and various degrees of hassles by gendarmes of whatever species. I don't know that there's much more to say than, "Be careful and keep your eyes peeled." The same advice I would give a Mexican planning to visit New York City, or, for that matter Denver, or, for that matter, Summit County, Colorado, where I live.

Just remember, keep your cool if the scene gets tense. If you have a problem with the police or the military, keep a smile on your face. Be verbally deferential. It will not help matters if you lose your temper and start threatening how they can't do this to you because, by God, you're an American! And, of course, the more Spanish you know, the better.

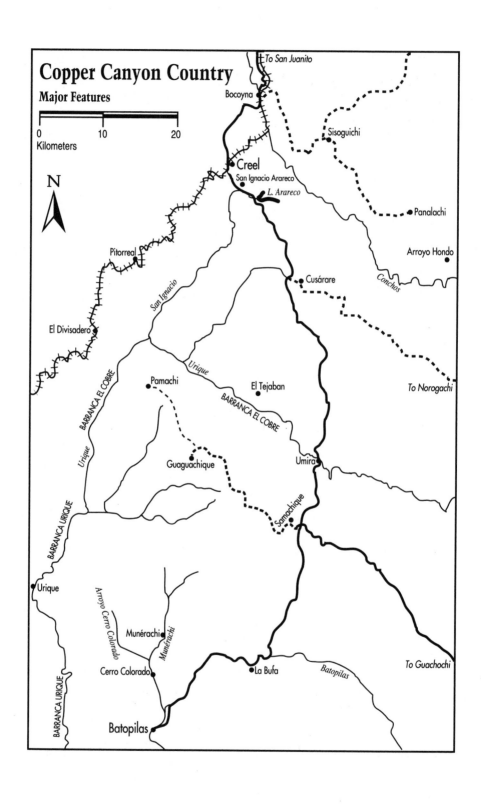

Copper Canyon Country

Major Features

0   10   20
Kilometers

N

To San Juanito

Bocoyna

Sisoguichi

Creel

San Ignacio Arareco

L. Arareco

Panalachi

Arroyo Hondo

Pitorreal

San Ignacio

Cusárare

Conchos

El Divisadero

Urique

Pamachi

El Tejaban

BARRANCA EL COBRE

To Norogachi

BARRANCA EL COBRE

Guaguachique

Umira

Urique

Samachique

BARRANCA URIQUE

Urique

Arroyo Cerro Colorado

Munérachi

Munérachi

To Guachochi

Cerro Colorado

La Bufa

Batopilas

BARRANCA URIQUE

Batopilas

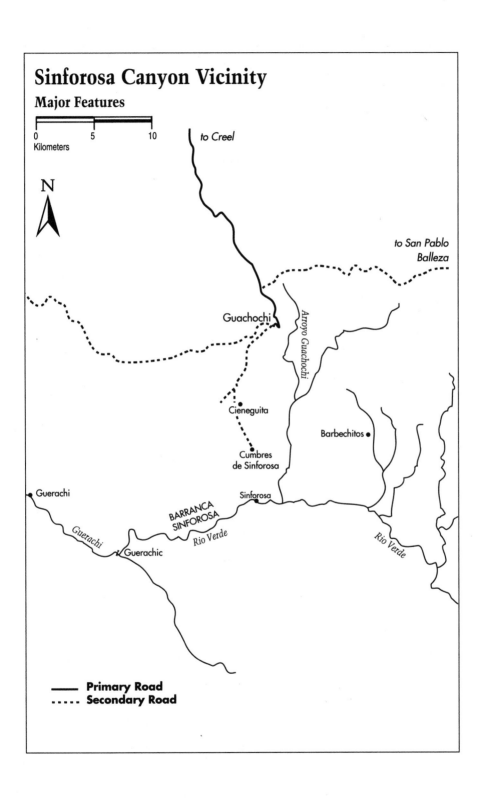

Sinforosa Canyon Vicinity

Major Features

0   5   10
Kilometers

N

to Creel

to San Pablo
Balleza

Guachochi

Arroyo Guachochi

Cieneguita

Barbechitos ●

Cumbres
de Sinforosa

Guerachi ●

Sinforosa

BARRANCA
SINFOROSA

Guerachi

Rio Verde

Guerachic

Rio Verde

——— Primary Road
..... Secondary Road

Mexicans are overwhelmingly wonderful people. They love their country and are usually very flattered that you have decided to pay them a visit. Most will go out of their way to help you at the drop of a hat.

Okay, technicalities.

At the border, you will need to get a tourist card, which is free and usually good for however long you ask for, up to six months. You will need to show proof of national origin. While in theory, you can use a birth certificate or voter registration card, you are well advised to get a passport and bring it with you. I have heard border officials are beginning to lose patience with voter registration cards because they have no photograph. If you don't have a passport, your local post office can start you in the right direction.

If you are just visiting a border town, you won't need a tourist card. But, if you are going into the interior—and Copper Canyon Country fits that bill—you must pick a tourist card up at the border. Unlike the U.S., you cross into Mexican border towns—on foot—without ordinarily being stopped. You have to go out of your way to get officially processed into the country. Immigration offices are located at all border crossings and processing usually takes only a few minutes, though it can certainly take longer if there are people ahead of you in line, or if the immigration people are shooting the breeze over a cup of coffee. (Remember, keep smiling and be as friendly as possible.) If you are traveling through Mexico to another country, you will need to buy a transmigration visa as well. Cost is about $15 U.S., though I have crossed into Mexico several times on my way to Central America and found Mexican Immigration offices on the the U.S. border where they couldn't find the transmigration visas and simply let me pass through after obtaining a free tourist card.

About 30 to 50 miles south of every border town, there are customs (*aduana*) and immigration stops. If you lack a tourist card, you will almost certainly be sent back to the border to rectify the situation. It is important that you don't lose your tourist card because, on your way back into the States, you are supposed to surrender it. Also, if you get into any sort of legal flap while in Mexico, you will have to produce your card.

In all likelihood, your gear won't be checked at the border unless you drive into the country. When you check your gear at the bus or train station, the local customs agent may ask you to open your pack. You are not being hassled here. This is normal procedure. Generally speaking, Mexican customs and immigration employees are very pleasant and efficient.

If you drive into Mexico, things are slightly more complicated. You must have Mexican insurance, which you can buy at most American border towns. Sanborn's is the big company—(512) 682-1354. This is important. Your U.S. coverage is not valid in Mexico. For full coverage, expect to pay about $4 a day. The Mexican government strictly controls insurance rates, so you don't have to worry about getting ripped off by the carrier. Also, expect to get searched a little more thoroughly if you drive into the country. Mexican customs officials are generally looking for consumer goods that, they fear, you may be looking to peddle south of the border. So expect scrutiny if you try to bring thirty VCRs in. They are also very serious business about guns. You will get into more trouble if you are caught with a gun, especially a handgun, in Mexico than you will if you're caught with drugs.

Okay, there are technicalities regarding processing your vehicle into Mexico. And these technicalities, in an effort to help stem the tide of stolen vehicles passing the border on their free-and-easy drive south, have become more stringent in the past several years. They have also changed several times in the past several years. There is no reason whatsoever to expect that they won't change again in 15 minutes. So, if you are going to drive into Mexico, you need to get in touch with Sanborn's to find out what the latest pertinent skinny is. Sanborn's, by the way, offers a thing called its "Mexico Club," which is worth asking about, because it includes all sorts of little fine-print bells and whistles, along with the insurance policy.

As of November 1993, this is what you have to do: You have to have a notarized copy of your title, or else, if there is a lien on the vehicle, a letter from whatever entity it is that holds the lien (a bank, finance company, or someone named "Vito") saying it's all right for you to bring said vehicle into Mexico. You also have to have one of the three credit card biggies: MasterCard, VISA, or American Express. And which of those you intend to use has to have an at least $500 worth of open credit available. Your other alternative is to bring $500 in cash, which you will post as bond at the border. If you do not bring the vehicle back out of Mexico, you will be considered to have sold it in Mexico, and you will either have $500 added to your credit card, or you will forfeit your $500 bond. This means, of course, that you have to make certain you process out of the country. The whole border is linked by computer, which is a mighty odd thing to consider in light of how Mexican border posts were even a decade ago.

The other thing to remember is that, in the early 1990s, Mexico essentially issued pink slips to a significant percentage of their customs employees and replaced them with a corps of mostly young, idealistic, educated, *Viva*-Mexico types who have the reputation of being uncorruptable. If you do not have your ducks in a huddle, paper-work wise, when you attempt to drive into Mexico, you will be turned away without prejudice. You may also be asked to show proof of Mexican insurance by the customs people. As complicated as this sounds, if you have all your paperwork in order, crossing the border with a vehicle should take little more than an hour.

Road quality in Mexico varies from as good as anything in the States to stuff that looks like the surface of Mars. The main highways are by and large good by anyone's standards. The main problem with driving in Mexico is gas. You can purchase only over-priced, terrible-quality, very low-octane gas only from nationally owned Pemex stations. Once you get off the main highways, you will be unable to buy unleaded (*magna sin*)— only regular (*nova*) and diesel. While the Mexican government is working hard to offer *magna sin* at every gas station, it will likely be well into the next century before those efforts make their way into the overwhelmingly boondocks regions this book deals with. (As of November 1993, the closest place to Copper Canyon Country where you can buy *magna sin* is the town of La Junta, between Cuauhtemoc and San Juanito, on the road to Creel.) If your vehicle needs unleaded gas, contact the EPA in Washington (202-233-9080) for special permission to have your catalytic converter temporarily removed. (Leaded gas ruins catalytic converters, and catalytic converters are not cheap things to replace.) This, I'm afraid, is a lot harder than it used to be, because Mexico is now listed by the EPA as a country that offers unleaded gas from sea to shining sea. The last time I had my catalytic converter removed, in the summer of 1993, it took a half-dozen phone calls before I could convince the EPA people that Copper Canyon Country is unleaded gasless. In 1988, it took me one phone call and one letter, a process that lasted maybe ten working days. If you can wangle EPA permission to do so, go to a muffler shop to get your catalytic converter removed. The cost is about $100. You will need to put the "cat" back in upon your return to the U.S. If you ask the muffler shop to weld flanges to the pipe that will replace the cat, instead of just welding it directly to the exhaust pipe, you will be able to re-install it yourself—as well as be able to remove it again the next time you drive south of the border.

Though this is less of a concern than it was, say, twenty years ago, I recommend that you always carry extra gas with you while driving in Mexico and top your tank off at every opportunity. Most small towns, like Creel (Chapter 3), only have one Pemex station. Sometimes they run out of gas for a day or two. Also, buy a bunch of octane enhancer in the U.S., and use some with each tank of Mexican gas. Octane enhancer (*aditivo*) is sold in Mexico, but it is expensive. Gas prices as of October 1993 were a ridiculous $1.60 a gallon.

I recommend only high-clearance vehicles, unless you plan to stick to paved roads. In Copper Canyon Country, this means driving no farther than 60 or so kilometers past Creel on the way to Batopilas and zero kilometers past Creel on the way to Divisadero. (Though it should be noted that the Chihuahuan government is butt-deep in a road-paving frenzy in Copper Canyon Country, so, by the time you read these words, there will likely be even more kilometers of paved roads in the area.) Four-wheel-drives are necessary in some places, and those places are noted in the appropriate chapters.

Getting There
Thousands of people visit Copper Canyon Country every year. More and more are coming all the time. Like most places,

the vast majority of these pose little in the way of a tranquility threat to the backcountry user because they never get more than about six feet from the closest road.

There is no way to quantify this, but I would guess about 95 percent of all visitors to Tarahumara-land arrive via the famed Chihuahua-Pacific Railway. Almost all of the newspaper and magazine press the Copper Canyon region has received has centered on this train. My favorite line, and I have read this more than once in reputable publications, is that the C-P Railroad runs *through* Copper Canyon. Now, there is no doubt this railroad is an engineering marvel, but it does not go *through* any of the major canyons in Tarahumara-land. From only one spot on the train route, the overlook at El Divisadero, which translated means, very poetically, "overlook," can you even see any part of any of the canyons traditionally lumped into the *Las Barrancas del Cobre* system. The train, going both ways, stops at Divisadero for 15 minutes so passengers can hop off to snap a few photos of Urique Canyon, at this point, 1,300 meters deep. This view, it should be noted, is one of the best you will ever see in your entire life.

The C-P train route starts in Ojinaga, across from Presidio, Texas, but, for our purposes, it runs between Chihuahua City and Los Mochis, where it connects with Mexico's major bus, train, and plane routes. The Chihuahua-Pacific covers almost 1,000 kilometers (620 miles) between Ojinaga and Topolobampo. It is joined by two other passenger train routes—one connecting Juarez/El Paso with Mexico City and one connecting Nogales with Guadalajara via Mazatlán. If you are connecting to the C-P train in Los Mochis and Chihuahua City, each of the lines uses different stations, necessitating taxi rides.

This train ride is among the most beautiful in the world, though in order to appreciate it in world-class terms, you need to board in Los Mochis. If you travel east to west, you pass the most beautiful scenery—between Divisadero and Los Mochis—at night, unless you are traveling in the dead of summer. The scenery between Chihuahua City and Divisadero is nothing to sneeze at, but it's just not quite as splendid.

The Chihuahua-Pacific train route was completed in 1961. The construction process, to this day, is considered one of the engineering marvels in the history of North America. The route boasts thirty-six major bridges and eighty-seven tunnels. The C-P train route even has a double loop west of Creel to gain altitude.

There are two classes of trains in Mexico, *primero* and *segundo*—first and second. When you buy your ticket (*boleto*) in Los Mochis or Chihuahua City, the ticket agent will probably automatically assume, if you are a gringo, you want to travel first-class. You probably do, because second-class trains can be quite crowded, real grubby, and downright glacial in the forward-progress realm. Ticket prices for the C-P have gone up dramatically in the past few years, ever since the Mexican government dumped the railway line and it was purchased by Estrella Blanca. As of October 1993, a first-class ticket from Chihuahua City to Creel, the main jumping-off point to Copper Canyon Country cost about $15. Ditto for Los Mochis to Creel. It will cost a few dollars more to travel from Chihuahua City to Divisadero, another prime canyon jump-off, two hours west of Creel. Conversely, from Los Mochis to Divisadero will be a few dollars less. Second-class is about a third the cost all the way around, and I have been told by semi-reliable sources that ticket prices are negotiable on second-class trains.

The first-class trains leave Chihuahua City and Los Mochis at 7 AM, followed an hour or so later by the second-class train. First-class trains usually have dining cars. Food vendors—selling everything from sodas and beers to enchiladas and potato chips—usually hop all trains at all stops, so you won't have to starve if you decide to travel second-class. With the exception of Divisadero there are no stops along the route of a long enough duration to hop off the train to eat. If you are bypassing Creel in either direction and find yourself in need of basic supplies, there's a small store directly across the tracks from the station.

For more information on the Chihuahua-Pacific Railroad, write to the International Map Company, University of Texas at El Paso, Box 400, El Paso, Texas 79968-0400. The cost for a nice pamphlet is $2.50.

You can connect directly from the U.S. to Chihuahua City by plane on AeroMexico or Mexicana. Or you can fly to El Paso and hook up with a commuter airline (Aero Lopez) from there to Chihuahua City. Or you can fly to El Paso and cross the border to Juarez. People at the airport will tell you that there's no alternative to the $15 to $20 taxi ride to the border. They lie like nine rabid dogs. If you don't mind walking a few blocks, you can catch the public bus, unless you arrive on a very late flight. Just walk out the main terminal entrance, south to the second traffic light, until you see a bus stop on the right. The bus will take you to the plaza, which is about a mile north of the border. Cost: A dollar or so. (See, I just saved you the cost of this book!)

From Juarez, you can fly, bus, or train to Chihuahua City. I recommend the bus, mainly because of the frequency of departures. After passing through immigration, hail a taxi. It will cost about $2 to the bus station. Buses leave for Chihuahua City every half hour or so. First-class buses—which most often have restrooms—will cost about $10. It's about five hours to Chihuahua via a brand-spanking-new four-lane *autopista*.

Trains from Juarez leave at 7 AM, meaning you will have to spend the night in Juarez if you decide to choose that mode of transportation. The trip to Chihuahua takes about six hours, and you will need to hire a taxi from the border to the train station.

No matter how you arrive, you will want to get to Chihuahua City the night before you plan on hopping the train to Copper Canyon Country. Since there are no hotels near the C-P station, plan on staying at one of the several decent hotels downtown. (I like the Hotel Apollo, at least partially because it boasts a decent-enough cafe and one of the tackiest little bars this side of a Bill Murray skit in *"Saturday Night Live."*) Make arrangements with a taxi driver to come pick you up at your hotel the next morning in time to get you to the train station. Offer him $5 extra and make certain that the driver understands clearly which train station you want.

If you arrive in Chihuahua City in the middle of the night and you don't want to spend the money on a hotel room for only a few hours, then get a taxi from the bus station directly to the C-P train station, which was completely refurbished in the late 1980s. You can just hang out there until morning. I've done this more times than I care to remember. Remember: never take your eyes off your gear in this neighborhood. I don't think there's much chance of someone robbing you, but there's always a chance someone could heist your gear.

Buses also connect Chihuahua City with Creel. Inquire about times at the main bus terminal, also brand-spanking-new, when you arrive from Juarez. Buses to Creel take about five hours, compared to six for the train, but it's nowhere near the experience. One thing though: Chihuahua City's new bus station, which is the size of several European countries put together, is located about a million kilometers outside of town. It'll cost you $7 or so to take a taxi from the downtown area to the bus station. There are five or six buses a day connecting Chihuahua City and Creel.

And, don't forget, you can easily drive from Chihuahua City—or from Hermosillo, if you are coming from the western U.S.—to Copper Canyon Country. Both roads are paved road all the way to Creel with several big towns in between, although it should be noted that the road from Hermosillo does not access Creel directly, but, rather, in a roundabout way, through Basaseachi. If you contact Sanborn's Mexico Club, they can tell you all about the route, as well as laying almost up-to-date maps on you.

There are less options coming from Los Mochis. For one thing, there is no road from there to Tarahumara-land. Well, actually, there is a dirt road all the way through now, but, as of yet, there is no bridge across the Rio Fuerte, which is a big enough river that things like bridges are sort of important. There is, however, a ferry, so, if you are adventuresome and you have a reliable, high-clearance, four-wheel-drive vehicle with plenty of extra gas, you could drive from Los Mochis all the way to Copper Canyon Country.

But, most people will decide to take the train. Just remember, the C-P train station is a half-hour by taxi from the Los Mochis city center. So, once again, make arrangements for your taxi ride the night before.

There are several ways to get to Los Mochis. From Nogales, Arizona, you can bus or train, though connections from the rest of the world to Nogales will necessitate a changeover in

Tucson. From there, you can take a Greyhound to the border, 60 miles south. You can also fly from either Tucson or Nogales to Los Mochis. And you can catch a ferry from La Paz, on the Baja, to Topolobampo. From there, it's only a few minutes by city bus to beautiful downtown Los Mochis.

If you are coming from southern Mexico, connections to both Los Mochis and Chihuahua City will be very easy, whether you travel by plane, train, bus, or car. Basically, if you want to get to Chihuahua City, start in Mexico City. If you want to get to Los Mochis, start in Guadalajara.

On your way home, plan on spending a day in either Los Mochis or Chihuahua City. Though neither is your classic tourist destination, they are each very interesting. I especially like Chihuahua City, at least partially because it has a great plaza and cathedral. Check the bibliography for *South America on a Shoestring*, which includes Mexico, for some specifics about these cities.

Languages

Spanish and Tarahumara. Don't expect to find much English once you get to Copper Canyon Country. A few of the employees at some of the lodging facilities in the area—the Parador de la Montaña in Creel, Las Cabañas del Cobre-Sierra in Cusarare, the Hotel Divisadero de las Barrancas in Divisadero, and Bustillo's in Batopilas, among maybe one or two others—speak varying amounts of English. Once you head out into the backcountry, expect to rely totally on *Español*.

No one should bypass a trip to Mexico because they don't speak a lick of Spanish. Though, of course, the more you can learn before you head south of the border, the better. With less than six months of diligent study, you will not only be able to order a beer with flair and aplomb, but at the same time, you will be making a cultural statement to the locals. Americans are perceived, rightly or wrongly, as being linguistically, as well as culturally, arrogant. A little Spanish will go a long way towards modifying that perception.

And, besides, Mexicans are the antitheses of Parisians. They are the most patient and helpful people in the world when it comes to learning their language. They are extremely flattered that you are making the effort. They praise your attempts mightily. And, if it becomes necessary, they will usually correct your foul-ups very gently. It's a great scene as you're boneheading your way through a simple "subject/predicate/direct object" sentence.

Most Tarahumara men speak Spanish, though it is their second language. So you'll be on equal footing. Tarahumara women, especially the older ones, may only speak Tarahumara, although this is almost inconsequential because they're generally too shy to speak to strangers, especially big, ugly, gringo strangers.

I have tried repeatedly to bone up on my Tarahumara. Lost cause. My tongue, lips, and larynx will not physiologically do some of the things required to get even the most basic Tarahumara words out. And the mainframe of my brain will not make enough room for the words. They visit, and they move on.

If you find yourself in the company of Tarahumaras, by all means ask them to teach you a few words and phrases. They get a little shy about this sometimes, but they seem to think it's amusing to listen to gringos mispronouncing their language. You'll point to the fire and ask, "*Como se llama?*"—how is this called?—while pointing to the flames. They'll smile coyly and, very softly, say "*ickwiiijzjzjwak*"—mixed with several guttural embellishments. You will attempt to repeat the word, and all the Tarahumaras present will giggle at you and consider you less-than-scholarly.

The Tarahumara Mission Store in Creel sells a Spanish-Tarahumara dictionary, and the map that Dr. Schmidt sells contains a small English-Spanish-Tarahumara glossary.

A few backpacking words to add to your list:

English	Español
to hike	camionar
to camp	acampar
trail	camino or sendero
How far is it to. . . ?	Cuando hay de aqui al . . . ?
highway	carretera
pavement	pavimento
far	lejo
very far	muy lejo

English	Español
close	cerca
very close	cerquita
boot	bota
backpacker	mochilero (a)
backpack	mochila
white gas	gasolina blanca
kerosene	keroseno
backpacking stove	estufa de acampar
sleeping bag	bolsa de dormiendo
tent	casita de acampar
guide	guia
map	mapa
cold beer	cerveza fria
rum	ron
cigars	cigarros puros
Fill 'er up.	Lleno.

One last note about languages. Don't worry about messing up. Everyone does it. Some people even go so far as to say that you can't get on with the business of learning a second language until you've embarrassed yourself major league at least once in front of several dozen people.

There was the time a buddy of mine ordered a *"perro caliente"*—a hot dog, he thought—from a street vendor. Everyone for nine blocks was immediately rolling on the ground with laughter. Come to find out the Spanish term for hot dog is *"jot dog,"* pronounced exactly as it is pronounced in English. *"Perro caliente"* means "bitch in heat," which, knowing that particular buddy, may have been what he really was ordering.

My buddy didn't even bat an eye. He just continued his quest to become bilingual, secure in the knowledge that he had already screwed up as badly as a person could possibly screw up without getting locked up.

The Tarahumaras
We don't call Copper Canyon Country "Tarahumara-land" for nothing. This area is the home field for the world-famous,

long-distance-running Tarahumara Indians. The Tarahumaras are the second-largest North American Indian tribe after the Navajos. Best guesstimates put their numbers somewhere between forty and fifty thousand, though I've never been able to determine how those best guesstimates were achieved.

When you visit Copper Canyon Country, it is nearly the same as entering an American Indian reservation, although the legal set-up is more fragmented. You must consider your every move in terms of how it will likely impact the Tarahumaras. This is their land, and "we" have no right to be there, except the right that they give us.

The Tarahumaras migrated to Copper Canyon Country from the high plains around modern-day Cuauhtemoc about five hundred years ago, after the Spanish Conquistadores started enslaving them to work the local silver mines. It wasn't a mass migration in the Exodus sense, but, rather, a very gradual process that took place family by family. As households got fed up with having their children enslaved, they moved west, into the canyon country. The conquistadores sometimes gave chase, only to find themselves looking down into the majestic depths of Copper Canyon. This, they decided, was simply not worth it. So, the Tarahumaras, were pretty much left alone, although isolated pockets of forced labor continued to plague the Tarahumara culture, especially around Batopilas and the almost-dead village of Barranca del Cobre.

After a while, the descendants of those conquistadores who stayed in Mexico began settling on the edges of Tarahumara-land. After all, there was lots of stuff they wanted in that neck of the woods—silver, gold, timber, and land. The Tarahumaras have lived on the fringes of the Mexican-run extractive industries ever since, interacting with it sometimes, ignoring it, and being ignored by it, at other times.

The Tarahumaras have been known to get riled and come out of the woodwork. During the Mexican Revolution of 1910–19, both sides came to an understanding that battles would no longer be fought in Tarahumara-land. Seems the peace and tranquility of the Tarahumaras' scene was threatened by the fighting. To demonstrate the depth of their irritation, the Tarahumaras would frequently sneak into whichever side's camp was handiest—the Tarahumaras didn't give a hoot in hell who was in power in Mexico City—and drench the slumbering soldiers with gasoline and set them on fire. Fullbody hot-foots.

The Tarahumaras wanted nothing more than to be left alone. This, my friends, is the best way to characterize the Tarahumaras and their culture. When you see where some Tarahumara families live, you will be convinced of the validity of this observation. They just want to be left alone.

Tarahumaras are, towards outsiders, very aloof, standoffish, and shy. This is not to say that they aren't basically friendly people. Neither is it to say that many Tarahumaras aren't very gregarious towards non-Tarahumaras. Some are. Most are not. It is to say that you should always assume, until provided ample reason to believe otherwise, that the Tarahumaras' privacy is sacrosanct. They cruise through life with a privacy force-field around them and around their property.

I don't know that Tarahumaras have developed culture-wide feelings about whether gringos are "good" or "bad." Our invasion of their turf is still too new. I do know that they have made judgments about some of our peculiar ways. Some good. Some bad. So, we are at the fragile point in the meeting of cultures where "we"—Americans, gringos, tourists, backpackers—can make a good impression for a change. Here are some things.

If there's any way to avoid it (and oftentimes, there is not), you should never pass onto a Tarahumara's land uninvited. Tarahumara dwellings do not end at the front door. They end at the fence surrounding their land. When you walk up to a Tarahumara's house without being asked to do so, it's the same as someone walking up to the foot of your bed without your permission. (Thanks to my friend Skip McWilliams for that observation and phrasing.)

If you want to talk with Tarahumaras—to ask directions, for instance—the mannerly thing to do is to sit outside their property fence, within sight of their house, and wait. If they want to talk, they will come to you. Eventually.

Never photograph Tarahumaras without asking their permission. Most Tarahumaras will tell you, politely but firmly, that they would rather not be photographed. Certainly, this is their right.

You should also be very careful about taking photos of Tarahumara dwellings. Tarahumaras consider their houses and their land to be extensions of themselves. So, if you photograph their *casita*, you are, at the same time, taking a picture of them. Again, you can ask, but, if they say no, don't try to talk them into it. And certainly don't try to bribe them. This is justifiably insulting and speaks poorly of our culture. If you have asked a Tarahumara to take their picture, and if they have answered in the affirmative, you can offer a tip after you take your shots. This you should do respectfully, making certain that they know that you know that they have done you the favor, not the other way around simply because some cash changed hands.

As well, there are plenty of old missions located in Tarahumaraland. The Tarahumaras are all basically Catholic, though many are far less Catholic than they let on to be. Either way, they take their churches very seriously. You are generally welcome to walk around inside (although many are locked). Remove your hat. And leave a small offering, perhaps one new pesos, on the altar.

When you are hiking in the backcountry, you may find yourself on a collision course with a herd of goats. If there's any way to do so, try to not disrupt the proceedings. Tarahumara goats are used to people. So, if you just stand still, they will pass around you with no problem. If the herd spooks, some poor Tarahumara girl will have to, with the aid of her dogs, run up and down steep hills until she rounds the herd up. She will think poorly of you and yours for the inconvenience.

Also—and please forgive me if this sounds overly didactic in tone—you may stumble across Tarahumara artifacts, especially pots, in the outback. As tempting as it may be, these should be admired, photographed, and otherwise left alone. The owners may plan on returning to the place where you find a pot, and they may plan on using that pot again. Also, by leaving pots behind, you give me the chance, if I stumble onto that spot, to admire it myself.

The Tarahumaras are some seriously primitive people. They are often referred to as "genuine cave dwellers" in the prints, in a tone that borders on "ain't that precious." There are plenty of Tarahumaras who do, indeed, dwell in caves, though a small percentage of the population. (And they *are* precious.) Many Tarahumaras are semi-nomadic people. Tarahumara families will have as many as five residences. One might be located near the place they grow beans. Another next to some good fall goat-grazing territory. Each of the places has a specific use.

The Tarahumaras are also near-puritanical in their day-to-day life. You don't, for instance, want to skinny dip in front of a Tarahumara homestead. They dress modestly, and it is polite for you to do the same in their presence. The one exception to this shy, puritanical attitude is when the Tarahumaras commence to drinking. I have read that the Tarahumaras are drunk most of the time. This is simply not the case.

The Tarahumaras drink mainly during ceremonial occasions called *tesguinadas*. During *tesguinadas*, which usually last two or three days and are by invitation only, Tarahumaras consume vast amounts of *tesguino*—corn beer ingloriously described by Skip McWilliams as tasting like spiked creamed corn mixed with a bushel of grass clippings.

During *tesguinadas*, most anything goes, especially if it has to do with spousal-exchange programs. When the festivities are over—meaning when all the corn beer is gone—the Tarahumaras dust themselves off and stumble back to the straight and narrow.

During the winter, Tarahumara men, with little else to do, spend more time drinking in non-*tesguinada* environments. Tequila is the beverage of choice during non-ceremonial imbibathons. And they drink a lot of tequila when the chance presents itself. Say it I must—the Tarahumaras make for some seriously nasty drunks. They may be fun to each other, but they are certainly not fun to gringos, even if the gringos are equally as drunk. It's best to avoid being in the company of Tarahumaras when the drinking gets serious. If you are invited to a *tesguinada*, try to show up the exact nanosecond it's scheduled to commence. That way, you can hang out for a few hours, check the scene out and sashay before the sobriety landscape gets littered with ugliness.

Otherwise, you will likely have no problems with the Tarahumaras. They are kind and gentle people, and I get to like them more every time I visit Copper Canyon Country.

Land Management

Almost all the land in Copper Canyon Country is part of Mexico's *ejido* system, established by Pancho Villa after he and his followers won the Mexican Revolution. Villa sent representatives into the countryside who gave communal title to land traditionally occupied by the local indigenous population. This is one of the most noteworthy land reform programs ever initiated in the history of the world.

This is where Tarahumara "reservations" differ from American Indian Reservations. Title was given on a village-by-village basis, rather than on a tribal basis. Therefore, though the cumulative acreage of all the *ejidos* in Tarahumara-land would make for a good-sized chunk of land, it is broken down into communally owned smaller parcels, each of which is governed by an elected tribal council, which may or may not be the real local power center. Some *ejidos* put more stock in their traditional chief/shaman concept.

You enter an *ejido* by the grace of the people of that *ejido*. And you enter the next *ejido* by the grace of the people of that *ejido*. No sort of permit system has been established, though that may be forthcoming in the next decade. Several *ejidos* are already charging admission fees to visit some of the more popular sites in Tarahumara-land. I'll tell you about those when and where appropriate. Just remember this about those fees: First, they are generally token. Second, from what I have seen, the small amount of money raised from those fees is used for good purposes, like building greenhouses and schoolbooks.

It is a mannerly thing, when camping near a *ranchito*, to let someone know what you're up to and, out of courtesy, ask for permission. If there is a mission nearby, make a small donation. Never camp on fenced property without permission, and always offer to pay a few pesos for the privilege. By the way, there are no signs welcoming you to whatever *ejido* it is you're about to enter. And they're not marked on maps.

Money

New Mexican peso. In 1993, the Mexican government dunked its age-old peso in favor of the *"Nuevo Peso."* All this dunking did was take a few zeros off of the old peso, meaning

100,000 pesos suddenly became 100 *Nuevo Pesos*. This new system was instigated at least partially for hyper-inflation PR purposes, but, more importantly, it was initiated so that coins could once again make their way into circulation. The new peso was valued at about three to one U.S. dollar in November 1993. Although the peso has remained fairly stable for several years now, you never know when a devaluation will occur. To hedge my bets against future uncertainties, I give most cost information in U.S. dollars.

The Mexican government allows businesses to change dollars into pesos and vice-versa. Usually, your best rate of exchange will be at a bank, because there is no black market for currency. Banks will usually charge some kind of commission on all transactions, especially if traveler's checks are being used.

If you can't find a bank, look for a *casa del cambio*. Your rate won't be as good as the bank, but you usually won't be charged a commission. Again, rates can be slightly lower for travelers checks than for cash at *casas del cambio*.

If all else fails, walk into a grocery store or hotel and ask if they buy dollars. If you have cash, this will be very easy. With traveler's checks, it can be more of a hassle, but certainly not impossible. Many places, banks especially, will want to look at your passport when changing traveler's checks. Of course, you will lose money when you want to change pesos back into dollars, so try to time it so you run out of pesos the same time you're leaving the country.

Personal checks are generally a no go, unless you've been hanging out in one place long enough that people have got to know you. Credit cards are accepted by many larger hotels, stores, and restaurants in the bigger cities. But, once you get off the beaten path, you'll have little luck with plastic. Carry small denominations of currency. Small change is often in short supply in the boonies.

Staying Healthy, Including Water Purification
You don't need any shots to visit Mexico, though there are those (like me) who would recommend getting a gamma globulin shot for infectious (type-A) hepatitis. This shot, which you

can save yourself some bucks by getting at a public health facility rather than a private doctor's office, leaves you stiff-hammed for a few days, but it is well worth it. Nobody says it is perfectly effective, and it only lasts about three months. Hepatitis is probably the biggest health concern for Copper Canyon Country, except for falling off a cliff or drinking bad tequila. Type-A is spread through contaminated water, or by eating food handled by a carrier or someone who has come in contact with contaminated water. The best prevention is to consume only purified water and eat raw fruits and vegetables only when peeled by you and rinsed with purified water.

Many people will avoid eating salads because a contaminated person might have cut the lettuce. If you're only going to be in Mexico for a week, maybe that's not a bad idea. But, if you're there for a longer period of time, it will start having serious digestive implications if you avoid salads entirely. You'll just have to take more chances than you would normally like to take. I have just said to hell with it. I eat anything in Mexico and have had nothing worse than, ironically enough, constipation. My time is coming, though, and I know it.

It should be pointed out here that Mexico is very definitely entering the late twentieth century. The government works hard, through its various health service entities, to teach good hygiene habits to its citizens. There are TV commercials, for instance, that preach the gospel of cleanliness. So, increasingly, restaurant owners are using purified water to clean food, dishes, and themselves. Also, purified bottled water is becoming increasingly available, even in very small towns. When purifying water yourself, remember, hepatitis is viral. You cannot rely on your backpacking water pump. There are only a couple of brands with any pretensions whatsoever of taking care of hepatitis virus. One is the $240 Swiss-made Katadyn. This is, by far, the best backpacking water filter on the market. I carry one, and I have also used a First Need, which, through much cheaper and somewhat lighter, is nowhere near as thorough, and is much more inconvenient in the long-run. The First Need has a disposable filter element that, once clogged, is useless. I have had a couple First Need filters clog up on me, under admittedly extreme circumstances, but circumstances, nonetheless, that I found myself in need of clean water—after only a few uses. You can back-flush the filter to prolong its life, but once it is clogged, it's history.

The Katadyn utilizes a filter that is ultimately disposable, in that it reaches a point where it no longer works and, therefore, needs to be tossed and replaced. It's just that it can be used over three years in the worst situations imaginable on a day-to-day basis before its days are done. The ceramic filter unscrews from the pump mechanism. All you do is clean the filter with a brush that comes with the unit and re-assemble the housing. You're back in business.

Herb Koelble, who is head of Katadyn's American distribution center, told me that his filter is able to take care of stuff down to .2 microns in size. Viruses are way smaller than that. But, Koelble says, viruses generally hook up with something a little larger, like a bacteria or amoeba—both of which are larger than .2 microns. Therefore, the Katadyn takes care of things. Even for those viruses that prefer to cruise unattended, the way is not smooth because the Katadyn's filter pores are zig-zag shaped. So, the virus can get caught up before it hits your water bottle. Then, it will perish because the filter is impregnated with some silver stuff that apparently spells doom for viruses.

But this, again, is no guarantee. So, Koelble suggests, if you are in an area known to have viral contamination lurking about—and this information can be found from a call to the U.S. State Department—that you add about a half a dose of iodine-based tablets, sold in outdoor stores with the brand-name "Potable Agua," after filtering it. He says that iodine latches onto the murk in murky water as enthusiastically as it latches onto little goobers that carry disease. Iodine is not intelligent life. So, the more muck you remove from the water, the less confusion factor for the iodine molecules.

Just remember, though you can get away by using a lot less iodine after filtration, you still need to let it work for however long it says on the bottle. If you have no filter, you will have to rely solely on either iodination or boiling. Boiling is inconvenient as hell, and you should not drink iodinated water for more than a few days at a time, as the iodine starts killing the bacteria that has called your digestive tract home for your whole life. Either way, bear in mind that this is hot territory. You will have to suck down lots of water. Whatever you do, don't go thirsty because it is a hassle to purify water.

There is a chance you might catch a case of the runs. This is almost always caused by the introduction of regional-dwelling bacteria into the ol' intestines. It will take about three days for your system to get used to the local micro-critters, which can jump into your here and now via food, water, soft drinks, a contaminated fly landing on your fork, whatever. This doesn't imply that a given country is unclean. Mexicans likewise get Uncle Sam's revenge when they're visiting the States. It's just a matter of what your system's used to.

Should you find yourself going through toilet paper at a major rate, just make sure that you keep drinking plenty of water. Dehydration is not good. It is generally considered preferable to avoid anti-diarrhea medicine, unless things get way out of hand, or unless you're scheduled to be sitting on a bathroom-less bus for half a day. If you suspect you only have Montezuma's revenge, you should let the beast pass from your bowels.

Dysentery, in both amoebic and bacillary forms, is also a concern, but, by taking the same precautions you are taking to prevent hepatitis, you should have no problem with it. You will need some medications you probably won't have in your first-aid kit to take care of amoebic dysentery. So, if you notice blood and/or mucus in your stool, you might want to seek medical care.

A surprising number of people suffer from constipation when traveling. As hard as it may seem since raw fruits and veggies are suspect, you need to keep up your roughage intake while on the road. Buy fruits and veggies from food stores and cleanse them yourself. Don't eat too much white flour and lay off the Mennonite cheese if things start clogging up.

You will also want to read up on heat exhaustion—a type of shock caused by the body's attempts to cool itself—and heat stroke—when the body's internal thermostat goes on the blink. Check out the book, *Wilderness Medicine*, listed in the bibliography.

One more thing. The most common cause of premature death among the Tarahumaras is tuberculosis. I heard a second-hand story, wherein the person telling me this had been told by a public health nurse that, in twenty-some-odd years of working with the Tarahumaras, *everyone* she had tested was a TB carrier. The temptation would be to recommend that you not participate in any passing-of-the-bottle-around-the-campfire or passing-of-the-cigar rituals. But, in addition to that being somewhat socially awkward at times, it would also deprive you of some good experiences. I have seen Tarahumaras wipe the mouth of the bottle after having it passed to them, so it is socially acceptable to do the same, though it will probably be a waste of time if any TB slime is on the bottle. If you do notice a Tarahumara coughing a lot, I would avoid sharing a water or tequila bottle with him—the stuff that they cough up being the point of concern. Other than that, travel in this part of Mexico with no more caution that you would travel in your own country.

Staying Alive

There are some critters and plants around here that could prove inconvenient. Just about every group will have at least one member who will have an encounter with a rattlesnake. One member of my party once had a three-foot rattler just about crawl directly into her lap while we were sitting around the campfire one night. Another person I know found himself sitting next to a six-foot rattler.

The good thing about rattlers, as opposed to some of the other more slimy, nightmarish species like mambas and vine snakes, is that they *rattle*. I mean, they rattle like birds tweet. You wouldn't believe what an effective reflexive deterrent rattling can be to progressing any further with the physical act you are currently engaged in. You don't even have to think about it. The deep recesses of your evasive action control have matters well in hand before you even know what's going on.

Rattlers are, despite their fierce, macho image, a very weenie species—maybe even the biggest weenie reptile species in the world. Lower than box turtles. I mean, what other intensely fearsome critter has evolved a body part that amounts to nothing more than a purely audible version of a human wetting in his or her pants from fright?

A rattler, when rattling, is pleading for mercy—telling you in no uncertain terms that it doesn't mind one bit being branded the most cowardly creature in the canyon. Yes, give a rattler the chance to high-tail it, so to speak, in the opposite direction, and it will take it.

You just need to make certain you give it the chance to do just that. If you get too close or touch it, you are going to get bit. And, even though envenomation fails to transpire about a fourth of the time, those aren't my kind of odds. So, don't put your appendages anywhere you can't see. That simple precaution will all but totally ensure that you will not suffer snakebite—unless, of course, one crawls into your lap while you're sitting around the campfire.

There are also coral snakes in Copper Canyon Country, just like the American Southwest. Because they are burrowing snakes, I have never heard of anyone even seeing one. Either way, I suggest you read *Wilderness Medicine* before entering the backcountry. It goes into some detail on snakebite.

There are poisonous spiders around—black widows, tarantulas, and maybe brown recluses. Another local fun lover is called an "assassin bug." I kid you not. *Wilderness Medicine*, likewise, goes into detail about this little critter. Many people feel a lot more comfortable sleeping in a tent when in the deep canyons, where more of this poisonous stuff lives. (I am increasingly becoming one of those people.)

And Copper Canyon Country is home to lots of cactus, as well as mesquite groves. Bushwhacking can sometimes require blood transfusions. For those of you allergic to poison ivy, there is some in the deep canyons. But that's about it. No more bad stuff than the Carolinas. And probably even less.

Maps

There are two topographical series, the 1:250,000-scale "San Juanito" map and roughly six to eight—depending on where you draw the boundaries of Copper Canyon Country—1:50,000-scale maps. The appropriate maps are listed in the

"Particulars" section of each chapter. Remember that these maps will be in kilometers and the contour intervals in meters. (One mile equals about 1.6 kilometers and one foot equals about .3 meters; or, one kilometer equals .6 miles and one meter equals 3.3 feet.)

These maps are geophysically accurate, as far as I can tell. The topographic data undoubtedly came straight from U.S. satellites. But the trail and town data is often way off. Do not rely too heavily on trail markings on the maps. Become familiar with the landmarks in your area and then look, on the ground, rather than on the map, for your trail. Also, many of the ranchitos marked on the maps are in the wrong place. Some by a long distance. (Sitagochi and Huacoybo come to mind.)

All maps of the area, with the exception of the map covering Basaseachi Falls, are sold at the Tarahumara Mission Store in Creel, although sometimes their stash gets hit hard by the tourist hordes. If you're coming through Chihuahua City, it would be a good idea to stop by the INEGI office (Paseo Bolivar No. 5, telephone: 16-15-17). The INEGI people are very competent and helpful, and they generally have every map you could ever want. I have yet to hear of a successful attempt to purchase these maps in advance through the mail.

A Note on Place Name Spellings

It is common for the little backcountry dots on your Tarahumara-land maps to end in "chi." Pamachi. Tehuirichi. Panalachi. Sitagochi. I guess this means "ville" or something. You may also see, or hear, these names with a "c" tacked on. Pamachic. Panalachic. Don't be confused. The "c" ending is just a slight Spanish-ization of these Tarahumara place names. Basaseachi is the same place as Basaseachic.

Guides

Though I am hardly an expert on the subject of guided trips, I still, somewhat old fashionedly I'm afraid, feel that trip planning and preparation are an important part of the wilderness travel process. By studying the maps for hundreds of hours and packaging your own food back in the bleakness of civilization, you are establishing an important pre-trip bond with the place you are heading to. That, I believe, causes you to arrive on the scene more mentally prepared for the trip.

As well, and again I know how 1950s-Boy-Scout-like this sounds, I think there's a higher level of post-trip gratification if you and your buddies pulled the trip off without professional help. I understand that many people disagree with me on this, or at least don't agree to the extent that they're foregoing any guided trip as a result. I just want you to understand that Copper Canyon Country is very available to you if you have any semblance of trip-planning ability. I also want you to understand that, at least a half-dozen times, I have found my lame butt lost as lost gets in the middle of the outback of Copper Canyon Country wishing like the dickens that I'd had whatever combination of more brains and less ego that it would have taken to get me to hire a guide before I ever left civilization. At the same time, some of the most memorable trips I've ever taken into the outback of Tarahumara-land have been those with a certain directional discombolulation factor factored into the story.

If you decide, for whatever reason, that you'd prefer visiting the area with a guide, here are a couple of suggestions, though I want to point out that I have been on the trail with none of these companies/people. Therefore, though I have a good feeling about them, I take no personal responsibility whatsoever for guide services.

> Sol y Luna, P.O. Box 02, Shafter, TX 79850
> *Info desk:* (915) 229-4541
> *Phone-in reservations:* (800) 597-4168
>
> Chihuahua al Pacifico Tours Apdo. 84AU9
> Chihuahua City, Chih., Mexico 31410
> *Phone:* 011-52-145-14-68-11 *FAX:* 011-52-145-17-38-04

The Sol y Luna folks—Chris and Wendy—actually live in Copper Canyon Country (the 'burbs of Creel, to be exact). They check their messages in Shafter frequently. They also have a working arrangement with Margarita's Casa de Huespedes (see Chapter 3). So, with Sol y Luna, you can either set something up in advance, or you can set it up after arriving in Copper

Canyon Country. I've met Chris and Wendy numerous times, and they seem like the real thing, guide-wise. They organize a wide array of standardized and custom burro-supported trips. Rates are very reasonable, and Chris is a very good cook, as well as being a very entertaining character.

The Chihuahua al Pacifico people are Mexican. Their head tour operator, Pedro Palma, grew up in the Sierra Madre, and he really knows the area from soup to nuts. He is able to organize everything from burro-supported backcountry trips to car itineraries that mix in dayhiking with sightseeing.

I also know of one company that organizes photography expeditions to Copper Canyon Country.

> *Contact:* Joe Carder
> 1507 W. Sendero Seis, Tucson, AZ 85704
> (602) 742-3928

There are also other guide services, covering the gamut from backcountry tours to mountain bike trips to photography seminars, operating in Copper Canyon Country, some of whom are surely very good. Peruse the classified sections of *Backpacker*, *Outside*, *Sierra*, and *Summit* magazines. There are usually guiding services listed in each of these just about every issue.

While in Copper Canyon Country, you may wish to hire a Tarahumara guide, for your whole trip or just one segment. Understand several things before you do so. First, if you hire a Tarahumara guide, you are responsible for setting the trip up in a conceptual manner. You are also responsible for arranging any necessary surface transportation, whether that take the form of car, train, or bus. Also understand that these people have no great tradition of embarking on wilderness forays with relatively affluent gringos, like Nepal's Sherpas. They don't always manage to figure out what it is you want of them. And I don't know if many Tarahumaras have it figured out why we are there. I've asked several if they know why we pay them to take us out into the boondocks, just so we can come back three days later. The response has amounted to massive shoulder-shrugging.

You need to let your Tarahumara guide know that you want to take the best trail, rather than the most direct trail. *"No*

queremos un camino feo. Queremos un camino mas facil."
("We don't want an ugly trail. We want an easier trail.") should
do the trick, although you may have to repeat yourself more
than once during the trip. You must also ask them to lead you
at a slower pace, because the Tarahumaras flat out fly on the
trail. If you try to keep up with them, you're doomed. *Ande
mas despacio*—"walk slower"—and *nos espera*—"wait for
us"—should work. Also, remind your guide to let you know if
you pass near anything interesting, like abandoned mine shafts
or a spring.

You will be able to hire a Tarahumara guide by just asking
around in Divisadero, Cusarare, or Creel. Expect to pay about
$10 a day, with you supplying the food. You need to know some
things about this food part.

One of the main reasons Tarahumaras hire out as guides—
and many do not—is because they are interested in checking us
out. They are especially interested in our food. Tarahumaras
have some proud appetites. They will eat every item they can
get their hands on. I have witnessed a group of Tarahumara
guides threaten to quit a trip if the food offerings did not
improve. This despite the fact that the reason the food situation was not up to snuff was because these same Tarahumaras
had been eating everything in sight for the last three days.

Once when dividing up supplies, I stupidly had my Tarahumara guide carry the lunches and snacks. Two days later, we
realized that he had been hiking up ahead and diving into the
food bag. With two days left in our trip, we found ourselves
going without lunch.

So, you've got to establish a workable food disbursement
plan. Before the trip gets underway, lay the food out in front of
your guide. Make certain that he understands that what
he sees before him is the total food supply. Ask him if he thinks
it's enough and if there's anything else he can think of that you
might need. Tell him what your basic chronological meal consumption habits are. Point out that you will stop for several
snacks per day on the trail, for instance. This way, if any problems do arise on the trail, you can refer back to this conversation.

If you pass around a bag of candy, the best procedure is to
either say how many pieces each person gets, or to just hand

over the correct number. This goes for serving supper out of a communal pan. You need to make your guide understand that you are on relatively limited rations; that you, as a group, can only eat certain amounts of certain foods at certain times. This should cause no friction, as long as the rations are interesting and reasonably ample. If they are not, you may lose your guide mid-trip.

You will also be expected to buy your guide cigarettes. He will be responsible for his own blanket, although I have procured an inexpensive Wal-Mart sleeping bag that I bring with me to Copper Canyon Country for whatever guide I may hire. (I have had Tarahumara guides turn back on dead-of-winter trips because they got cold at night, so the sleeping bag thing is a good idea.) You also need to dig up a cheap bowl, spoon, and cup—easily accomplished along the main drag in Creel.

If, before leaving home, you are certain that you are going to hire a Tarahumara guide, you may want to bring an extra pack and sleeping pad. Whatever guide you eventually hire would be mighty pleased to have use of them. Just make certain he understands that it's a loan—*un prestamo*. And, if for whatever reason you don't end up hiring a guide, you can just ask the proprietors of whichever lodging facility you stay at in Creel to hold onto the extra gear while you're in the backcountry.

Okay, having said all that, there is one person, Sahuaripa (saw-wah-REE-pah) Gonzales who, if ever a Tarahumara was genetically predisposed to guide gringos into the boondocks, it is he. Sahuaripa, who has, over the years, become a good buddy of mine, instinctively interfaces with the gringo backcountry way of thinking better than any Tarahumara I have met, and I have met a lot, on trail and off. He lives about a five-minute walk from Las Cabañas del Cobre in Cusarare (more on this place later), and everyone who I have ever talked with who has hired Sahuaripa has come away mightily pleased. He speaks no English, and he is a little bit timid, but he has hiked enough with me that he knows what he's doing, gringo-wise. If you are interested in hiring Sahuaripa, just get yourself to Las Cabañas del Cobre and ask one of the management-level employees to send someone to his house to fetch him. Sahuaripa can set you up on anything from an over nighter to a five-day foray through the heart of Copper Canyon Country. He knows a lot of routes, and I have never met anyone who remembers trails as well as he does. I've even used him in areas he has never visited before and, through a combination of deductive reasoning, great trail-finding, and asking directions of the locals, he has always managed to lead me to our destination.

Several of the lodging facilities in Tarahumara-land provide guide services. Most have a set price, regardless of the number of customers, up to the point that there's no more room in the vehicle. Whenever one of the hikes described in this book can be accessed by a tour out of Creel, I make mention of that fact.

Gifts

This is something you might give some thought to before leaving home. It is tradition with American travelers that we go out and buy balloons or jellybeans or sewing needles or cigars or costume jewelry to give away to locals we meet·on the trail. As well, many people decide to lay gifts or tips on their guide after the trip.

Some places have well-established guidelines for gift and tip giving. Since Copper Canyon Country is new to this game, it does not. Therefore, "we" have the opportunity to establish some sane ground rules. Unfortunately, I have no definite ideas on what those ground rules should be.

I am tempted to suggest that candy not be given, for health reasons, mainly. But, hell, what harm's a few peanut M&Ms going to do to a Tarahumara who will never visit a dentist his entire life and gets sweets maybe twice a year? If some Tarahumara children hang around my camp, I can't resist giving them a cookie or some candy. You almost feel like Santa Claus if you pass something out.

At the same time, it would be a drag if the Tarahumaras got to expecting handfuls of goodies every time a gringo passed by. (The children in some of the Mexican villages around Batopilas and Urique are already doing this—running out in droves and asking if you could spare some *dulces*—candies—as you pass by.)

With the Tarahumaras, this concern is not too far-fetched. I have seen gabillions of Americans (Europeans do not seem as prone to this habit) who have brought full bags of trinkets, baubles, and curiosities, with the intention of just handing it all out. This only encourages outright begging, which seems to be on the increase as well, though we're still talking small potatoes compared to urban Mexico.

I guess the only thing to do is stick to your personal beliefs about gifts. If it makes you feel good at whatever level, do it. If it makes you feel as though you are aiding and abetting the corruption of a pure society, don't. At the trinket level, costume jewelry, candy, tobacco products, sewing supplies, and brightly colored cloth are popular. You may want to give someone—perhaps your guide—something more substantial than a trinket or candy. Things that any Tarahumara family would appreciate include good quality knives, axes, and clothes.

Physical Preparation

We both know I have to write this part, and we both know you have to read it. At the same time, we both know that it will likely not induce you to get in shape before coming to Copper Canyon Country, any more than it will induce me. We'll both continue to practice those twelve-ounce curls right up until the day we leave for Mexico. But, let's go through the motions.

Hiking around Tarahumara-land is physically demanding—all the more so because it can get unbelievably hot. Multi-hour, steep ups and downs are hard on the legs, especially the feet, thighs, knees, calves, ankles, shins, Achilles tendons, and toes. You are well advised to embark on a fitness/diet regimen at least a couple of months before your visit. Steve Ilg's book, *The Outdoor Athlete: Total Training for Outdoor Performance,* listed in the bibliography, is the best I have seen for getting backpackers in shape. Or, at least for making us feel guilty about the fact that we've blown it off again.

Seasons

For deep canyon trips, dead of winter is best. The deep canyons are too hot except from late-November to early March. Even as early as mid-March, the daytime highs regularly exceed 100 degrees F. Nighttime lows in the winter necessitate three-season bags only. As well, the biting flies get bad towards summer. Avoid the rainy season, mid-July to mid-September, because of the flash flood danger. Best time for photography is just after the rainy season ends, because then the countryside is at its most verdant. From that point until the rains return next summer, things get browner and browner. For trips in the mountains, just about any time of year is good.

I personally prefer the end of the rainy season, because the rivers are warm enough to swim in very comfortably—especially if they are near any hot springs (*aguascalientes*). Nighttime lows in the dead of winter in the high country will always be below freezing. It can easily get below zero at night. And it can snow. Daytime highs are usually in the sun-drenched 60s or 70s F. Come prepared for the extremes.

Fires

There's plenty of driftwood along the rivers in the deep canyons. In such locations, building fires is probably okay. Away from the rivers, you're going to have to make a judgment call. It can be argued that the thin dry soil of Tarahumara-land is extremely reliant on the organic matter from felled trees and branches. At the same time, the Tarahumaras rely on the local wood for survival. So, it would probably be better if you used a stove.

If you are camping with any Tarahumaras, though, you'll have a fire regardless of what you may think of the matter. A Tarahumara would look at you very funny if you told them they ought not build a fire there in the middle of Tarahumara-land. These people are fire magicians. They revere flames. They love sleeping with their heads near 'bouts in the coals. You may be able to convince them that it's more practical to cook on a stove, but they will be listening to your arguments while cozying up to the fire they have just built.

Wildlife

While Copper Canyon Country is geophysically and culturally as wonderful as any place on the continent, alas, when it comes to wildlife viewing, it is no Yellowstone. I have seen a huge flock of parrots, a few snakes, a few squirrels, a coatimundi, a raccoon, and herds of goats, cows, chickens, and children.

Besides lizards, that's about all you're likely to see. Animals are very wary in Copper Canyon Country. Tarahumaras will attempt to kill and eat just about anything with a heartbeat. You may lay eyes on fox, wild turkey, eagle, mule deer, bighorn sheep, mountain lion, jaguar, peccary, or, if your karmic affairs are in very good order, a Mexican wolf or a grizzly. The latter two may be extinct in Tarahumara-land, but who knows?

Gear

For average backpacking trips of less than a week's duration in Copper Canyon Country, you don't need to run out and buy thousands of dollars worth of new gear. At the same time, you don't want your gear falling apart on you at the bottom of Sinforosa Canyon. Focus most of your attention on footwear. After that, in descending order of importance, come water purification system, pack, sleeping bag, tent, raingear, and stove.

Once you determine what time of year you will be coming to Tarahumara-land, and whether or not you will be heading into the deep canyons, you can draw on your own experience as to what you'll need. Some specific recommendations:

- *Hat.* Get a good one that will keep your face from getting sizzled; the sun in this area can be intense. Keeping the sun out of your eyes and off your nose is not the only concern here. You also want to keep direct rays off your noggin. So, dump the tennis visor and get a real, head-covering hat.
- *Sunglasses.* Same thing; get good ones with 100-percent UV protection.
- *Backpack.* I recommend a medium-sized (4,500- to 5,000-cubic-inch capacity) internal-frame pack—preferably one that is no wider than your body and no taller than your head. The latter of primary concern if you end up doing any bushwhacking. That said, I have been using a Lowe Frame Pack Deluxe, with a capacity of about 6,100 cubic inches—mainly because I am often overloaded with camera gear. My wife carries a Mountainsmith Frostfire II internal-frame pack. She loves it.
- *Raingear.* We usually just carry a Gore-tex shell. No rain pants. A cheap poncho would do you fine.

- *Sleeping Bag.* For winter camping in the high country, you need a bag rated to at least five-below. For winter camping in the deep canyons, a 45-degree rating should do it. For summer camping in the high country, a 40-degree rating will be sufficient. All non-winter camping in the deep canyons requires nothing more than a fiber-pile tropical bag or a bedsheet.
- *Sleeping Pad.* This is desert country with lots of stickery plants. Be careful with your self-inflating pad. Always lay it on a groundcloth and keep it inside your pack when hiking.
- *Boots.* Make sure you have good boots in good condition. I once had a pair of soft boots blow out on me in the worst possible situation in Tararecua Canyon. My back-up shoes were some cheap running shoes with badly worn tread. I don't want to go through that again, and neither do you. You can do worse than using new, soft boots, like Hi-Techs. The problem with soft boots is that people believe they do all the same things as sturdier, mid-weight boots, but that they just wear out faster. False. They do not provide the same amount of support, especially on rough trails with heavy weight. Very light, soft boots are made for on-trail dayhiking. If you use them in Copper Canyon Country, especially on the steep downhill grades, with a week's worth of food in your pack, you are probably going to suffer from very sore feet. I recommend mid-weight books, like the Asolo Super Scouts. They cost more—almost $120 at last look—but they will last a lot longer and they will be much easier on your feet.
- *Back-Up Shoes.* Don't overlook this. I always recommend that people bring camp shoes that they can hike in, in case there are problems with their boots. Trail shoes, such as the Nike Air Yewtahs, would fit the bill nicely, though they are a little on the heavy side. New running shoes, with knobby tread, will do just fine. These you will wear for river crossings. Teva sandals are very useful. Both my wife and I carry Tevas, for river crossings and camp shoes. They can also be hiked in in a pinch.
- *Tent.* In the high country, the frost can be intense in the winter. I always use a tent then. I used to never use one in

the canyons. I always just brought a groundcloth and a tent fly, in the unlikely event of rain. Because of recent experiences with snakes, scorpions, tarantulas, and assassin bugs, I am starting to feel more comfortable in a tent, even though the temperature and precipitation concerns do not generally merit carrying one. Go with something very light weight. After all, you are not likely to be tent-bound for three days in Tarahumara-land. You won't need a vestibule. I've been impressed recently with the Sierra Designs Clip Flashlight and the North Face Tadpole for deep canyon trips, though neither are really appropriate for the high country in winter, unless you carry a really warm bag.

- *Water Purification.* See section in this chapter sub-titled "Staying Healthy."
- *Water Bottles.* Carry at least two liters worth of water bottles. Hikes out of the deep canyons can take most of the day. You may walk for hours on end with no shade, in direct sunlight, with temperatures well over 100 degrees F. I always carry a three-gallon water bag for camp use, as well as for those extremely long ascents, where two liters of water simply is not enough.
- *First-Aid Kit.* Carry as much of one as you can. See *Wilderness Medicine* for specific recommendations.

Just remember the old sailor's adage: "Go cheap, go light, and go NOW!" Don't get overly caught up in gear acquisition. You can hike in Tarahumara-land with your old Kelty Tioga. Iodine will do if you don't have a water filter. You don't need to buy a bunch of new stuff, unless you are looking to upgrade your gear anyhow.

The Jesuits

The Jesuits are a very powerful political, as well as spiritual, force in Tarahumara-land. They have been in these parts for a long time, they speak Tarahumara, and they have a death grip on Tarahumara salvation. The Tarahumaras take the Jesuits very seriously and they fear them. Most Tarahumaras who have had any formal education, studied under the Jesuits. And, for the last decade or so, they have been taught in Tarahumara. The Jesuits role in your visit will probably be minimal, but don't underestimate their influence with the Tarahumaras. I'll be offering some insights into this important aspect of Tarahumara life throughout the book.

Some Final Observations

- *Tarahumara Ranchitos.* You will notice lots of dots on your maps with place-names. Do not assume these are little towns. They are, for the most part, ranchitos—little Tarahumara settlements with usually no more than a handful of dwellings. Do not count on buying anything at a ranchito. This is not to say that you might not be able to buy a little food, if you really need it and they really have it. Just don't plan on it. A couple of the small Mexican outback villages have very tiny stores selling soft drinks, crackers, and sardines.

- *Thievery.* I have near-perfect confidence in the honesty of the Tarahumaras. You want to be careful in and around Mexican settlements, but no more so than around rural settlements in the U.S. Several popular tourist destinations in Tarahumara-land are starting to get hit with rip-off problems. I will make mention of these places when appropriate.

- *Rainy Season.* Between about mid-July and mid-September, it rains a lot in Copper Canyon Country, usually in the form of late afternoon cloudbursts. In addition to watching your rear for lightning in the high country, keep a lookout for high water in the canyons—even very small ones. During rainy season, river levels are much higher on a day-to-day basis. You will not be able to cross the Urique below Divisadero, for instance, until several weeks after rainy season ends. At the same time, flash floods are the most powerful natural phenomenon in Tarahumara-land. A bone-dry, fairly small arroyo can suddenly became a major-league torrent with little notice. It doesn't even have to be raining or even cloudy where you are. As long as it's raining up-canyon from you, you're in danger. Never camp in canyon bottoms, no matter how small, no matter how dry, during rainy season. I have lived for almost twenty years in flash-flood territory, and I have seen unbelievable damage caused by seemingly innocuous little creeks. Likewise, just because a river, like the Urique, is flowing fast and strong in flood stage, doesn't mean that it is immune from relative flash flooding. Water levels, even those that are already very high, can rise very quickly. And very fatally. Please take this seriously.

- *Drugs.* In some places in Copper Canyon Country, especially around Batopilas and in Sinforosa Canyon, this can be a serious situation. But, if you act intelligently, you will have no problems. The main drug of concern in Tarahumara-land is marijuana, though none is cultivated, that I have seen, near any of the route itineraries I have described in this book. The people who grow this weed, if the tales be true, all lack senses of humor. They carry weapons, and I have no doubt they would use them under the right circumstances. Should you find yourself in the midst of a pot field, you need to act NOW. This is not the time to thank Buddha for your good fortune, while setting up camp with one hand and stuffing sticky buds into your pocket with the other. You need to leave the area immediately. Retrace your footsteps, no matter the inconvenience factor. If you are confronted, play stupid. They will likely suspect you of being a Yanqui Fed. (The U.S. Drug Enforcement Agency operates big time in Copper Canyon Country.) You need to convince them otherwise. If you succeed in convincing them that you are nothing more than a disoriented tourist, who has NOT SEEN anything suspicious and who would not know it if he/she had, then you will likely just be escorted away rather briskly.

The military presence can be strong in this area, especially on the road between Creel and Batopilas, in Batopilas itself, and in Sinforosa Canyon. I have talked to many people, some so straight-looking that you can't help but giggle when they relate their story, who have been stopped at military roadblocks and questioned, sometimes with weird little macho threats thrown in, about whether or not they are carrying vast amounts of drugs in their pockets.

I have not personally met with any military checkpoints in this part of Mexico, though I have had to deal with three or four of them in the state of Guerrero. Despite the fact that they are very strange in a lot of ways, the checkpoints are to be taken seriously. Don't break into any monologues about them not being able to do this because, by damn, you're an American citizen!

A good thing to do in Batopilas, and this is a good thing to do in small towns all over Mexico, is to ask around town if there are any areas that the townsfolk would recommend visiting and any that you should stay away from. You will be told exactly what areas are off-limits.

- *Sun.* Be extremely careful of sunburn, even in the dead of winter, maybe even especially in the dead of winter because many visitors from northern climes will be arriving on the scene seriously white. I am a person who tans easily and burns only under extreme circumstances, and I have been scorched in Copper Canyon Country. Protect yourself with hat, sunscreen, and long-sleeved clothing.

Enough of the preliminaries, let's hit the trail.

3

Creel, Your Gateway to Copper Canyon Country

Creel is a dusty—or muddy, depending on the precipitation situation—slag heap of a boondock burg that just happens to be sitting smack dab in the middle of one of the most geo-physically and culturally wonderful places in the known universe: the Sierra Tarahumara, 10,000-foot, plus or minus, rounded mountains that are part of the Sierra Madre Occidental.

Creel is not, despite what many tourist-type magazine stories have said to the contrary, mere spitting distance from any of the barrancas. The closest canyon view is at least 12 miles away (the headwaters of Tararecua Canyon). It is, however, the most noteworthy orientation point for Copper Canyon Country, even if you start your hike from somewhere else, which you probably will.

Nor is Creel "hip" in any sense of the word. There are no funky bistros with interesting travelers from all over the planet sitting around swapping lies about exotic locales with unpronounceable names—a la Panajachel, Guatemala, or Cuzco, Peru. Creel is no oasis of the road. It *is* the road.

This is not to say that Creel is totally without its redeeming values. Quite the contrary. I have come to love this place—but, like my love for heavy ales and Mozart's "Requiem," it was an acquired taste.

Creel is the kind of rough-and-tumble frontier town that those of us who shop for clothes solely at places like Banana Republic and L. L. Bean envision—maybe even fantasize—ourselves feeling perfectly at home in. (By the way, it is tempting to pronounce Creel as a two-syllable word: CREE-uhl. In Spanish, it is distinctly a mono-syllable, pronounced CRIL, with the "i" having an almost piercingly long "e" sound.)

Because Creel is on the world-famous Chihuahua-Pacific Railroad, about six hours, depending on the mood of the railroad gods, from Chihuahua City and eight from Los Mochis, on the Pacific coast, thousands of gringo tourists, covering the gamut from hard-core backpackers to senior citizen travel club members, end up spending time here. But a fairly low percentage of these visitors really tap into Creel's potential. They do little more than get off the train, go to their hotel rooms, take a short, guided daytrip or two, rummage through a couple of Tarahumara gift shops and get back on the train, sometimes very eagerly, a day or two later.

In part, that's because Creel's roots lie not in catering to visitors, but, rather, in silver mining and timber harvesting. The natural resources-based economy has made Chihuahua one of Mexico's most affluent states, and, since Creel can be considered, at the very least, a vertebra in the backbone of Chihuahua's wealth, there never has been much of a need to cultivate a tourist trade. As a result, Creel's first paved road—which actually bypasses this town of about eight thousand residents—was only built in the mid-1980s.

Founded in 1907 as a railroad town, Creel (full name: Estacion Creel) was named after Enrique Creel, who was twice governor of the state of Chihuahua. Until 1961, when the C-P Railroad was finally completed through to the west coast, this was the end of the line and thus, the embarkation point for those residents of Copper Canyon Country bent on making a foray out into civilization, usually meaning Chihuahua City, which is not exactly Paris.

When your average visitor hops off the train in Creel, you can almost hear them mutter, "*This* is Creel?!" as the local herds of piglets, curs, and snotty-nosed children immediately start sniffing around their luggage. And, in addition to what we will tactfully term a "lack of spit and polish," the attitude of the townsfolk towards visitors has traditionally fallen considerably short of the *mi casa es su casa* mind-set prevalent in much of rural Mexico. There are those who may even go so far

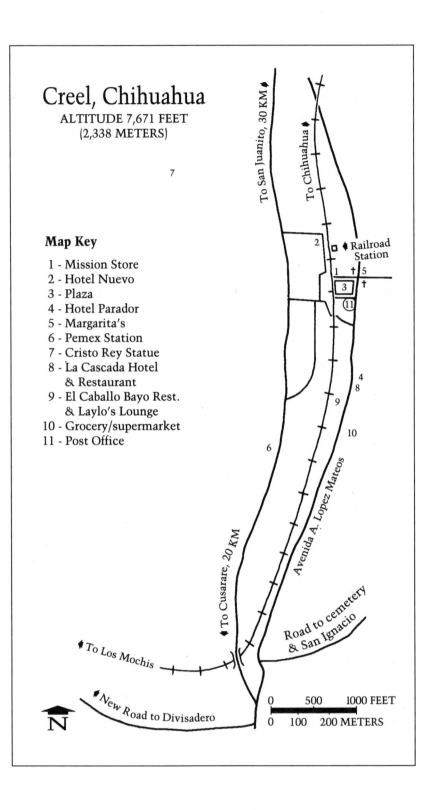

Creel, Chihuahua

ALTITUDE 7,671 FEET
(2,338 METERS)

Map Key

1 - Mission Store
2 - Hotel Nuevo
3 - Plaza
4 - Hotel Parador
5 - Margarita's
6 - Pemex Station
7 - Cristo Rey Statue
8 - La Cascada Hotel
   & Restaurant
9 - El Caballo Bayo Rest.
   & Laylo's Lounge
10 - Grocery/supermarket
11 - Post Office

To San Juanito, 30 KM

To Chihuahua

Railroad Station

Avenida A. Lopez Mateos

To Cusarare, 20 KM

Road to cemetery & San Ignacio

To Los Mochis

New Road to Divisadero

N

0   500   1000 FEET
0   100 200 METERS

as to say that the folks who live in and around Creel can be standoffish to the point of surliness.

With regards the Tarahumaras, few of whom actually live in Creel, though hundreds roam its streets daily, this standoffishness can be forgiven. Like most Indians in Mexico, the Tarahumaras "enjoy" secondary citizen status—to the degree that they are not exactly encouraged and sometimes even "discouraged" from entering many of the area's eating and drinking establishments, although this is changing—ever so slowly.

What all this amounts to is that Creel has managed to remain, for better and for worse, a *real* town, despite its proximity to the Chihuahua-Pacific Railroad, and despite the ever-increasing gringo hordes. That, of course, to many of us, is what makes Creel such a compelling, even refreshing, place to visit and hang out in.

The silver and timber industries have, in the past twenty-five years, fallen on relatively hard times, caused at least partially because the raw materials necessary for the viability of those industries—namely sizeable trees and rich, easily accessible ore—have been exploited to the point where it's becoming harder and harder to exploit what little is left. (If you have not already done so, please read the preface to the second edition for more about the timber industry.)

As a result, the hitherto-unmined, tourist-borne currency is looking better and better to Creel townsfolk at the same time that tourists—Americans, Europeans (especially Germans), and Australians, mostly—are searching far and wide for more ruggedly spectacular travel destinations.

A match made in heaven in the making. The town, consequently, has undergone something of a facelift in the past decade. Many of the adobe buildings along the main drag, Avenida Lopez Mateos (which was coincidentally cobble-stoned about nine minutes before Mexican President Salinas dropped by for a visit in the early 1990s), have been re-stuccoed and painted in the last few years. The main town plaza has been overhauled a couple of times, and a second, smaller plaza has been constructed behind the post office. Much work has been done on the town's water and sewer systems. Many of the backstreet potholes, which can easily be mistaken for one of the area's major canyons—I've seen tourists taking pictures of these things—are being filled in. Several nice new hotels and restaurants have been built, and several of the older lodging facilities and eateries have been upgraded dramatically.

At the same time, it seems the locals are becoming more friendly toward visitors. And I don't think it's faked in any, for example, Colorado ski town chamber of commerce sponsored "please-don't-hate-the-tourists-too-much" campaign. The first time I visited Creel, in 1983, my blue-eyed self was told in no uncertain terms by the proprietress of one of the nicest and most successful lodging facilities for hundreds of miles, that Americans are creatures more suited to four legs than two.

On that first visit, I walked into the local billiards hall, all ready to engage in some low-rent cross-cultural male bonding, took one look around the establishment, decided "wrong place, wrong time," and started to back slowly out as the patrons thereabouts, most of whom, if memory serves me correctly, had huge scars on their grimacing faces, sent a class-action telegraphic message that said, in no uncertain terms, "Best be heading up the road, gringo, lest ye be gutted briskly."

This irritated me. So I stormed back in, grabbed hold of the biggest, ugliest, *smelliest* guy in there and I slammed him against the wall so hard that it cracked the plaster and sent shockwaves throughout the town. (You can still see the damage today.) Just kidding. Actually, I just squeaked a pitiful "Oh, no!" and ran away from the place at a dead sprint.

Anyhow, that was years ago. In the interim, things have mellowed considerably. The local business community is reaching out to tourists like never before. Many of the store signs in Creel now have English translations hanging next to them. A few have German translations. And I even shot several fairly pleasant games of pool in that same billiards hall before it moved to a less-conspicuous, non-main-street location.

While many of us may look at this facelift and demeanor metamorphosis as a sign that the Creel we know and sort of respect is heading down the tubes towards civility and couth, there is little risk that outsiders will start confusing Creel with, say Ixtapa or San Miguel de Allende. The place is simply too fundamentally sloppy.

There's only a couple of near-fancy hotels in town—the Parador de la Montaña, the Cascada (with its new indoor swimming pool), and Margarita's new hotel. All are more on a level with a Quality Inn than with a Marriott. If you want to eat at a restaurant where the ambience will more or less not offend Denny's-honed sensibilities, again, you've only got a few choices—El Caballo Bayo (the nicest restaurant in town), the Parador, and La Cascada. And, if you want to go out for a night on the town, there's only three places: the Parador, La Cascada, and Laylo's Lounge, all of which are located within a stone's throw of each other towards the west end of town.

Many of these facelift features are not exactly threatening the preferences of those who liked Creel the way it was. The water and sewage improvements have raised the system up to the point of being unreliable only 75 percent of the time. Filling in the backstreet pot holes amount to a Sisyphusian task. As soon as one "lake" is transformed into something resembling a street, another mystically opens up a few feet away. The plaza, oft repaired, remains in a constant state of near-completion. This stuff is not exactly going to have the Club Med set pouring in, though Creel could certainly use a few dozen bikini-clad females wandering around in search of some serious hedonism.

So, what all this facelift talk amounts to is little more than an assurance that the average gringo traveler—and here I'm talking more group-tour types—can stroll in and around Creel's nooks and crannies while experiencing only a modicum of gut-wrenching trepidation.

The backpacker/rough-traveler type, on the other hand, will eat this place up. Facelift or no facelift, Creel still retains enough of a sleazy third-world gee-dunk backwater feeling that all but the most intrepid of us will feel like we've gotten our money's worth even before heading out into the backcountry.

And backcountry is what it's all about in Creel. While Creel is a sore sight for eyes, it sits in the heart of some sweet country. Located just west of the Continental Divide at an elevation of 7,669 feet (2,337 meters), Creel is in a high valley circled by wonderful rock formations. Pine forests surround the valley. A huge religious statue stands on a hill above town.

Even those on very limited time schedules should plan on spending at least one night in Creel. If you are heading to Batopilas, Humira Bridge, Recohuata Hot Springs, Guachochi, or El Tejabán, you will have no choice but to spend a night here, unless you are driving. And if you do have your own vehicle, stop here for at least an afternoon. Remember, this is your last semi-reliable gas stop until Batopilas, which is even less semi-reliable.

If you plan on starting your hike in Divisadero, Posada de las Barrancas, or Urique, I still advise a stop in Creel. If you are coming from Chihuahua City, stay over and then catch the first train heading west the following afternoon. If you are coming from Los Mochis, continue on to Creel, returning west to wherever it is you want to start hiking the next day.

Creel is the only town resembling an orientation point for Copper Canyon Country. On a practical level, Creel is the only place in Tarahumara-land where you can buy maps. The Tarahumara Mission Store, which is right next to the bank, generally has a good supply of 1:50,000 and 1:250,000 topographic maps for the whole area, except Basaseachi Falls. Sometimes they will be sold out of a specific 1:50,000 map, in which case, go with the 1:250,000 topo, which should get you through, unless, of course—this being Mexico we're talking about here— they're sold out of *those*. In which case, you cuss a little, angrily kick a few rocks, and go to plan B: ask around for some verbal input from other hikers and/or hire a local guide.

Though there are minuscule stores in just about every small town where there is a road, Creel is the only place with the capacity for stocking a backcountry trip of more than a few hours. But, more than just candy bars, instant soup, and beers, Creel affords backpackers the chance to rub elbows with others of their ilk. As I hinted in Chapter 1, in order to get the most out of Copper Canyon, this book will best be utilized in combination with your own route-finding abilities. That need not be limited to playing Daniel Boone in the middle of the woods. It can start right in beautiful downtown Creel—by chewing the fat with folks who have just returned from the backcountry, or with folks who have talked with folks who have just returned from the backcountry.

The best, maybe even the only place to do this is Margarita's Guest House (Casa de Huespedes), which is located right on the plaza. It's between the two churches and doesn't look anything like a guest house from the outside. If your urban orientation skills aren't up to snuff, worry not, because within a second of disembarking from the train, you will find yourself facing a minimum of several people—Margarita's employees—imploring you to follow them to Creel's best-known budget lodging facility. Margarita has been running her guest house since 1983. Two of my ne'er-do-well compadres and I were among her first guests, and therein lies a story best told past midnight in a watering hole.

Margarita's is a place where rough travelers from all over the world, most young, most on fairly tight budgets, bed down in clean, comfortable accommodations ranging from bunkbeds in a dormitory room to private rooms with private baths. Margarita's almost—almost—makes up for the fact that Creel lacks anything even resembling a funky travelers' pub.

Since Margarita's meals, which are part of the price—meaning just about everybody eats breakfast and supper there—are served communally, guests have ample opportunity to shoot the breeze with each other. And many of those guests are backpackers. There are maps on the walls and a community bulletin board for messages to people with exotic names who should be arriving by spring. You will very likely be able to get information not in this book, or at least some different perspectives. And, if you are of a mind to hook up with another party, this is the most likely place to do it.

Since Margarita justifiably asks her boarders to pipe down by 10 PM, you have to head out into the crazy Creel night if you're going to have any fun. This is not meant to get your hopes up too high. "Fun" in Creel, you must remember, is relative to "no fun" in Creel, or "fun" in a Burmese jail, rather than to, say "fun" Tonapah, Nevada.

Not to worry, for several reasons. First, if you've just come in from two weeks in the deep canyons, you will not be too choosy. Second, I have, through coincidence of cosmic magnitude rather than through any predisposition to being a mobile party epicenter, had some wacky times in Creel. And, third, once you hook up with a group of kindred-soul backpackers/ world travelers, you will, needless to say, need to find a place to wet your whistle, 'cause, you know, lie-swapping makes a person thirsty.

Okay, you're out on the town and, since they're the only places, you head either for the Parador, the Cascada, or Laylo's Lounge. I especially recommend Laylo's, which is attached to the Caballo Bayo restaurant. The bartender, Fernando, who I have known for years, is one of the nicest guys you will ever meet in your entire life. He speaks fairly good (and constantly improving) English, but will, like most Mexicans, go along with your pidgin Spanish up until the point where you do something like order a glass of spider web on wet dirt, at which time you will be gently corrected, before conversation instantaneously, if that is your preference, returns to Español.

The crowd in all three of Creel's imbiberies will be more middle-class tour-group-oriented than the crowd at Margarita's—meaning you can find yourself rapping one minute with a gaggle of hyper-Republicans from Sun City, Arizona, the next with a group of dirt bikers from outside Tulsa.

Locals also frequent these bars, especially Laylo's, so it's a good chance to learn some of the ins and outs of Tarahumara-land, most of which will be dead wrong. Mexicans in these parts, especially the older, more affluent ones you will meet in fairly pricey bars, which all of Creel's are (about $2 U.S. per carbonated beverage), are not good sources for backcountry information. They are quick to toss out tidbits about the canyon country terrain and the Tarahumaras that fall somewhere between innuendo and slander. But don't back out of a conversation just because someone obviously has no idea what he's talking about. After all, you're here to dial into every component of Tarahumara-land and the misconceptions of the locals who, although they have lived here all their lives, have never walked more than three feet into the canyons, is part of that.

And, besides, the locals are usually very quick to buy you drinks. If you are an "unescorted" female, you may want to be careful about accepting them, lest the wrong impression be given. Unfortunately, many Mexican men still subscribe to the misconception that gringas can be had for the price of a drink or two. Or, at the very least, if a gringa accepts a drink or two, then she is saying that she is in the market for a little sack action. Judging from what many women have told me, including my wife, dealing with this attitude can be inconvenient to the point of downright bothersome.

If you are male, you've got nothing to worry about. If some local offers to buy you a drink, toast his good health and drink it. Then, if you can afford to, buy him one. Mexico, is not like, say, the Dominican Republic, where, if you are a gringo, it is automatically assumed, by everyone except you, that you will be paying for all the drinks all the time.

Besides a few dayhike possibilities, that's about it for Creel on the practical level. While waiting for transportation, you will almost certainly take a peek inside the Tarahumara artisan stores, of which there are about five or six. This is well worth doing. If you are interested in buying Tarahumara-made goods, see a copy of *Material World of the Tarahumara* listed in the bibliography. Tarahumara arts and crafts, especially pots, are hot on the collectors' market these days, having infiltrated the hoity-toity markets of northern New Mexico. So, a little homework might be worth the effort.

Remember this about Creel: Its practicality as an orientation point for Copper Canyon Country transcends supply buying and networking. This town offers a good chance to lay eyes on large numbers of Tarahumaras. Check out the way they are, as best you can under the circumstances. A little eye-balling on the streets of Creel may come in handy later—on the trail.

Particulars

Hikes. There are several possibilities right out of metro Creel. On the hill just north of town is the sort-of-famous Cristo Rey statue. The view from there of the valley is very nice. It takes about 15 minutes to get up there from the plaza. Cross over the paved road on the west side of the statue-

adorned hill and follow one of the many paths to the top.
There are several small religious shrines below and around
the statue, and, often, there will be people up there tending to
those shrines and/or praying to the Saint of their choice.
I have learned over the years that raucous gringo gatherings,
replete with the kinds of beverages appropriate to a short dayhike, are viewed by praying people with a certain amount of
disdain. So, be prepared to pretend to be reverent, or failing
that, non-irreverent, at least until whatever praying might be
going on is over.

Many people hike the two miles to San Ignacio Mission,
which is actually on the other side of the ridge to the south
of Creel. To get there, follow Avenida Lopez Mateos—Creel's
main drag—south out of town, towards the cemetery. Continue past the cemetery and wind around behind the ridge.
A very easy walk. Mission is interesting. Scenery is wonderful. The Tarahumaras of San Ignacio *ejido* now charge admission to enter their lands, so be prepared to fork over a couple
of pesos to visit the mission. You can also hike about 8 kilometers via dirt road from San Ignacio to Lake Arareco.

The dirt road through San Ignacio continues east for
about 16 kilometers (10 miles), to a point where you can
overlook the Rio Conchos. From the overlook, you can bushwhack down to the river. It would be possible to hook into
several other hikes from this point (Chapters 7 and 18).
There are many, many trails intersecting with this dirt
road—good places to begin your own personal explorations
of Tarahumara-land.

Many people walk, hitchhike, or ride on a rented bicycle
to Lake Arareco, eight kilometers (five miles) south of Creel
on the paved road to Batopilas. I've talked to many people
who have been incorrectly informed as to how far the lake is
from Creel. If you are self-propelling, plan to take most of the
day to get there and back. And bring food and water. More
about Lake Arareco in Chapter 5.

Lodging. Creel is full of hotels, from exceedingly seedy to
almost fancy. I have not heard about any gringo staying in any
of the truly scuzzy-looking ones, but I know you can get basic
accommodations for about $3 U.S. a night. More respectable
alternatives are Margarita's, which starts off at about $5 U.S.
for a dormitory room bed and goes on up to about $20 U.S. a
night per couple for a private room with bath. Breakfast and

supper are included. Breakfast is usually fried eggs, beans, toast, tortillas, and coffee. Supper often consists of a stew or soup, some sort of starch, beans, and tortillas.

I've stayed twice at the Hotel Nuevo, across the tracks from the train station. Fairly nice. About $20 per couple, with a private bath, meals not included. Ask for the room with the fireplace (*chimanea*). The Nuevo also has a restaurant. The Korachi, across the tracks from the plaza, is about the same as the Nuevo, although they do offer some cheaper rooms without private baths.

The Parador and the Cascada are the most expensive and nicest hotels in town. Prices start at about $50 a night per couple, without meals. Each has a restaurant which is, likewise, among the most expensive in town.

Restaurants. Creel has more eateries than Carter's got liver pills. I like Lupita's and La Cabaña, which are both pretty cheap. Both are located right on Avenida Lopez Mateos, between the plaza and the Parador.

As far as I can tell, after the Parador and El Caballo Bayo, just about every restaurant in town offers about the same fare for about the same price with about the same type of ambience. Be forewarned: Some restaurants lack bathrooms and beer. Sometimes they lack bathrooms and beer only some of the time. And some restaurants don't have menus. You'll have to ask what they have. (*Que hay?*) Or you will have to ask if they have a certain dish, for example, enchiladas. (*Hay enchiladas?*)

Local dishes are very similar to what we call Mexican food in the States. Burritos, fried chicken, beef steak with salsa, scrambled eggs with chilies, quesadillas. You will not eat healthy here. Tough territory for vegetarians because beans and flour tortillas always have lard in them. Especially tough for vegans, because there's just not much on any of the menus you will be able to eat.

Mail Service. The post office (*correo*) is located in the building on the southwest corner of the plaza. Go in the main entrance, look for doors on the right. It takes as long as two weeks for a post card to reach the States. You are better off toting your newly bought souvenirs home with you. Postal rates are about the same as in the States.

Telephone. There is a long-distance phone office right next door to Margarita's. Collect and non-collect calls are easily

placed. Collect calls to the States aren't cheap—as much as
$25 for 15 minutes.

Banking/Money Changing. Banco Serfin is located on the
plaza, right next door to the Mission Store. Travelers checks
are cashed only at certain times of day, usually about 11 AM.
There's no problem with converting cash—dollars only—to
pesos, but I've seen people stranded for a day or two because
they've had problems changing travelers checks. (I have, sad
to report, been one of those people.) More and more, though,
Creel's business community is coming to understand that
travelers checks are basically the same as money. All the
hotels and some of the restaurants, as well as several of the
stores, will accept travelers checks as payment for goods and
services. You may even be able to talk local business people
into cashing travelers checks for you. Credit cards are even
making headway in Creel, though only at the nicer restaurants and hotels.

Groceries/Trail Supplies. There are at least a billion grocery
stores (*abarrotes*) in Creel, though only one real supermarket,
located about a block west of the Parador, on the same side of
the street. Made (or grown)-in-Mexico products are pretty inexpensive. Anything imported will be twice the cost as the same
thing in the States. Plan on buying fresh fruit in Creel. The
selection is extensive and cheap. Buy beer in *abarrotes* (there
are several in Creel with liquor licenses) rather than in restaurants. Tecate and Dos Equis, in cans (*en lata*), should cost about
70 cents a can. *Abarrotes* are also good places to buy spirits,
although liquor stores are generally cheaper. A good liquor
store is one building west of the Pemex station, on the same
side of the road. Best buys for trail purposes are Mexican vodka,
about $3.50 U.S. a bottle, and tequila, which can cost less than
$1 U.S. a liter. Buy the best tequila you can afford, for the sake
of your head the next morning. Remember, many places—like
Batopilas and Panalachi—are dry towns. No alcohol sold at all.

Hardware. There are several hardware stores (*ferreterias*)
in town. Here you will try, probably with little success, to
buy white gas (*gasolina blanca*) or, with more success,
kerosene (*keroseno*).

Gas. The Pemex station is on the bypass road, about a
mile past the turn-off to Divisadero. Prices for this, the
world's worst gasoline, have soared in recent years to about
$1.60 U.S. a gallon for Nova (regular) (1993 figures). No Extra

available, and unleaded is still several years away from Creel. Diesel is available. The station sometimes runs out of gas for a day or two and, frequently, lines are long. You will need to journey elsewhere for oil (*aceite*). The attendant will point the way. It's close. You will also have to buy octane enhancer (*aditivo*) at the oil place.

Car Repairs. There are several places in town. Mexican mechanics are very good, unless you show up driving one of those brand-new, sci-fi-looking jobbies, like a Lexus or something. Give a Mexican a 1978 Ford pick-up, and he will fix the hell out of it. Mexicans, unlike many American mechanics, actually *fix* things. They don't just replace things. Tires (*llantas*) can be purchased here, but are very expensive.

Tours. Just about every hotel in Creel offers generic and customized tours of the area, ranging in duration from a few hours to several days. When a certain hike is best accessed by one of these tours, I make mention of it in the appropriate chapter.

And remember, Creel's businesses are big fans of siesta time, usually about 1:30 to 3:30 in the afternoon.

4

Cusarare Falls and Environs

Twenty-two kilometers (13.8 miles) south of Creel on the road to Batopilas is a road sign pointing the way to the mission of Cusarare (koo-SAH-rah-ray), which is one kilometer off the highway to the left (east) if you are traveling south. About half a kilometer further south on the main road, on the right, you will see another sign, this one to *Las Cabañas del Cobre*—the Copper Canyon Lodge, which is sometimes advertised as the Sierra Madre Hiking Lodge.

Take a right a few feet past the sign on a rough little dirt road that looks like it is probably heading back to someone's whiskey still rather than to a highly recommended, thirty-one-room lodging facility. Cross a small creek that borders a Tarahumara homestead. To the left, within 100 yards of the main road, there is a small log cabin housing a Tarahumara gift shop and a gate. The large wooden building on the opposite side of the parking lot is the lodge. You can't miss it. There's a big sign on the roof.

The parking lot is, essentially, the trailhead for the 45-minute (one-way) hike to Cusarare Falls (*La Cascada del Cusarare*). Dozens of people—some lodge guests, most not—stroll to the falls daily. This is probably the most-hiked stretch of trail in all of Tarahumara-land, because the trail is not only used by lots of gringos, but also by Tarahumaras heading into or out of the outback. If you're here at the right time, you can pass a whole Tarahumara clan—the men and boys traveling as a group several hundred yards ahead of the brightly clad women and girls.

What many people do not know, however, is that the Copper Canyon Lodge is also the jumping off point for numerous other short hikes—one of which leads to some wonderful and seemingly abandoned Tarahumara cave dwellings. I say "seemingly" because you can never tell how long Tarahumaras might be gone from a dwelling.

The Copper Canyon Lodge is owned by Skip McWilliams and his ex-wife and still-business-partner, Suzanne Rossi, of Troy, Michigan. They bought the place in 1986 after hearing it was going to be turned into a disco, which, if you've ever set foot in a Mexican disco, you can understand why they jumped into action.

Many businesses might be displeased at the thought of dozens of non-customers using their parking lot to gain backcountry access. The staff of the lodge, however, operates under the assumption that their facility is a social gathering place for the entire Cusarare area. Non-guests are invited to hang out and sip a beverage. The lodge has one of the best late-afternoon reading porches I have ever utilized. And, despite the fact that the lodge has no electricity, there are chilled Coronas in the dining room.

You can also eat supper at the lodge, unless all the rooms are full—meaning there won't be any extra seats at the tables. A good idea is to plan an afternoon walk to the falls. Stop in the lodge before you leave and make reservations for dinner. Time it so you return by happy hour, about 6 PM. Dinner is served at seven. Margaritas here are excellent. And local music legend, Rafael Morquecho, provides nightly entertainment.

The trail to the falls—which are almost 100 feet high—initially follows the creek downriver on the same side as the lodge. Shortly after the first bend, it crosses the stream on a small bridge. From there on, it remains on the left-hand side as you walk downriver.

After the trail goes uphill for a few hundred yards, it intersects with a primitive logging road. Almost immediately after intersecting this "road," you will be asked to pay one Nuevo Peso per person to pass. At this point, you should stop and make a mental note of this intersection. There is no sign and it is easy to miss your exit on the way back—especially if you return towards dusk. It's not like you'll fall into a massive vat of decomposing yogurt byproducts or anything if you cruise by the trail junction on your way back. It'll just make it easier to get to those margaritas back at the lodge if you don't.

The trail to the falls is a cakewalk. You should be able to follow it all the way without any problems. At that, I should point out that we heard of one male human, a professional tour guide, no less, who, after being told by yours truly that, one, the trail sticks to the left-hand side of the river as you are walking downstream, and, two, it's so obvious a clam could follow it, still managed to find himself on the wrong side of the stream after losing the trail. One of the members of his tour related the story some hours later, as he was warming his wet feet by the fire.

At one point, the trail forks, with the right-hand fork crossing the river and entering a small arroyo. This occurs about halfway between the falls and the lodge, at a point where there's a monstrous rock on the other side of the river. If you follow that arroyo for a mile or so, you come to a wonderful little Tarahumara ranchito—its name I either forgot or never knew. This is also the point where you begin the Cusarare to Recohuata Hot Springs hike described at the end of Chapter 5.

Anyhow, the trail to Cusarare Falls makes for a pleasant, hands-in-your-pockets and song-on-your-lips, by-the-babbling-brook kinda stroll. Absolutely perfect for those lacking a lot of extra time, those who are not in good shape, or those who want a mellow introduction to Copper Canyon Country.

The canyon formed by Cusarare Creek is only a couple hundred feet deep here. At almost any point, you could scramble up either side for a view. The creek flows for about 25 miles, until it runs into Copper Canyon itself, less than three miles upriver from the great bend of the Urique. By the time it joins the Urique, Cusarare Canyon is over 4,000 feet deep.

You don't want to follow the river that far down unless you are seriously hardcore. I have been to the intersection of the Cusarare and the Urique, but I got there the "easy" way—by walking down from Divisadero. I had no desire to hike up the Cusarare. The canyon bottom is simply too tight and boulder-strewn. Very dangerous. *Not* mellow. Completely unlike our walk to the falls.

Depending on the water level, you may not be aware that you are nearing the falls. No major tributaries enter the Cusarare between the lodge and the falls. The water you see is the water you get. Unless it is rainy season or shortly after a storm, Cusarare Falls is not very voluminous. And, thus, you will hear no roar well in advance.

The flood plain is fairly wide—maybe 50 yards—but only a few ribbons of water, each a couple of feet wide, form the falls for most of the year. Before we hiked to the falls for the first time, my wife, Gay, and I met a gentleman who had just returned from the drop and couldn't believe how unimpressive it was with regards volume of water being dispatched. The falls were, we were told, hardly worth visiting—at least to one who "has an intimate familiarity with Niagara Falls."

This knowing soul made the decision to visit the falls based on photos that were taken during the late-summer flood season. Gay and I headed out ready for disappointment, because all the photos we had seen were also taken at high water. It was midafternoon in early November. Temperatures were somewhere in the high 70s. The sky was crystal clear. The walking was easy. It was such a relaxing stroll that we didn't give a hoot if Cusarare Falls was dry.

Halfway there, we passed a couple of teenage Tarahumara females selling sashes on the side of the trail. Seemed like it was their regular retail space—which should give you some indication of how busy this trail is. (Since that time, the number of Tarahumara vendors alongside the Cusarare Falls trail has increased dramatically.) Then, before we even worked up a good sweat, there we were—at the falls. Relative lack of water or not, this place is hip. When the flow is so minimal, you can, without much danger, walk to the very edge and peer over. At the bottom, a stand of scrub oaks was showing its fall colors. Down below, we noticed a couple of nice turquoise pools that looked very swimmable. The trail continues downstream from the top of the falls to a couple of overlooks from where most of the highwater photos of this place were taken.

We followed the last remnants of the trail, still sticking to the same side, down to the bottom. We rock-hopped over to those pools, stripped off in the hot sunshine, embraced lovingly, stuck our big toes in the water—COLD—said the hell with this, got dressed, ate lunch, and drank a few luke-warm Tecates.

This coldness situation should not deter you from enter-taining the dip potential of this place, but Gay and I are profes-sional weenies when it comes to cold water. So, you may stick *your* big toe in while standing naked with *your* naked partner and reach a different conclusion than we did. The pools are attractive enough to justify some swim-oriented rumination.

About two months after this dayhike, two solid days of rain and snow broke over Tarahumara-land. Cusarare Creek rose several feet. Gay returned to the falls to check it out. Though the water was still not nearly as high as it is during rainy sea-son, the entire flood plain was filled to overflowing. The pools at the bottom were inaccessible. And you wouldn't have been able to stand at the top to peer over without being swept into the afterlife. So, with highwater, you get power and splendor to stand and ogle at. With low water, you get wonderful pools that you can skinny dip and drink beer in. Your choice.

This is the extent of most folks' visit to this part of Copper Canyon Country. They walk to the falls. They walk back. A nice dayhike, for sure, but just the tip of the overly used metaphoric iceberg. Just upriver from the falls, on the same side as the trail, you pass under a blown-down tree with names carved all over it. Right there, to your left if you are heading downstream, you will notice a small side canyon. On the left side of that side canyon, as you are standing with your back to Cusarare Creek, you should be able to make out a very faint trail. It becomes more apparent a little farther up, though it is never as well worn as the trail to the falls.

Follow this up for a couple miles and keep your eyes open. On your left, you pass several small side canyons with impres-sive rock formations. Many of these sport Tarahumara cave dwellings. As well, there are a few set up on cliff faces that are not part of any side canyon.

If you cross the main side canyon and make your way up to the opposite rim, you can walk out and get a good view of Cusarare Canyon. While up there, you may stumble across a few Tarahumara campsites. We also found a spring thereabouts.

This is an area that has more than its fair share of Tarahumara artifacts, but everything you see belongs to someone who probably plans on coming back one day to find it there. Please don't add anything to your pack.

Gay and I have also descended into this dry side canyon several miles up from the trail from the lodge to the falls. If you look out from the front porch of the lodge, you will see a Tarahumara homestead on the other side of Cusarare Creek. This is the home of one of the lodge's longtime employees, Patricio, who you will hear more about in Chapter 17.

Walk to the other side of the creek and make your way up the ridge. There will be a faint trail that doesn't really seem to go anywhere even if you find it—so don't worry if you don't. Follow this ridge west for a half hour or so, then descend the back side. We went down into a heavily wooded bottom, climbed up and over the next ridge, and then down into the side canyon that, if followed down, will intersect with the trail to the falls right where the blown-down tree is. Unless you stumble onto the same spring we found, this is a dry hike. Including putzing around a slew of Tarahumara cave dwellings, it took us about three hours to make our way from the lodge to the falls via this route.

The hot springs at Basirecota are about five hard hours downstream from Cusarare Falls. We have been told that there is no continuous trail. We have also been told that the going is fairly tough, but not dangerous. You will have to pick your way along, sometimes hiking on river level, sometimes going up a few hundred feet. This section is a very good introduction to following rivers in Tarahumara-land.

You can also get to Basirecota by hiking around through the mountains. Hire a Tarahumara guide in Cusarare—my aforementioned amigo, Sahuaripa, knows this route well—and follow the first day's itinerary for Skip McWilliam's "Canyon Crossing" trip. (Chapter 9) Then, if you feel like looping, return via Cusarare Creek. This should take about eight hard hours, so, you will probably want to camp at Basirecota. From there, you can see a couple of caves high on a cliff face. At least one of these caves is a Tarahumara burial cave.

Another trip from Copper Canyon Lodge is the day-long hike to El Tejabán, which is a Tarahumara ranchito perched on the rim overlooking the Urique River. The photos on the main advertising posters in the lodge were taken at El Tejaban. From there, you can descend into Copper Canyon in a few hours because the canyon is not that deep there—only a few thousand feet. (Please see Chapter 8 for more on El Tejabán.)

Two last notes on the Cusarare Falls area. First, Gay and I poked our noses into seemingly abandoned Tarahumara cave dwellings before we fully understood that such an act is considered to be bad manners at the very least and trespassing at worst. We have since modified our behavior. If a cave dwelling looks like it has been unused for some years, we will get close enough for a good look inside, but only a look. If the cave dwelling looks from a distance to be even seasonally occupied, we move on without intruding any closer. Good advice.

Second, don't drink the water in Cusarare Creek unless you purify the hell out of it. You can top your water bottles off from a well house behind the Tarahumara gift shop near the lodge.

Particulars

This area is covered by the 1:250,000 San Juanito map or the 1:50,000 Creel map.

Both Margarita's and the Parador offer transportation from Creel to the Copper Canyon Lodge parking lot. The fare is cheap, but the trip is contingent on there being enough people riding along. Though this is easier with regards transportation, you will be locked into a half-day trip—plenty of time to make it to Cusarare Falls and back, but not enough time to explore the area properly. You may want ride out with a tour group and then hitch back. Or, if there is no tour on a given day, hitch both ways. It should be pretty easy, though I have seen some people stranded for a few hours trying to get back into Creel. If there's traffic, you should get a ride fairly quickly.

As always, taxis are available on the plaza in Creel, across from the Mission Store. If the cabs are out on a run, you may have to wait a while.

The Copper Canyon Lodge staff meets every first-class train arriving in Creel, as well as some of the second-class trains. If they have room, you may be able to catch a ride to Cusarare with them. Offer to tip the driver a couple bucks. You may even want to stay at the lodge instead of in Creel. It is somewhat pricey compared to Margarita's, but, if you've got the bucks, it's a great place to stay. Meals are part of the deal and the lodge serves the best food I've eaten in Tarahumara-land—by far.

The staff will also pack a lunch for your dayhike to the falls, though again, this is somewhat pricey. Other than that, the only thing you can buy here is beer, cocktails, Mexican wine, which is quite good, and sodas. So, come prepared. That said, there is talk about building a small cafe at the falls. This could be done at any time, so ask at Margarita's about the situation.

5
Recohuata Hot Springs and Tararecua Canyon

This part of Copper Canyon Country holds more memories, good and bad, for me than any other part. Gay and I first visited Recohuata Hot Springs in late September 1984 with Norbert Bame and his wife, Lori. We had arrived in Creel the day before, like many people before us, with a burning desire to check this area out—but with no idea where to begin. At that time, the only map available in Creel was the Schmidt publication which, though well worth the money, is hardly the kind of map American backpackers are used to planning trips with. For one thing, it is not topographic—a handy feature in canyon country, where multi-thousand-foot-high cliffs dominate the landscape.

We hitched out of town on the road south to Batopilas. We knew from Schmidt's map that Lake Arareco was only a few miles outside of town, so we thought we would camp there for a night before cruising off in an as-yet undetermined direction. Our only desire was to at least lay eyes, if not boots, on the famed Copper Canyon.

We got a ride from an American expatriate who had lived in the area for years. This was good luck. He told us that, about a kilometer past the lake, we would come across a dirt road off to the right (west) that would lead us to Recohuata Hot Springs. (There is a road sign there now.) He laid a quick series of directions on us, laced with ten or twelve "lefts" and "rights" at places "we couldn't miss" before speeding off. We jotted down what we remembered of the directions, knowing full well that it would take a direct intervention by the luck gods for us to find the hot springs.

We hiked into the woods on the north lakeshore, set up camp, and proceeded to swim and sun the afternoon away. This lake is actually a small reservoir and supplies much of Creel's drinking water. It forms the headwaters of the Rio San Ignacio, the creek that flows by Recohuata Hot Springs and forms Tararecua (tah-rah-RAY-kwa) Canyon.

Arareco (which means "horseshoe" in Tarahumara, in reference to its shape) is one of the most beautiful small lakes I have even seen. It is surrounded by rugged rock formations and pine forests. You can spend most of a day hiking around it, though if you were gung-ho, you could make it around in a few hours. This is one of the more popular dayhikes for visitors to Creel who lack the time, inclination, or knowledge to venture further into the interior. (By the way, it now costs a few pesos to camp near Arareco, and you can even rent boats there.)

We got up early the next morning, mainly because we froze our glutes off all night. Since the four of us were on our way to Central America—this trip being but a small detour—we were carrying very light, fiber-pile tropical bags. At almost 8,000 feet (2,400 meters), this area can get right brisk at night, even in the late summer.

We began walking south on the road to Batopilas, which, at that time was still dirt. Just past the concrete 10-kilometer marker (the distance south of Creel), on the right-hand side, we did indeed spy a sad excuse for a dirt road heading off in the correct direction. We waited on the side of the road for a few minutes until a logging truck drove by. I flagged it down and asked if this was the way to Recohuata. The driver told us it was and proceeded to draw us a primitive map.

It wasn't long before we were all convinced that the driver of that logging truck was soon sitting in a bar in Creel with his cronies laughing his fool head off. Everyone was buying him beers and congratulating him on his expert job of sending the gringos on a wild hot springs chase.

The dirt track wound its way through dry pine forests, up and down rocky hills, past a few Tarahumara homesteads, along a dry creek bed or two—everywhere except down into a canyon. The guy who had picked us up hitching the day before had told us it was a six-kilometer walk to the rim.

This is a common problem with folks who have lived for long periods of time out of the U.S. They start getting their miles and kilometers confused. In 1988, Gay and I finally drove this route and measured the distance from the now-paved main road to the rim of Tararecua Canyon at 6.5 *miles*. Because Norb, Lori, Gay, and I were all mentally set for a mere four-mile jaunt, the extra two-and-a-half miles seemed interminable—especially because we had no idea whether we were anywhere near where we wanted to be.

Finally, towards late afternoon, we said something along the lines of "copulate this!" We had Schmidt's map, which we had been orienting all along. The jeep track we were hiking on was paralleling Tararecua Canyon—at least on paper. A few times, we were able to peer through the thick woods well enough to see what appeared to be the opposite rim of a canyon, though, from what we could see, not a very deep one. Since our map was not a topo, we had no earthly idea if our destination was in the bottom of some 2,000-meter-deep monster or at the head of some weenie little bugger that you could jump out of with a half-hearted running start.

It didn't really matter at this point whether the canyon we had seen through the trees was the right one or not. We were out of water, and it was getting late. So, at the first opportunity, we swung west. In a few minutes, we were staring down a side canyon to the one we had seen through the trees. There was a well-worn trail, so we headed down. Soon after, we could see what appeared to be a fairly good-sized stream flowing past a nice meadow.

The trail down was a maze of steep switchbacks. It took us about 45 minutes to get to the bottom of the side canyon. We crossed over the stream bed, found a camp littered with several years worth of trash, and made our way down to the main stream, which was clearly warmer than it "should" have been. We crossed and headed downstream because the canyon was more open in that direction.

Less than a quarter-mile later, we found ourselves, through no skill of our own, at Recohuata Hot Springs. The remnants of an old dwelling sat next to a crumbling old bath house. The water was perfecto. Not as hot as some of the springs in, say, the Gila National Forest of New Mexico, just comfortable enough to sit in for hours on end.

At this point, the campsite options were fairly limited, but, being pretty tired, we decided to sleep near the bath house anyway. Our plan was to hang out in this vicinity for three nights before retracing our footsteps back to Creel. Though we estimated the descent to Recohuata at only about 250 meters, the temperature had increased dramatically. While autumn was going full-swing on the rim, we were basking in summer in Tararecua, with daytime highs in the upper 90s. At night, those tropical bags were plenty sufficient.

Just downstream from the decaying bath house began a series of swimming holes on par with any I had ever seen outside the tropics, which, bionomically speaking this place is, despite the fact that latitudinally, it is not. We spent the best part of the next morning investigating said swimming holes in some detail.

After lunch, we packed up and hiked about a mile downstream. The trail goes up and over a spur that begins right behind the bath house. We passed a beautiful meadow, the best potential campsite in this area, although I have never camped there because the place is frequented by multitudes of our bovine amigos who have thoughtlessly left several generations worth of their ever popular chips on the ground—meaning this otherwise pleasant little park was swarming with flies.

Just a little further on—where a large, waterless side canyon intersects with Tararecua on the right (facing downstream), there's an industrial-strength swimming hole that is ushered in with a ten-foot cascade. On the downstream side of this particular hole, there is a sunning rock to rival all sunning rocks. Driftwood, shade trees, and tent sites abound. We stayed.

This campsite—which I have used many times in the intervening years—is only about 30 minutes from the bathhouse. It is also less than five minutes from what may be the best swimming hole on the entire Rio San Ignacio. Just downstream, a floodplain-wide cascade drops five feet into a pool that looks like something right out of Tahiti.

So, here we were in this hip canyon lolling around in 80-degree water for hours on end. We started feeling a tad guilty about our slothfulness. After all, we had a three-month Central America trip ahead of us wherein we planned on doing a lot of backpacking. We decided, therefore, that we should at least go on a dayhike. So, we headed down toward where Tararecua Canyon joins the Urique. We "thought"—and I use that word very loosely—that it would take us no more than two hours to reach the junction.

We left camp in early afternoon. The "trail"—and I use *that* word very loosely, as well—stuck to the right side of the river. Several times, whenever the canyon boxed up, we had to climb up and around spurs. Every 100 yards or so, we would pass *another* wonderful swimming hole. The hike was amazing.

Finally, after two hours of walking, we came across a side canyon pouring a 10-meter ribbon of a waterfall into a deep pool that drained into the San Ignacio. This was supposed to be some seriously rough country and we just weren't seeing such a thing. It struck us more as a desert version of J.R.R. Tolkien's mythical Shire, where the Hobbits lived.

Though we were positive that the Urique was just up ahead, probably around the next bend, we were getting a little paranoid about leaving our gear unattended for so long. We had our passports and money with us, but if our camping gear was lifted, the rest of the trip would be ruined.

So we returned upriver to camp. Our gear was undisturbed. High above us, passed a Tarahumara man, who waved and moved on. He was the only person we saw in four days in Tararecua Canyon.

After a second night camping next to the pool, we packed up and hiked out. It took us less than an hour to hit the rim, and another three hours to make it to the main road. Within 15 minutes, we got a ride in the back of a pick-up truck and, 15 minutes later, we were sucking down cold beers in front of a grocery store in Creel.

When the train came, we hopped it to Los Mochis and, two days later, we were tromping through the jungles of southern Mexico. But, we found ourselves talking quite often about following Tararecua Canyon to the Urique and then following the Urique downriver for a week or so. Sounded plausible.

A year and a half later, in mid-March 1986, Jay Scott and I decided to pay Tararecua a visit with the intention of, you guessed it, following it down to the Urique. Then we would follow the Urique down to the village of Urique. We'd take our time. Since we estimated the total distance at no more than 40 miles, we knew for a fact we could make it in six or seven days. We camped our first night beside the same swimming hole I had camped next to eighteen months before. The next morning, after returning to the bathhouse for a soak, we started downriver. By mid-afternoon, we were snacking next to the waterfall where Norb, Lori, Gay, and I terminated our downstream exploration.

Two hours or so downstream from there, another big side canyon joined the Tararecua. This place is incredible. Not only are there several hot spring pools that put Recohuata to shame, but across the river there's a warm spring pouring right out of the side of the cliff, like a shower. The views were splendid, which, as you might have guessed, is a phrase, and a reality, that will perhaps become redundant in this book. But, what can I say?

If you are attracted to canyon country on whatever level, these hot springs, which we named "Jay and John Hot Springs," after two great guys long overdue to have something named after them, and the surrounding area are heaven. This is the place to stay forever. The place where religious types should come to figure out all kinds of deep stuff. The place some sort of little Utopian monarchy should be formed—with Jay and me as monarchs. That kind of place.

On the hill above the springs were some Tarahumara homestead ruins. Rock walls surrounded some of the fields. And, I'm afraid, there were some cows hanging out. I hate cows. I hate just about everything about cows—the way they look, what they do to the environment, how their carcasses taste. Their only redeeming value is hiking boots and even that is rapidly being replaced by synthetics.

But these are Tarahumara cows, and if you tried to lay the argument on a Tarahumara that they would be much better off in many ways if they did away with their cattle, they would look at you as if you were as dumb as they suspected you were before you even opened your mouth. Not only do Tarahumaras measure their personal wealth by the number of livestock they own, but they also enjoy the hell out of a good steak.

Meat, especially dead cow, is not something Tarahumaras get to munch very often. And, when they do have the chance, they jump on it like flies on cow pies. And they are, for the time being anyhow, happy people as a result. So, when you're in Tarahumara-land, you might as well grit your teeth when it comes to cattle-related pet peeves.

During the hike from Recohuata to Jay and John Hot Springs, we passed one place that, in retrospect, should have tipped us off to what we were getting into with all this talk about hiking to the Urique. At one point, we were forced to make a move that, if not executed properly, would have resulted in a broken, bleeding gringo or two laying 100 feet or so down in the river. We were just humping along, not paying much attention to route finding, when all of a sudden, the path we were following became a clump of roots protruding from a cliff for a distance of 20 feet.

We made it across without incident, but Jay said later that this was the place that scared him more than any other dangerous spot on the rest of the trip. Since we weren't scouting routes very well at this point, perhaps there would have been an easier way to traverse this section. I do know that if I had been with my wife, I *would* have been scouting alternative routes. She would not have attempted that section, and I wouldn't have wanted her to try.

Jay and I have done a lot of hiking together. Many of our hikes have been relaxed affairs, but, believe it or not, most of them have been reasonably serious, insofar as we have made a reasonable attempt at knocking off a predetermined route in a predetermined amount of time. To that end, we generally get up before dawn and hit the trail less than an hour later.

This we did at Jay and John Hot Springs—after a shower across the river, of course. This early-on-the-trail habit would serve us well over the course of the next week because, right around the very first bend past the hot springs, the mellow

Tahitian ambience of Tararecua Canyon instantly transmogrified into the backpacking equivalent of the movie "Aliens."

From that point on, for the next five days, we did not *walk* another step. We raised and lowered our packs over slippery, house-sized boulders wedged between dozens of other slippery house-sized boulders that perched precariously above labyrinthine watercourses. We rock-hopped on slippery little pointed rocks where one misstep would have resulted in, at the very least, death. We often waded through chest-deep water with our packs on our heads, unable to see the rock-strewn bottom because of the sun's glare. We broke our way through bamboo thickets, tripping on the exposed roots. We tip-toed across cliff faces. We built a raft out of bamboo and sticks to float through one box canyon, nearly freezing to death in the process.

Several miles after our raft-building experience, we were again faced with the multi-hour prospect of making yet another raft, because, once again, the canyon boxed up. The water in the box was way over our heads and the cliffs on both sides were several hundred feet high. This time, though, there was not enough wood around to pull off another Huck Finn project. We considered trying to swim with our packs, but they were simply too heavy.

Because I had predicted a very easy trip, we had way too much stuff. When we left Creel, we each were carrying at least 50 pounds—not much by mountaineering standards, perhaps, but way too much for this kind of traveling. Especially when you consider it didn't rain the whole time we were there and the nighttime temperatures never dropped below 50 degrees. We carried a tent, winter sleeping bags, heavy food, extra long pants, binoculars, the whole nine yards.

We started hiking up and around the box canyon. After an hour, we hooked into a surprisingly well-worn path. For a while, it looked as though we were in for an easy time. Then the path did something I will never forgive the Tarahumara culture for—it crossed a cliff face hundreds of feet high. Some Tarahumara had chipped footholds into this cliff, each just deep enough to wedge the edge of a boot in. It is tempting to say that whoever chipped those footholds was not carrying a 50-pound pack, but, in all likelihood, he was. I have seen Tarahumaras carrying hundreds of pounds on tumplines across very hazardous terrain. They are magical in this regard.

I went first. The only thing between the footholds and the river was one century plant rooted to the rock. So, on the way down, I would be shish-kabobbed by a century plant before falling to my death on the rocks below.

Halfway across, I realized on all psychic levels—from basic adrenaline-enhanced fear all the way up to a calm intellectualism that was entertaining how it would feel to float through thin air at near terminal velocity—that I was not going to make it. Jay said later that, when he saw my knees start shaking violently, all he could do was hope that the century plant was ready to snag a *homo sapiens* pop fly.

I really don't know how I made it. I don't remember the moves. I just remember Jay scampering across—I'm convinced that Jay is part Tarahumara—and immediately suggesting that I find a cool piece of shade to rest in for a spell. I felt cold and clammy at a time you could have fried an egg on my forehead.

My life had been changed. To this day, I have a fear of heights that I did not have before. It's not to the point of a phobia, but, for the rest of this hike, it approached vertigo. Even harmless grades would jump up into my psyche and send my head spinning. This was bad because the hiking did not get any easier.

Also, this little episode altered our trip dynamics considerably. I have always been cursed with a personality that causes me to always want to be the leader, to be first. This I know about myself and, when hiking with a close friend like Jay, it is not usually a problem because he knows this about me as well and, being a laid-back New Mexican, he doesn't really care who is first. But, from this point, Jay became the group leader, almost to the degree that he had to hold my hand for the rest of the trip. He scouted our routes. He would rock-hop across the river first and stand patiently while explaining to me what I should do to follow. He started carrying more than his fair share of the weight.

It was a sobering experience for me because I was well aware that it was happening. On one level, I felt somewhat embarrassed and probably would have been if I had been in the company of strangers. With Jay, I was able to be completely honest with him, and with myself. To do otherwise might have been fatal because there is no doubt my judgment was impaired. I hadn't realized until then how important my miserable little life is to me.

And we still had three full days left in Tararecua Canyon, though, of course, we did not know that. Every time we saw a side canyon up ahead, our hearts raced, hoping against hope that we were about to hit the Urique. Always, we were let down. The worst part was the growing fear that, if things got much more difficult, we would have to turn around. Or else try to escape from the canyon over one of the rims which, by this time, were over 1,800 meters above us.

During all this, we saw a fair number of Tarahumaras. Whenever the canyon opened up to more than six feet, sure enough, a Tarahumara ranchito would be there, complete with herds of goats and cattle and fruit orchards.

We asked every Tarahumara we saw if it was physically possible to follow the Rio San Ignacio, by now a fairly good-sized river, as far down as the Urique. Everyone answered in a perplexed affirmative.

Finally, at about lunchtime one day, we ran into a Tarahumara man who told us he had left the Urique that very morning. We had been picking our way through a particularly nasty boulder jam that forced us to lower our packs with rope to a small ledge before we could lower them to the ground. That done, we collapsed from exhaustion on a small beach. We rested for about 10 minutes, during which time we snacked a little. When we got up to leave, we saw the Tarahumara man. He had been sitting less then 15 feet from us the whole time.

Much to our relief, this man told us the walk to the Urique was a cool breeze. Even factoring in an intense idiot gringo factor, we figured we would be able to make it by the next day.

We watched as the Tarahumara man headed upriver, from where we had just come. He took a completely different route, however, and the section that had taken us almost half an hour to traverse, he knocked off in less than half a minute. We were getting deflated. But, at least we thought we were getting there. By tomorrow, we should make it to the Urique.

We made it the day after—almost two full days to cover a distance the Tarahumara man had covered in half a day. During those days, we stopped talking about all the usual things male backpackers talk about when they're away from females out in the woods, which is mainly, of course, females. As a matter of fact, we almost stopped talking altogether. Our hike became a purely mechanical operation designed entirely for survival. Though we would occasionally comment on a particularly nice agave or an exceptional swimming hole, our appreciation of Mother Nature in this context was limited to awe at her power rather than happiness at her creative abilities.

Our last night in Tararecua Canyon, though at the time we did not know it was our last night, was long and restless. The canyon walls were so close we felt claustrophobic. The air was still. At dawn, we both talked about our dreams. Both of us had dreamt that we would not make it out of Tararecua Canyon.

My recollection of those dreams was intensified by the fact that before retiring for the night, I had noticed that one of my boots had ripped out somewhere along the line. The sole was hanging halfway off. I tied it back on with a spare bootlace and hoped for the best— always a stupid hope. We decided then and there that, if we did not reach the Urique by nightfall, we would attempt to climb out over the rim.

That morning, I went up a small side canyon to talk to a man about a dog. Halfway through the process, I looked over and found myself staring at a Tarahumara burial cave. Inside was a clothed Tarahumara corpse in an advanced state of decomposition. In the history of humankind, no man has finished the biological elimination process with more vim and vigor. Within seconds, I was back in camp ready to get on the trail.

The day started badly. We picked a route through thick undergrowth down the right side of the river. After 30 minutes, the route petered out, and we were forced to return almost to where we had camped and start over, this time following the left bank.

And then it happened. We passed out of Tararecua Canyon and entered Copper Canyon proper—six full days after we left Creel. I guarantee that Moses and the Hebrew hordes' reaction to finally seeing the Promised Land was tame by comparison.

We whooped and hollered and danced around for 15 or 20 minutes—all the time being scrutinized by a Tarahumara goatherd on the hill behind us who probably thought those damned gringos have been stealing our peyote again.

There were several Tarahumara homesteads on the Urique. We walked up a steep hill to the first one we saw. At this point, all we wanted to do was get out of the canyon we had worked so hard to get into. Though we still had plenty of food, we decided to pass on the downriver walk to the village of Urique. This, I learned later, would have been one mighty tough hump anyhow, because the Urique canyon boxes up so tight that it is near-bouts impassible for about 32 kilometers without wetsuits and flotation devices. (Please see more detail about this subject in Chapter 19.)

At the time, we did not know that it is very bad manners to simply walk up to a Tarahumara abode. But, had we known, we wouldn't have cared. We *needed* to find out how to get to the train station at El Divisadero, social graces be damned, just this one time.

The man of the house was not home. His wife and mother-in-law were. Bad news. Most older Tarahumara women don't speak any Spanish. We tried hard, but were unable to communicate with them. They, however, were able to communicate with us. They wanted us to split, pronto. Dejected, we cruised.

Shortly thereafter, we stumbled onto Marcelio Bautista's spread, a place I have visited several times since. Marcelio is a good ol' boy, then in his 30s. His winter estate is a paradisiacal 20-by-20-foot, one-room rock hut on a mesita just above the Urique. Behind the abode there is a multi-thousand-foot cliff face and, in front, there's a 10-meter deep, 30-meter-by-15-meter swimming hole. Just a few days back, I had thought the Rio San Ignacio sported the best swimming holes in the known universe. The most minuscule holes on the Urique put the San Ignacio's best to shame. And this is no insult to the San Ignacio.

Marcelio lives here during the winter months with his wife, his mother-in-law, his ten children, seventy-five goats, several burros, fifteen head of cattle and a large flock of chickens. Because of his livestock, Marcelio is one well-to-do Tarahumara. Like all Tarahumaras who dwell in the canyon depths, the Bautistas head for the high country come late spring because, from then until mid-September, the heat becomes unbearable, even for a Tarahumara.

The fact that we had backpacked down Tararecua Canyon was one of the funniest things Marcelio had heard in months. When he related this to his family in Tarahumara, they all laughed long and hard. When they finally settled down, they looked at us quizzically, like all the rumors they had heard about the fairhaired nabobs from the north were proven to be the gospel by this one data transmission.

Despite having lived his whole life close to the mouth of Tararecua Canyon, Marcelio had never hiked up there. "Too rocky," he deadpanned, implying that we were, perhaps, not exactly Rhodes Scholar material.

We couldn't have cared less what they thought. We wanted information, pure and simple. Could we hike to Divisadero from here?

Yes.

Which way?

Walk down the river a ways, take a right, and climb out of the canyon. Can't miss it.

Okay.

We unloaded our excess food on the Bautistas and gave the children a couple gifts—pen and paper, candy, a whistle. I knew from the train trip to Los Mochis that, from Divisadero you could see the Urique, but just barely. So it only figured that, from somewhere on the Urique, you could see Divisadero. All we had to do was walk until we found that place.

At least here we *could* walk. Quite an improvement. That aside, we both knew we were doomed. There was no way, the way this trip had been going, that we were going to stroll mellowly down the second-deepest canyon on the continent for a few hours, until we spied a speck of a hotel 10 miles away and 1,700 meters up.

Then, to top everything off, we both had a mirage. Right there on the side of the river was a small backpacking tent. We walked over and touched it. It was a serious, professional mirage, because it was tactile as well as visual. Then, three Mexican men walked around the corner. They were as surprised to see us as we were to see them—especially because, judging from their body language, these men were far more than just drinking buddies. They were seriously smooching as they walked. We wanted to run over and kiss them on the lips just for being alive and here in the bottom of this huge canyon, but, under the circumstances, we decided that act might be misinterpreted. These poor guys just stood there and stared, their heretofore passionate embraces falling by the wayside. They must have been wondering where in the *hell* do you have to go to get some privacy.

They happily pointed the way to Divisadero. We walked back upriver and set up camp. Before dawn the next morning, we were hiking out of Copper Canyon. Ten hours later, we were staring down from the scenic overlook above Divisadero. (Chapter 6 details the route.)

We had managed to make it there before the last train. Jay's pants were torn so badly that they were indecent, so he quickly pulled them off and unloaded everything out of his pack looking for his spare pair. The exact second he had everything out, the train pulled up. Jay threw his stuff back in the pack and we commenced sprinting. This is something our bodies did not appreciate. But, at the same time, our bodies did want beers and tacos. So, we made it, with three minutes to spare.

By the time we plopped down into our seats on the train, we were talking about the ridiculous nature of the entire avocation of backpacking. Copper Canyon, which we had started referring to as the "Valley of Death," had whipped us bad. We were beaten men. For several days I had been shouting oaths to any cut-rate deity dumb enough to lend an ear. Stuff like, "Just get me outta here in one piece and I swear I'll give up vodka and beer and tequila and skirt chasing and cigar smoking and poker and you will never ever see a pack on this back again because I'll be spending all my spare time helping homeless people and praying in church. . . ."

Well, as we all know, backpack junkies tend to put little stock, once they're out of harm's way, in duress-induced oaths. Both of us knew we would be back. Copper Canyon is just too special a place to let a little lesson in humility jade one's view forevermore.

Particulars

Let me say, first, that, out of all the chapters in the first edition of this book, this one generated the most reader input, both positive and negative. First, the bad part. I have received several letters and phone calls from people who had their gear ripped off at Recohuata Hot Springs. From what I have heard in and around Creel, it was one man doing all the heisting (more than twenty packs, all told), and he has since been arrested and jailed. Still, I would advise you to keep a close eye on your gear while visiting Recohuata.

Also, I have received a lot of input over the years from people who decided to follow my directions and visit Jay and John Hot Springs. Most of that input amounted to variations on the "this was one tough hike" theme. Many people told me they made it to Jay and John Hot Springs, but only after the most arduous hike of their lives. Others told me they simply could not make it.

Well, let me at least partially defend my direction giving, or lack thereof, by saying that the first edition incarnation of this chapter was the only one I penned without knowing, while I was on the trail, that I would be writing a book about Copper Canyon Country. So, I did not pay as much attention to trail details as I did with the other chapters.

That said, in the fall of 1993, I revisited Jay and John Hot Springs to learn if there had been some sort of geophysical calamity since Jay and I were last there. It ended up being easy as pie, at least partially because, in twelve years of hiking in Tarahumara-land, I've become fairly adept at figuring out routes. I have come to the point where I can ask myself, "Where would a Tarahumara go now?" and actually be right most of the time. This ability would probably make for an easier hike from Recohuata to the Rio Urique, but I don't think I'm that interested in finding out. Call me a sissy.

So, here is the skinny: Between Recohuata Hot Springs and Jay and John Hot Springs, you never go more than about 75 feet above river level. You stay on the same side of the river as Recohuata for about an hour and a half, cross over for about an hour, then cross back over for about half an hour. There are no hard sections, as Jay and I experienced. Also, you will need to pay ten new pesos when you pass Recohuata. (Yes, even in the boonies, toll collectors are at work.)

Also, the last time I visited Recohuata, I hiked from the Copper Canyon Lodge in Cusarare with my buddy Sahuaripa and a crazed Canadian named Charlie. It took us about three hours one way. You definitely need to hire a guide, because there are a lot of trail junctions. You end up descending into Tararecua Canyon at exactly the same spot as you would if you drove from Creel, but the hike is very pleasant and fairly easy. I really recommend this if you plan to camp anywhere near Recohuata. (A Cusarare-Recohuata round-trip would make for a long day.)

Okay, you will need the 1:50,000 Creel and San Jose Guacayvo (sometimes indexed as "San Luis") maps, or the 1:250,000 San Juanito map.

It is very difficult to describe how to get from the highway between Creel and Batopilas to Recohuata Hot Springs because new logging roads are cut in there all the time. I have been back along this route four times, and each time, the route looked at least slightly different. But, here goes.

Take a right at the Recohuata road sign, a couple of kilometers south of Lake Arareco. You will not, at this point, be on an interstate highway. Stay on the main track. At 4.5 kilometers (2.8 miles), take a left at the fork. At 5.6 kilometers (3.5 miles), you will be able to see glimpses of Tararecua Canyon through the trees on the right. At 6.4 kilometers (4 miles), you pass close to a couple of cabins in a small valley. Bear right and cross over the creek bed. Follow the track up the hill. At 8 kilometers (5 miles), take a right at the fork. At 9.6 kilometers (6 miles), take a right. Continue straight to the prominent side canyon, where the route from Cusarare intersects. From here, the trail down sticks to the right side of the canyon as you look into it. If you are driving here, you will definitely need a high-clearance vehicle. Four-wheel-drive is also handy.

Your best bet is to hook up with a group at Margarita's in Creel, or to hire a guide in Cusarare. Margarita runs tours to the canyon rim—about 45 minutes walking distance from the hot springs—almost every day. Cost is only a few bucks. Then, whenever you want to come out, you can catch a ride back with that day's tour group. If for some reason you have to walk out, pay attention on your way in. And, remember, the walk out is long, hot, and dry. Unless it rains. Or snows. Then it will be long, wet, and cold. Either way, the hike out will not be the highlight of your trip. Hitchhiking back into Creel once you get to the main road should be easy.

I have never tried hiking to Recohuata by following the Rio San Ignacio all the way from Lake Arareco, but I have heard from one group that it can be done, and from another group that it cannot be done. Maybe you want to check it out for yourself.

To visit the lower reaches of Tararecua Canyon, where it enters the Urique, leave from Divisadero. This route is described in Chapter 6. Also, the route from the Copper Canyon Lodge to Divisadero—"Canyon Crossing"—intersects Tararecua Canyon. See details in Chapter 9.

Remember, any time you follow rivers in Copper Canyon Country, you are asking for a tough row to hoe. This is fine, if that's what you're looking for. If it is, you need to pack very light. Bring some good rope for lowering your packs. If you have good climbing skills, you should be able to follow Tararecua Canyon all the way to the Urique. Wear good, lightweight boots with new soles. And, most importantly, keep your wits about you just like you would if you were scaling a major peak.

If you are not looking to risk life and limbone one hundred times a minute, don't follow the Rio San Ignacio downstream any further than Jay and John Hot Springs.

6

Rim to Rim, from Divisadero to Pamachi via the Río Urique

When I first proposed a story about the Copper Canyon region to the editors of *Backpacker*, they were a little skeptical. Although enthusiastic about the fact that this area is relatively unexplored and presents the opportunity for any and all Type-A readers to risk life and limb forty-three times a second, the editors were casually wondering, based upon my account of our Tararecua trek, whether they should be actively encouraging families of four from the 'burbs to go within 1,000 kilometers of this place.

Doing my best to get the assignment, I did the only thing any mercenary writer anywhere would do: I lied like six pigs. "Oh, yeah," says I, "Tararecua Canyon is but one of the myriad of options down there. There's *plenty* of easy hiking to be had in Copper Canyon Country."

All this time, I, myself, am experiencing a near-terminal case of sphincter puckering at the very thought of going back into the "Valley of Death." This fear was multiplied by the fact that, having stretched the truth in my communications with *Backpacker's* editors, I was certain to experience a serious karmic retaliation of monumental proportions the instant I so much as stuck my big toe back in Copper Canyon.

At the same time, I knew that I would have to come up with a story titled something like "Fifty Easy Copper Canyon Nature Strolls for Brownie Troops from Toledo," because the *Backpacker* editors had made it very clear that the story had to make the place seem attractive and accessible to your average pack-schlepping schmuck and schmuck-ette. Yet, there was no doubt in my mind, after I got the assignment, that my tale would be written from the intensive care ward in Chihuahua City because I had performed a screecher off the very first cliff.

I'll jump ahead of myself here and say that this attitude was a waste of good fear. It was almost as if the Tararecua Canyon trip was an initiation rite. All of my subsequent wanderings in Copper Canyon Country (and we're talking about a lot of wanderings here) have been far more laid back when it comes to adrenaline output. I'm not a man who is keen on adrenaline abuse. Occasional recreational use, yes. But that's it. I swear.

Right now, Jay Scott, Norbert Bame, and I have camp set up on a beach next to the Urique right across from the gaping maw of Tararecua Canyon. The hike from Divisadero down to the Urique was, though certainly strenuous, very pleasant. We experienced a very special day of hiking. For me, it was just good to be on the trail with two old friends. For Jay and Norb, it was an opportunity to make new friends, because, as much as they had heard about each other over the years, they had never met.

The only damage on this hike so far has taken the form of three sets of very stiff, steep-descent-racked thighs. And the dayhiking we have been doing along the river for the past three days has been very mellow, involving just enough in the way of river crossings and easy scrambling to keep us on our toes.

Without those six days in Tararecua Canyon to twist our perspectives, this place shines in a whole different light. It's about 10 AM in the clear-sky morning and we have been hitting the bottle pretty hard, because, we have decided, today is laundry day—meaning, we don't plan on doing *any* hiking, not that we have exactly been killing ourselves the past few days. Perhaps I should point out that we are drinking only in the interest of ethnological research, although that won't make any sense for several more pages.

We boarded the train for our Copper Canyon return engagement in Chihuahua City. We hopped off in Creel only long enough to stock up on Tecates.

The plan was to get off in Divisadero and descend into the canyon via the same route Jay and I had climbed up from the Rio Urique exactly one year before. We would set up camp at the first comfy-looking stretch of beach we laid our eyes on. After a day of rest, we would dayhike down the Urique a few miles. Then, after another day of rest, we would move camp upriver near the mouth of Tararecua Canyon. From there, we would dayhike upriver a ways, before returning to our original camp the night before hiking out to Divisadero.

After getting off the train, we set up camp among the junipers right next to the canyon rim above Divisadero where the scenic overlook is located—the same overlook that saw Jay's naked self frantically trying to get his fashion act together before the train pulled away, twelve months prior.

We had arrived in Chihuahua City on the bus from Juarez at about 2 AM the night before. We laid our sleeping bags down in a back alley near the train station, and tried to sleep the rest of the night. No go; the city was simply too noisy, and we were simply too wired from the trip. So, by the time we arrived at the overlook above Divisadero, we were some bleary-eyed hombres, so we sacked out for the afternoon, dragging our carcasses out of bed only long enough to cook supper and watch the sunset.

This mesa is a very good place to experience both dawn and dusk. And if you've done a good job of orienting your map, you can pick out the great bend of the Urique—where Tararecua Canyon meets Copper Canyon.

Once again, we froze all night. When you're in Copper Canyon Country, you often have to make a choice of carrying too much sleeping bag down into the canyons for the sake of staying warm the one or two nights you may be camping on the rim, or of freezing on the rim because you're using a light bag with an eye towards the warmer temperatures below. I recommend the latter, unless it's mid-winter, when you have no choice but to sleep in a warm bag up high.

At dawn, we broke camp, confident of quickly locating our route down to the river. After all, it had only been a year since Jay and I had been exactly here. Of course, we being us, it wasn't going to be that simple.

When Jay and I ran into the three Mexicans camping on the Urique who pointed the route to Divisadero, we forgot to ask them whether we turned right or left to find Divisadero once we made it to the rim. We zigged and zagged at every opportunity, hoping against hope to catch a view of the hotel sitting perched on the rim. So, we covered a lot more ground than we would have had we been making a beeline for Divisadero. Meaning, that the three of us this go-round should not have been looking for the route we were so studiously looking for because it was not the most direct route to the river. To complicate matters further, Jay and I were suffering from acute memory failure.

Each of us was certain beyond the shadow of a doubt that the other one was dumb as a clam. I *knew* where we needed to go. And Jay *knew*. It's just that what each of us "knew" was different. So, we ended up arguing the whole way down about whether this one 15-foot stretch of goat path was the very place where we tromped, disoriented, the year before.

The ironic part of all of this idiocy is that there is a good trail all the way from Divisadero to the Urique. We were just too bull-headed to open our eyes and look for it. A couple of times, through no fault of our own, we stumbled onto the trail, only to part ways with it before long, because "this isn't the way we came last year!"

Despite the fact that Jay, Norb, and I were making Pathfinder, Deerslayer, and Daniel Boone all roll over in their graves at the same time, the trip down from Divisadero was fairly straightforward and easy. We made it down to the river in six hours, whereas Jay and I had needed ten to ascend to Divisadero the year before. On the surface, it would seem that the time differential would be caused by nothing more than simple downhill dynamics versus uphill dynamics—going with the flow of gravity rather than fighting it—combined with a slightly improved familiarity with where it was we were heading in the first place.

But, in canyon country, the grades can be so steep and the footing so treacherous that, all other things being equal, like pack weight, there's usually not that much of a difference between the time it takes one to hike out of a canyon and the time it takes to hike down into it. The main difference is how you feel the next day. Recovery from steep uphills is much shorter than for steep downhills. By weeks.

About an hour from the river, in the middle of the hardest part of the descent—thick undergrowth, steep grades, and poor footing—we met a Tarahumara family. They had left Divisadero two hours earlier, meaning they were traveling more than twice as fast as we were. Even while understanding that they, one, obviously didn't have to spend as much time as us looking for the trail, and, two, weren't stopping every few minutes to take pictures, this was still a very sobering situation.

Despite our propensity, jointly and severally, for misadventure, the three of us look upon ourselves, jointly and severally, as seriously bad backpacking jocks. Our group resume, though not nearly world class, at least partially backs that up. Jay has spent something like fourteen seasons building trails and fighting fires for the U.S. Forest Service. He has hiked hundreds of miles in the Gila National Forest of New Mexico—tough terrain in its own right—and in Idaho, Arizona, and Montana.

Norb, who lives in Washington State, spends his free time playing around on glaciers like a crazy human. He has climbed Rainier, Baker, and Hood. He and I spent several months hiking in Central America, and we've hiked together in China, the New Territories of Hong Kong, Puerto Rico, and the Dominican Republic. In addition, I've hiked the entire Appalachian and Colorado trails. I don't want all that to sound like it undoubtedly sounds. I just mention this experience thing to point out how little it all amounts to in a place like Copper Canyon when you find yourself hiking near Tarahumaras.

This Tarahumara family, which was herding fifteen goats at the time, consisted of a fifteen-year-old wife (whose name we never quite memorized) toting a newborn baby, her fifteen-year-old husband, Cruz, and his thirteen-year-old sister, Candelaria. At the time they caught up with us, we were resting. Though the descent was relatively easy, it was still over 1,700 steep meters, and we were carrying eight days worth of supplies. Jay and Norb seemed like they were merely tired. Your humble narrator, on the other hand, who had been living a cushy city life for several years, was one hurting cowboy. My thighs felt like they were going to explode, implode, and melt down all in one fell swoop.

This Tarahumara family made things a little easier by pointing a trail out to us. They slowed their pace so the dumb gringos would have a fighting chance of keeping up. This also gave the dumb gringos the opportunity to check out Tarahumara walking technique close-up. These people moved as fluidly on rough Copper Canyon trails as highly trained runners do on an indoor track. They wasted no energy whatsoever. And their footing seemed perfect. These people moved like they were *part* of the rugged canyon environment. We, conversely, felt like the stumbling lummoxes from hell—where, only minutes before, we had been feeling right good about ourselves.

I had read quite a bit about the Tarahumaras' perambulatory prowess during the previous year. The Tarahumaras' on-foot cruising abilities, probably more than any other aspect of their culture, have been well documented by academicians, journalists, and casual observers.

For instance, Bernard L. Fontana in *Tarahumara: Where Night Is the Day of the Moon*, relates, "One 28-year-old Tarahumara man was found who was able to run continuously in hill country over a period of four days and three nights without sleep. 'Probably not since the days of the ancient Spartans,' observed one of the doctors making the measurements, 'has a people achieved such a high state of physical conditioning.'"

That is hardly an isolated example. Some other pieces of Tarahumara endurance trivia:

• Two Tarahumaras gained a certain amount of notoriety in the 1968 Mexico City Olympics when they competed in the marathon. They lost badly, both complaining about the shortness of the distance and the fact that they were required to wear shoes during the competition. No matter how hard the Mexican coaches tried, they were unable to convince their Tarahumara marathoners that such a short race was worthy of serious attention and effort. The Tarahumaras wondered why, since they were not sprinters, they were entered in a sprint? A 26-mile sprint.

  The Tarahumaras' reputation was so firmly entrenched in the minds of the Mexican Olympic team, that they didn't even do any sort of tryouts. They simply went to Tarahumara-land and asked who the best runners were. That was their marathon team.

- Get this one! Whenever the Tarahumaras feel like a little venison for din-din, they go out, find some deer sign, and proceed to run the hapless beast to death—a process that can last four days. I talked with a man who witnessed part of such a deer hunt. He told me that one of the Tarahumara hunters was actually carrying a rifle. My friend asked the Tarahumara why he didn't just save himself some time and effort by shooting the deer. The Tarahumara responded that bullets cost money. Running is free.

- Most Indian tribes in these parts refer to themselves, in their own tongue, simply as "The People." The Tarahumaras, on the other hand, call themselves "Raramuri"— the Runners. Their national pastime is a game called *rarahipa*—sort of a kickball relay race that covers a course between 12 and 26 miles in length. An NBA-playoff-caliber *rarahipa* will last three days and two nights, nonstop. The players will each cover several hundred miles in that time.

What makes all this all the more interesting is that the Tarahumaras are among the most serious drinkers in the world. You could hear the gears turning in my head when I dialed into that reality.

Quoting Fontana again, "It would be almost impossible to overstate the importance of corn beer and corn beer parties in the lives of the Tarahumaras. Anthropologist John Kennedy . . . estimates that each adult spends about 100 days out of each year . . . directly involved in the preparation, consumption and recovery from the effects of this national drink."

This makes for a captivating paradox. To many of us, the "problem" with adopting a healthy lifestyle lies not so much with trading the rapture of a bacon double cheeseburger for the staid nutritional maxims of the late Nathan Pritikin while simultaneously spending enough time on a Lifecycle to merit inclusion in a doctoral dissertation proving a direct evolutionary link between caged hamsters and educated Americans.

Rather, the problem comes from trying to figure out how to do all that while still managing to consume the U.S.D.A. Adult Minimum Daily Requirements of beer and cigars.

Up until I started researching the Tarahumaras, the best argumentative reconciliation I had been able to come up with in this context was something along the lines of "I'm in pretty darned good condition for someone who drinks at least a case of Stroh's a week." Then I learn about the Tarahumaras—drinkers nonpareil who can, according to Pritikin in his book, *The Pritikin Promise*, "run 500 miles in five days" and "carry 80 percent of their body weight . . . 110 miles in 70 hours." And, suddenly, I have a vision. A vision of an athletic drunkard's cult. With teams of Bacchus schmoozers laying waste to world records in every sport. And me as their Don King.

We could even have running events where the participants were given alcohol tests before the race. "Oh, sorry, you didn't have enough beer in your blood, so we're going to have to disqualify you." Or we could organize all kinds of athletic competitions wherein participants would be given "drunkenness factors," much like divers are given "difficulty factors." You know: "Well, Fayhee finished an hour after Jones in the half-marathon, but, since Fayhee consumed three beers before and five beers during the race, while Jones only consumed a total of two beers, Fayhee wins by nine hours—a new world record!"

It would be impressive enough if, one, the Tarahumaras upon whose feats the data quoted above is based lived in Kansas, and/or, two, those kinds of statistics were the equivalent of Tarahumara world records, and/or, three, there was one segment of Tarahumara society comprised totally of the drinkers, while the other part was comprised totally of the runners, and somehow all the scientific data overlapped.

But, none of these is the case. The Copper Canyon area is at least as tough to traverse as the Grand Canyon and the figures Pritikin cites come from everyday Tarahumara life. We are not simply dealing with athletic feats being performed by the Tarahumara *creme de la creme*. Rather, we are dealing with all Tarahumaras—including old folks and children. And all of them drink heavily.

All of this impressed Pritikin enough that, essentially, he based his hyper-low-fat diet on Tarahumara fare—which, not surprisingly, consists mainly of vast amounts of complex carbohydrates. There are seven separate references to the Tarahumaras in *The Pritikin Promise*—the first of which occurs in the book's fourth paragraph.

So, it was with great joy that I ran into Fontana's references to the Tarahumara's drinking prowess. In *Tarahumara: Where Night Is the Day of the Moon*, Fontana, who is a University of Arizona ethnologist, dedicated as much verbiage to the Tarahumaras' drinking abilities as Pritikin did to their endurance capabilities.

Fontana points out that the Tarahumaras have raised the entire concept of getting frequently ripped to the gills to a quasi-religious art form—to the degree that ethnologists have concluded that these corn beer binges are crucially important to the overall health and well-being of their culture in every regard from grape-vining to baby making. (You can just imagine slews of Tarahumaras getting a good chuckle out of that one: "Sorry I'm nine weeks late for dinner, honey, but me and the boys had to get together for some academically sanctioned and culturally critical debauchery.")

Meeting this Tarahumara family, the Bautistas—Cruz being Marcelio's first cousin—on the trail was mighty good luck in more ways than one. First was the fact that we got to watch them walk close-up for an hour. Most times, if you meet Tarahumaras on the trail, they will blow by you so fast that you will not have much chance to study their walking technique.

Second, on my first two trips into Copper Canyon, I hadn't had the chance to engage in the kind of cross-cultural interaction that makes for colorful retrospective Third World-born yarn spinning. I had seen lots of Tarahumaras, but hadn't known quite how to go about becoming buddy-buddy with any of them. The Bautistas, perhaps because of their young age, were very amiable and invited us to camp near them almost immediately. They were, like us, planning on just hanging out next to the river for a few days.

And, third, because of that friendliness, we knew we would be able to do some serious drinking with some genuine

Tarahumaras. We had ample ammunition, in the form of several liters of 151 rum. Which gets us back to the scientific research part of why the three of us are sitting here well before noon with blurry vision.

By the time we met Cruz and his family, the three of us, after discussing the Tarahumaras' ability to drink heavily and simultaneously perform unbelievable athletic feats, had decided that there must be some kind of "secret" that the Tarahumaras had managed to keep from the gaggles of academicians who have studied them over the years. We had decided to dedicate our lives to finding out what this secret is. We would become rich.

The plan was to learn the secret and smuggle some of whatever it turned out to be back to the States with the idea of opening a franchise-ready bar/fitness emporium. If the Bautistas were up for it, we would lay a nice cut on them.

With Cruz in the lead and the rest of the clan pulling up the rear, we continued down to the Urique. We had been catching good views of the river for the last few hours. It seemed tantalizingly close. The temptation is always to sprint the rest of the way once you lay eyes on the river. This is a bad plan. Canyon descents should always be done fairly slowly, especially if you have been sitting on your tail for the last nine months. Because, remember, unlike mountain climbing, you will be carrying the most weight while heading downhill. This is very hard on the feet, knees, and thighs.

I speak from experience. The very last 15 yards of trail follows a small cliff face. Cruz, Jay, and Norb had already descended while I stood above them knowing full well that my next act would rank as one of the most humiliating backpacking experiences ever recorded in the history of mankind.

By this point, I no longer trusted my legs' ability to resist gravity. I was forced to lower my pack by rope over about a three-foot drop-off. It was a choice of that or fall flat on my face. Cruz was bewildered. Norb and Jay proved once again that they are sensitive, caring sorta guys, by questioning my masculinity, boisterously in two languages. I love being a guy.

Cruz and family trooped off to a campsite about 50 yards downriver. We dropped our packs right where we stood, on a perfect stretch of beach that was catching the afternoon sun very nicely. Though we had managed to get fried to a crisp during the last several hours on the trail, we still planned to spend the rest of the daylight hours getting scorched further. After all, one is supposed to return from south-of-the-border places sunburnt and bug-bit, and we intended to do just that.

The Urique is my favorite river in the world. It would be my favorite river if it were located on the bleak eastern plains of Colorado. That it is located at the bottom of one of the continent's deepest canyons makes it all the more appealing.

The temptation, if for no other reason than to establish a point-of-reference that is palpable to Americans, is to compare Copper Canyon with the Grand Canyon. While such a comparison may be useful in some ways, it hardly does either of the canyon systems justice, because, once you've noted that they are both huge and arid, the similarities end.

Copper Canyon, in my opinion, is not as breathtakingly spectacular as the Grand Canyon, mostly because it lacks the intense color contrasts of the Grand's geological striations. Just a few miles downriver from our camp, though, it is almost 300 meters deeper. And, unlike the Grand, over yon ridge lies another canyon almost as deep. And, beyond that, lies yet another.

At the same time, the physical scenery here is surpassed, in my experience, *only* by the Grand Canyon. There are all the multi-thousand-foot cliff faces, rock spires and deep side canyons you would ever hope for. Copper Canyon is literally so massive that there are mountains within the canyons.

But, the most important difference between the Grand Canyon and Copper Canyon comes from the nature of the rivers that carved them. At the bottom of Copper Canyon, there is no swiftly flowing, muddy brown river that serves as a gift from heaven for rafters, while playing the part of a back-country Berlin Wall for hikers. The Urique, very much unlike the Colorado, is a fairly small, placid stream that sports, one right after another, giant aquamarine pools that might as well have neon signs alongside them flashing "Swim Here! Swim Here!" Some of these pools approach the size of small lakes bordered by white sand beaches and bamboo thickets. The Urique is your reward for humping it down from the rim. And it is your golden memory while you're humping it back up.

Ordinarily, I would have, by this point, decided that I had already fulfilled my journalistic responsibilities to *Backpacker*. I told them this place was okay for average hikers. I had set out to see if I was merely a lying piece of spent trash, or a prophet. It must be the latter, which is what I'd always predicted about myself. But, concerns for my assignment with *Backpacker* aside, we still needed to find some answers. How do the Tarahumaras manage to drink so much and run so far so fast over such heavy-duty terrain?

I mean, Marcelio, who has been visiting since we arrived, Cruz's friend, Patricio, and Cruz are certainly as drunk as we are right at this very moment. Maybe even more so. Yet, every hour or so, one of them will jump up, sprint 300 meters or so up the side of a canyon wall, check on the goats, sprint back down, and resume drinking. The three gringos, on the other hand, are having heated arguments about whose turn it is to stand up and mix the next batch of drinks—the "standing up" part being the bone of contention.

While all this drinking was going on, the Tarahumaras smoked every cigar we gave them. They smoked cigarettes. They smoked marijuana. They shared big ol' bags of candy. They did *everything* you're not supposed to do. The same as us. Yet, we knew that they would be able to hoist a pack at any moment and hike farther than any of us could on our best day if we had been in serious training for a year.

As time passed, we started seriously querying our Tarahumara buddies about this secret of theirs. They were all well aware that their tribe was near-famous for both its drinking and running prowess. Cruz told us in no uncertain terms that, yes, there was a reason why his skinny-as-a-rail, thirteen-year-old sister could run circles around all but elite-class American runners. He told us that he would be glad to share some of this substance with us this very night.

He left and came back a few hours later—with a full plastic bag. You should understand that we of the seriously bad gringo backpacker contingent were getting a little nervous by this point. First of all, what if he had brought some nightmarish hallucinogenic tuber that would put us out on our backs for the next 75 hours?

Okay, we thought. We could handle that; we've been there before.

But what if it was the food item from hell?

All of us who enjoy the Third World like to picture ourselves in a scene like in *Indiana Jones and the Temple of Doom,* where the natives serve up a nice hot plate of whatever it is they eat that's green and gooey and contains the internal parts of at least three species of dirt-dwelling invertebrates. We like to think that our only reaction under the circumstances would be to joyfully dig in, pausing in our mouth-cramming only long enough to compliment the chef on her provocative use of the eel slime marinade.

However, we all know better. We all know there are certain probably perfectly edible items that could be placed before us that we simply would not be able to eat. We can't predict, before the fact, what form this refusal would take—it could be a little white lie about how we are still full from lunch or it could be a power regurgitation. Whatever, one thing is clear: the item in question is not going into this mouth.

(Actually, this thing is always a joke. Native cultures eat Cap'n Crunch and Lean Cuisine, too. It's just that, whenever a khaki-clad gringo comes into the neighborhood, they take bets on what they can get us to eat and, to that end, they run gleefully through the woods harvesting anything and everything that is either slimy in texture or earthy in aroma. Then they mash it up, add some belly-button lint, and serve it. And we, being nitwits, eat it while being happy for the "experience.")

Cruz seemed attuned to our apprehension. He theatrically unwrapped this magical elixir that would, within a few weeks, have people like me doing shots of mescal before my weekly record-setting triathlon.

Meanwhile, I'm standing there thinking, "Just don't let it be eyes—anything but eyes."

A waste of good trepidation, because all it was, was thick corn tortillas liberally laced with the best refritos I have ever eaten. There was also a side of sweet potato and a side of squash.

Yes, you frenetic 10K junkies, Pritikin was correct. These people eat right—plain and simple—to the degree that super-human alcohol intake doesn't faze them.

So, all you have to do is never eat anything bad, unless there are gringos in town to corrupt you, move to an area where getting a drink of water can require a 700-meter vertical descent and get a herd of goats to chase around all the time, and you, too, can perform athletic feats that dazzle and amaze pundits and pontificators hither and yon.

We pulled ourselves together enough to dayhike both up and down the Urique a few kilometers. We even went a few hundred meters up into Tararecua Canyon—up to the first place where we would have had to start climbing. And, that was about it for this trip.

Jay hired Marcelio to carry his pack to Divisadero, because Jay had stuffed it with guapa-tree pods that weighed in at about 70 pounds. These pods, which explode like a sea of white fuzz when they're ripe, are used by the Tarahumaras to weave necklaces and bracelets. Jay is a creative artist-type, so he wanted to check out the weaving possibilities himself.

Halfway out of the canyon, we heard some faint drum beating way off in the distance. When we asked what the drums were all about, Marcelio told us that a bunch of the boys over yonder were having themselves a *tesguinada*—one of the Tarahumara's infamous corn beer parties. *Tesguinadas* are the type of native gathering that, if invited to one, you've got yourself a nice little addition to the ol' back-country resume.

The drumming, according to Marcelio, was a cross between party jams—boom boxes not having made in-roads in these parts yet—and a sort of audio smoke signal. Judging from the wry grin on Marcelio's face, the drummer was letting everyone know that Larry just passed out and fell in the fire.

Being the types who are always game for a little cross-cultural beer swilling, we asked Marcelio if the *tesguinada* was close-at-hand and, if so, would it be considered gauche if he brought a couple gringos by to enjoy the festivities.

This was more than just a casual inquiry, insofar as it was about 105 degrees in the shade with zero-percent humidity—

typical early spring weather in these parts. We were parched and, well, a couple of brewskis would have gone down right easy.

Marcelio responded that, yes, now that we mentioned it, the *tesguinada* was a mere four-hour jaunt "over there." His attitude was "right on, Jack, we'll sprint over for a few cold ones before heading on to Divisadero."

The conversation terminated with three-red-faced "Gee, heh, heh, heh, we really don't understand" kinds of shrugs when we found out where "over there" was. This, more than anything else, brought the Tarahumaras' endurance capabilities into clear focus. Despite all we had heard and read, all we had seen, it was still incomprehensible to us that Marcelio was seriously, yes, seriously, suggesting that we sashay on over to that *tesguinada*.

He was talking about toting our packs for four hours up and down at least 3,000 extremely vertical meters in a direction 90 degrees from where we wanted to go. For a beer.

Our jaws-agape negatory response wouldn't have been quite so humiliating if we had not been talking some serious *mierda* to Marcelio and the others down in the canyon for the last week. In that mature tone of voice that makes wives so enthusiastic about going to redneck pool halls with their hubbies, we assured them at every opportunity as we smoked cigars and sipped rum around the fire that, despite all the academic accolades to the contrary, we would match them drink-for-drink 'til the cows come home.

Tails between our legs, we passed on the *tesguinada* trek, though attending it would have been the experience of a lifetime. Instead, we continued our dry-throated, five-hour hump to Divisadero—where Marcelio proceeded to drink us under the table at the hotel bar to the tune of something like twenty-five Tecates to our fifteen. His smirk was the kind you see on a helicopter pilot's face after he has just power-dived you into retching terror.

As we crawled onto the train, Marcelio left to return to the Urique, some 1,700 meters below. In the dark. Next to cliffs and along talus slopes. After 600 gallons of beer. Whistling a tune like he was Ward Cleaver walking down to the local drug store for a paper.

As he was leaving, he mentioned that he might just stop by that *tesguinada* on the way home. No doubt, the drum beater would take great pride in letting the world know that, when it comes to partying down—count the gringos out.

The vista from the hotel bar in Divisadero is the best bar view I have ever seen. You stare directly down a giant arroyo— *El Ojo de la Barranca*, the Eye of the Canyon. This arroyo goes straight to the Urique, but because of a huge cliff halfway down, it has no trail to the river.

Directly across from the mouth of the Eye of the Canyon, also in plain view from the hotel, another huge arroyo—the name of which doesn't appear on any maps—begins its upward journey to the opposite rim and the *pueblocito* of Pamachi. Many times, I had sat in the bar at Divisadero looking over at the other side, wondering what it would be like to look back towards the north rim—to be part of the best bar vista in the known universe.

I had not heard of anyone backpacking rim-to-rim from Divisadero to Pamachi. So, being intense, Lewis-and-Clark sorts of folks, Gay and I, in December 1988, decided to do just that. We hired a teenage Tarahumara guide named Juan, who is from Sitagochi, though he hangs out in Cusarare a lot. He told us that he knew the way to Pamachi very well, because one of his sisters lived there. We learned later that the little bugger was lying through his teeth. He knew the way to Pamachi, all right, but from Sitagochi, not Divisadero.

I admired his chutzpah. Reminded me of me. Besides, by the time we figured out that he was winging it, we were already to the point where it was apparent he was pulling it off.

We caught the train from Creel to Divisadero—this time armed with topo maps not previously available in Creel. Within two seconds of getting off the train, we were adopted by a stray dog, who decided the instant my nose broke the plane of the train door to cast his lot with the Great Gringo-Tarahumara Rim-to-Rim Expedition.

We named this foul-smelling cur *Perro*—dog. As far as Tarahumara dogs go, Perro was okay, although his enthusiasm for American backpacking food combined with Gay's enthusiasm for stray quadrupeds left us a little short on grub.

After buying some snacks from the food vendors near the train stop in Divisadero, we headed up to the mesa above the scenic overlook to camp for the night. Since we had all consumed several Tecates on the train ride, the walk up the hill was "deliberate" in pace. Juan carried the full water bag and I carried two medicinal six-packs—extra weight that slowed us even more.

Perro couldn't have been happier. He not only had himself a couple of gringos laden with vittles, but, at the same time, he had himself a hiker—me—hiking slowly enough that he could easily get his mangy carcass entangled in my legs, causing slapstick disruptions to my alcohol-influenced walking. I went down three times before we topped out. Each time, I would chase this animal for a few yards, while he sprinted away grinning like a Cheshire dog.

We made it down to the Urique by 1 PM the next day—basically by the same route Jay, Norb, and I had followed. The only problem was Juan's preference for the most direct line of travel. I would explain to him in no uncertain terms that we were in no real hurry, that we would much rather take an extra hour to reach our destination via mellower trails. He would nod his head, promise to mend his ways, then jump over a 3-meter cliff and beckon us to follow.

This is the first time in my life that I find myself in the position of employer. I reflect, as Juan is totally ignoring my "commands," that I once harbored the fantasy of being a publishing magnate—hiring, firing, leading, and inspiring my minions like a latter-day Citizen Kane.

We set up camp on a nice piece of beach near where Cruz and family had camped two years before. While Gay and I just hung out, Juan headed downriver looking for bamboo. Over the next four days, he carved over fifty flutes with the idea of consigning them to the artisan stores in Creel. We suspect, in retrospect, that he was also scouting our route to Pamachi—hoping like hell that there *was* a route.

Within an hour, Marcelio was in camp. It ends up he is Juan's cousin as well as Cruz's. We invite Marcelio to dinner—vegetarian chile with jalapenos and cheese. During the meal, Marcelio tells us that, yes indeed, he did stop by that *tesguinada* after Jay, Norb, and I got on the train. We told him, "Oh yeah? That's nothing, pal. While you were dinking around at your quaint little *tesguinada*, we hiked all the way back to America that very night, stopping for at least 100 beers in every bar we passed." In truth, we were gone-to-the-world passed out at Margarita's within about an hour of our arrival in Creel.

The next day, Gay, Juan, and I hiked downriver a mile or so, until we hit a beach directly down the Eye of the Canyon from Divisadero. We had to cross the Urique three times. Only the first crossing was slightly bothersome. The next two crossings were knee-deep and smooth-bottomed.

This was a great day. After doing a little exploring, we spent the rest of the daylight hours laying back and reading in the sun. Since we had not brought any camp shoes because we were already overloaded with photography gear, we had crossed the river wearing our hiking boots. So, we were—and this is our excuse for our slothfulness—"giving our boots the opportunity to dry" before tomorrow's ascent.

The whole time we were lounging, Juan was carving his flutes. This boy is clearly an eager beaver in the financial sense. He had only recently learned about the monetary possibilities that guiding presented. Since, in the eyes of the average Tarahumara, one, gringos walk weenie distances in slow motion and, two, we eat good, guiding is considered easy money in Tarahumara-land. Much of Juan's conversation during this trip centered on what a young man would have to do to market himself to the gringo backpacking hordes. Short of taking out an ad in the classifieds of *Backpacker*, I told him I didn't know.

As well, he told us he would soon be heading down to the tomato fields near Los Mochis, where he would spend the next three months as a migrant worker—for about $4 U.S. a day. Plus, he thought he could make as much as $20 from those fifty flutes! I mean, we're talking stocks and bonds and yachts here.

Seriously, Juan was in the market for a wife. And he wanted to make certain he had enough in the way of fiscal resources to set up house and hearth before he popped the question to an as-yet-undetermined Tarahumara female. (Gay wondered aloud—much too aloud—why I had not approached our impending matrimonial bliss with such a responsible attitude.) Traditionally, newlywed Tarahumara couples take up residence in the bride's parents' house—where the bridegroom serves, essentially, as a gofer for his father-in-law. Juan had already articulated his disdain for that system. He was, he told me, looking to break with Tarahumara tradition in this regard—even if it meant leaving Tarahumara-land for the slums of Chihuahua City.

From what I have seen in my Copper Canyon Country travels, Juan is far from alone in this sentiment. What effect this attitude among the young will ultimately have on Tarahumara-land is hard to say. One thing is for certain. Under the old system, which is certainly still practiced by the vast majority of Tarahumaras, family survival needs were met because everyone pitched in with the food growing, the hunting/gathering, and the goat herding. Now, young Tarahumaras, instead of working the bean fields in the canyon depths, are going to places like Los Mochis to earn money—which they spend less on family needs than they do on new clothing and portable tape players. Same old same old, the world over.

Early the next morning, we followed the unnamed arroyo opposite the Eye of the Canyon up towards Pamachi. After a few hundred yards, the trail started switch-backing up the right-hand side, through thick brush. The next hour or so was uncomfortable because of the briars and brambles. It was here that we started questioning Juan's knowledge of this neck of the woods. He had told us that the route between Divisadero and Pamachi was well traveled by Tarahumaras. It did not seem to us that this section of trail was well traveled by anything, save, maybe, your occasional rattler.

An hour later, we crossed over the arroyo at a small waterfall—a good place to fill water bottles. Suddenly, we were on a trail that was fairly major. And it stayed that way for the rest of the hike. Juan looked relieved.

Our relationship with Juan began to deteriorate along in here somewhere. In his defense, Juan had only guided one trip before, and, even then he was more a toter than a guide. So, he may have simply not understood the nature of our arrangement.

Problems started when Juan tried to renegotiate his contract halfway between the Urique and Pamachi. This we thought unscrupulous, though we agreed he was not being paid top-dollar—5,000 pesos a day, which is about half what experienced guides charged in these parts in 1988. But he wasn't worth top-dollar. He was a third-round draft choice rookie just trying to make the team and we were poor people. So, we refused to up his pay, though we did tell him that if we were especially pleased with his performance, we might consider laying a tip on him.

Shortly thereafter, we realized that Juan had been hiking way ahead of us and hitting the group lunch and snack foods that were in his pack, to the point that for the next two days, we had no lunch stuff. As well, we had been trying to make him understand that he was expected to take part in all camp-related chores. He was dogging it on washing his eating utensils. He figured that, since we had a female along, why should his sixteen-year-old male self be expected to wash dishes? That went over real big with my then-thirty-four-year-old wife. Then he started dogging even the traditional male things, like gathering firewood.

He was sulking and it was bringing us down on an otherwise wonderfully successful trip. So, while Gay was off photographing the sunset that night, I had to read Juan the riot act. Man, I felt weird doing that. I tried to get to the bottom of what was bothering him. I tried to make certain he knew that his attitude was bumming us out. I asked if he wanted to settle things up now so he could simply leave. He said he wanted to continue working for us and that he realized it was poor form to ask for more money in the middle of a trip. But, he never really came back around until we returned to Divisadero three days later.

Just before we reached the "rock bridge" pass at the top of the arroyo—four hours after leaving the river—we came across a muddy spring. This was good because we were really hot. Perro did a swan dive. We soaked bandannas, washed our faces, and tried to snack. This is when we learned that all our snack foods were wallowing in Juan's digestive juices.

From the rock bridge pass, the view is astounding—one of the best I have seen. You can see straight up the Eye of the Canyon to Divisadero. From there, you are—finally—part of that great bar view.

On the other side of the rock bridge pass, you can see down another arroyo to the Urique and up the other side to the creepy looking mesa of Sitagochi. In between, is the great bend of the Urique. On the north side, we were looking at Copper Canyon, on the west, at Urique Canyon.

We walked around towards the head of a second arroyo descending into Copper Canyon. About halfway to the opposite side, we passed a lush spring. The vegetation was dense, cool, and shady. We filled up our three-gallon water sack and continued 30 minutes more. We camped at the saddle opposite the rock bridge pass. From there, we could look down on Pamachi.

From this point, we could have gone down to the Urique and then up to Sitagochi, where we could tie into the trail to Cusarare (Chapter 9). Or we could have hiked south to Guagauchique, where we could thumb out to the road connecting Creel and Batopilas.

We did none of those things. Next time. We retraced our footsteps back to the Urique the next day and, the day after that, we hiked back up to Divisadero. Though there was still a little tension with Juan, we had a great hike. Gay showed that she could handle the deep canyons. Four days out of five, and the last three in a row, we had either done a major descent or ascent. And the only part she did not like was crossing the Urique with a bunch of expensive camera gear in her pack. (You may want to think about carrying a dry bag—especially if you want to hike upriver from the point where the trail from Divisadero intersects the Urique, because there's one neck-deep crossing between there and the great bend.)

It took us five non-stop hours to descend from Pamachi to the Urique, then another half-hour to walk upriver to the beginning of the trail to Divisadero. And it took us five bust-ass hours the next day to hike out to Divisadero. We left as soon as it was even close to light enough to see. We wanted to catch the first-class train to Creel at 1 PM. We knew the Las Cabañas del Cobre staff meets all first-class trains in Creel, but only some of the second-class, which pass through Divisadero at 2 PM.

We made it by 12:30 PM. No problems. Perro abandoned us as soon as we reached Divisadero—about two minutes after we actually started thinking about adopting him. Tough noogies for the cur.

Then we got terrible news. The train had derailed between Los Mochis and San Rafael. No one was hurt, but delays the day before had been 18 hours. This day, the delays would be a mere 15-and-a-half. We caught the train in a driving rainstorm at 4:30 AM and arrived in Cusarare as the sun was coming up in a driving snowstorm.

Winter was coming to Tarahumara-land, but love was in the air. During the long wait for the train, Juan had exchanged chitchat with a gorgeous sixteen-year-old Tarahumara female. She giggled a little and he giggled a little. And then she left. On the train, Juan informed us that he now had a new girlfriend. He wanted to know if I had any advice about what he should do with his old girlfriend.

Updates

The Tarahumaras now have even more evidence to add to their running prowess tribal resume. In the summer of 1993, five Tarahumaras were brought by Richard Fisher to participate in the Leadville Trail 100 high-altitude ultramarathon, which takes place mainly along the Colorado Trail, about 45 minutes from where I live. The Tarahumaras took first, second, and fifth, despite the fact that the Leadville 100 is considered an elite race, meaning it attracts all manner of very serious gringo runners. The elevation in the race never goes below 10,000 feet, and it tops out at 12,600 feet.

The winner, Victoriano Churro, won the race by a solid 40 minutes. He wore guaraches through the whole race. At the mile-70 aid station, he was asked what manner of refreshment he would like. He asked for, and received, and drank, you guessed it, a Cerveza. He was fifty-five years old.

Several years after the rim-to-rim trip, I was hiking with several friends from Cusarare to Batopilas. We planned to pass through Pamachi, which we did. (Please see Chapter 17 for more details about all this.) It was not the same place Juan had led Gay and I to. It ended up that the place we had camped with Juan was a good, solid 90 minutes of mostly uphill hiking from beautiful downtown Pamachi. Where we had camped with

Juan was a part of Pamachi *ejido,* but not the village itself. Semantics, semantics.

I have run into Cruz several more times. The first time I ran into him after our experiences down on the Urique, I asked about the health of his family. The baby daughter he had with him while they were camping next to us had passed away before her second birthday. Such is life in Tarahumara-land.

Particulars

The 1:250,000 San Juanito map covers the whole trip from Divisadero to Pamachi via the Urique, but the more detailed 1:50,000 San Jose Guacayvo and San Rafael maps are better.

Catch the train to Divisadero. If you come at a time of year when the days are a little longer, and if you are gung-ho, and if the train arrives early enough, you could make it to the Urique before dark. I've never done this. I've never even thought about trying this.

I recommend staying either at the hotel in Divisadero the first night or on the mesa behind the scenic overlook, which is above the hotel to the east. If you pursue the second option, fill your water bag before you get on the train or from the tap on the train. You may want to purify this water. Since there are eight or ten food vendors in Divisadero, you'll want to stock up on gorditos, quesadillas, and tacos before kissing civilization good-bye for a few days. It's about 20 or 30 minutes of walking to a good camping spot next to the rim. Just continue uphill past the overlook until you reach the rim.

You will be out on a point. From there, look to your left, as you're facing the canyon. You will see another point jutting even further out, about a mile or two away. You want to make your way to that point, passing a school shaped like a Quonset hut. Stick to the rim until you get to that point. From there, you can see another, lower point to the southeast. Make your way down to it and then along the ridge that divides the Eye of the Canyon and another giant arroyo to the east, named Arroyo Rurahuachi. Stay on this ridge for quite a while—sometimes on one side, sometimes on the other, sometimes right on the spine. Eventually, you will switchback into Arroyo Rurahuachi, on your left as you are hiking down. About an hour from the river, cross this arroyo and stick to its left side all the way to the Urique. All this won't be too hard once you locate the main trail, which is a good, burro-train-quality trail. Do not descend the arroyo that drops straight down from the hotel in Divisadero (the Eye of the Canyon), as there is a huge cliff about halfway down. Impassable.

The entire walk down is dry, unless you stumble onto a small spring, of which there are several. But don't count on being able to fill your bottles until you reach the river. There are many campsites on the Urique, and driftwood is plentiful. A few miles upriver, you will come to the great bend of the Urique. The tight canyon entering on the left as you walk upriver is Tararecua Canyon. Just for grins, hike half a mile or so up there. It's powerful. The Tarahumaras call it the Canyon of Bad Dreams—as good a name for something as I have ever heard.

I have continued upriver on the Urique from the great bend for several miles and turned around only because of time, rather than impassibility. I have also walked downriver a couple of miles, again, turning back only because of time. Either direction, you'll have to cross the river several times. Bring a good pair of back-up shoes for the crossings. The rocks in the river can be slippery. And the glare of the sun off the water can make it hard to see the bottom. But, I've never had a mishap, nor been with anyone who has. (Knock on wood.)

If you want to go rim-to-rim, walk downriver until you get to the mouth of the Eye of the Canyon—the one with the view all the way up to Divisadero. You want to go up the arroyo directly opposite it. Start by following the bottom of the arroyo. Within 30 meters, look for a faint trail to your right. It is badly overgrown. Switchback on this trail until you come to the base of a cliff. Parallel this cliff, walking up the arroyo. Soon, you will head down towards a little waterfall, where you cross the arroyo. Stay on the left side all the way to the rock bridge at the top of the canyon. You will pass close to several Tarahumara dwellings. From the waterfall on, the trail is excellent.

Take a right at the rock bridge. (There's undoubtedly a geological name for this type of rock bridge—not an arch, but a little saddle eroded down to exposed rock. You can see this bridge from Divisadero.) Follow the obvious trail around the head of the valley beyond the bridge. The plan is to get to the base of the little hill on the opposite side of the valley. About halfway there, you will pass a spring. Fill up here. Go around to the little saddle at the base of the hill. The hill is actually a point jutting north towards Copper Canyon. The views are stupendous.

From the saddle, you can see a few Tarahumara houses to the south that are part of Pamachi *ejido*. There's a trail right down to them. From Pamachi, you can make your way south to Guaguachique, which is connected by road to Creel and Batopilas. Or you can hike back down into Copper Canyon via the first small valley to your left after you cross the rock bridge. You can see a trail on the other side of the valley heading down to the river. (Again, please see Chapter 17.) From there, you could hike to Divisadero via Tararecua Canyon, though that route is hard to find. Or you could hike to Cusarare. (Chapter 9)

If you return to Divisadero via the same route Gay, Juan, and I used, leave the river early enough that you can catch the last train at 2 PM to Creel, 4 PM to Los Mochis. If you miss the train, just fill your water bag at the hotel and head back up to the mesa immediately south of Divisadero. Or, again, you could simply splurge on a night in the hotel. Rooms in the hotel run about $60 U.S. a night per couple, including meals. There is also a small bar at the hotel that is closed most of the afternoon. Divisadero also sports a very small store, just down the tracks from the food vendor stalls.

You can figure to make it into or out of Copper or Urique Canyons in five to eight hours. On both sides, shade is minimal, direct sunshine is maximal. Bring at least two water bottles per person (three would be better), wear a hat and use sunscreen. Keep your eyes peeled for rattlers as you get down into the canyon.

You can drive from Creel to Divisadero in about 45 minutes over a recently improved dirt road. Be very careful about railroad crossings on this stretch. Several of them are blind and lots of trains run this line. The signs at the blind crossings tell you to stop, cut your engine and listen for a train. Please do just that.

There are a couple of other interesting hikes beginning in this area. About three kilometers west of Divisadero is

Posada de las Barrancas, one of the most wonderful hotels in Copper Canyon Country. The train stops at this hotel, which is actually two hotels in one (both owned by the same person). The first, Posada de las Barrancas-Ranchero, is right at the train station. The second, the Mirador, which was just opened in the fall of 1993, is perched on the canyon rim, about a half kilometer from the train stop. The Mirador sends a bus to pick up guests at the train station.

About halfway between Posada and Divisadero, right on the road, is a campground, owned by the same people who own the hotel in Divisadero. From this campground, a burro trail follows an arroyo down to the gorgeous little ranchito of Bacajipara. From Bacajipara, you have two choices. You can follow the burro trail over the ridge finger to the right. Once on the summit of the ridge finger, it's about three or four more hours of steep downhill climbing to a magical spot on the Rio Urique. I highly recommend this hike.

The other alternative from Bacajipara, which I have not taken myself, is to follow the ridge to the left all the way down to the Urique. From what several people have told me, you can then hike upriver until you intersect with the trail up to Divisadero. This hike should take three or four days.

I highly recommend getting a room at the Mirador upon your return. This is a very expensive hotel (about $70 per night per person, however, the price includes three meals), but well worth it. All rooms have balconies right on the rim. The hotel also boasts a nice little bar, for those few of you who have have an interest in that sort of thing. There are several short dayhike possibilities from the hotel, and the staff can dial you into those possibilities.

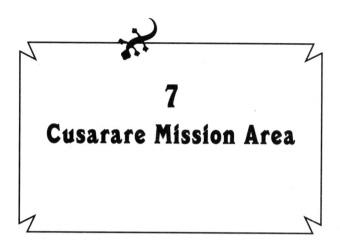

7
Cusarare Mission Area

Cusarare is one of the most conveniently located missions for visitors without cars in Tarahumara-land. It is one kilometer off the road connecting Creel with Batopilas. About 22 kilometers (14 miles) south of Creel, there's a sign on the left pointing the way east. The area surrounding the mission is perfect for dayhiking. It also offers up some overnighter possibilities that I haven't personally tapped into—yet.

The first time Gay and I pulled into Cusarare, a school teacher had his class of young Tarahumara children outside on the basketball court, making them practice their marching—a practical skill for any schoolchild anywhere, but especially for the offspring of Tarahumara-land, the military history of which rivals Prussia. Right. The teacher would shout the order for everyone to "jump." And everyone would jump. March, march, left, right, left, right, "*jump!*" march. It was too unreal.

The Cusarare school is run by the federal government and, from what I have heard, one of the best ways for a teacher to impress his or her superiors is to show them evidence that their Tarahumara charges are well disciplined and follow orders. I have asked various people—in a tone that indicates that perhaps I am not being objective in my thinking—why the Tarahumaras put up with this stupidity, why they don't demand that the government spend its time and money teaching their children something a little more important than marching?

A beautiful female teacher who I picked up hitchhiking one time told me that they do spend the bulk of their time teaching Tarahumara children important academic stuff. She said they would be able to teach them even more if they can get their unruly little carcasses to sit still for longer periods of time. That's where the marching comes in. Uh-*huh*.

Another person, a non-teacher, told me that the Tarahumaras really aren't that concerned about what their children are taught in school, because they have total confidence in their children's ability to separate the important from the weird, to pick up on the reading and math skills while filing away those orders to "jump." What Tarahumara parents really care about may be the fact that their kids get a free lunch when they're in school.

A couple of Tarahumara men were watching the proceedings, the same as us. The look on their faces as they watched twenty or so elementary-age kids hup-two-three-ing around the basketball court told us that they thought there was no end to the crap that Western society would heap on their people for no apparent good reason.

The whole educational system in Tarahumara-land is strange. All schools, and there are a surprising number of them, are run either by the government or, more often than not, by the Jesuits. The government schools are notorious for teaching the Tarahumaras that it is better not to be a Tarahumara. Tarahumara children are taught how backwards their people are, from a perspective that "backwardness" is a bad thing.

The Jesuits probably don't do that as much. They have managed to convince the government oversight bureaucracies that the Tarahumaras deserve to be taught in their own language and within the context of the culture. From what I have heard, the Jesuits have been so persuasive that the government has expanded this concept to other parts of the country.

In Cusarare, the school is right next to the wonderful old mission, built sometime about 1740. Cusarare Mission is one of the oldest around. There are more missions in Tarahumara-land than there are Jesuit preachers, so some of the priests play the part of circuit riders. Each mission hosts a mass about once a month.

Cusarare Mission is kept locked. So, on our first trip there, we were unable to get inside, however, that was okay because it was a fine day for a walk in the hills. We each packed a light lunch and a total of three liters of water because it was hot and sunny.

The plan was to hike east to the ranchito of Cochipachi via Gomirachi, either of which can be accessed more conveniently by simply following the road. But, so what? We wanted to walk through the rolling hill country surrounding Cusarare. We parked our truck next to the mission and headed out toward the little pass with the crosses, due east of the mission. You can't miss it, unless the locals remove the crosses, which is highly unlikely. We could have gone any number of ways, because this area is crisscrossed by very obvious walking trails. The area also sports plenty of primitive logging roads, so this would be good fat tire territory.

All things considered, this is a good area to acclimate yourself to Tarahumara culture and high sierra topography. It is also serious cross territory, with many of the small summits in the vicinity being adorned with the Christian penance symbol.

A Tarahumara man at the mission told us it would take but 15 minutes to get to Gomirachi. We would make certain it took longer than that. We walked through the mission cemetery, stopping to snap a few photos. After reaching the little pass with the crosses, we skirted a few Tarahumara homesteads. On the mission side of the pass, the Tarahumaras are used to seeing lots of gringo tourists, because Cusarare is on the local tour "A" list. But across the pass, even a few minutes walk from the parking lot, it was a different story. The locals here come running out of their dwellings just like they do when you pass a ranchito in the deep canyon country. When we reached Gomirachi—which, despite its proximity to tourist-"infested" Cusarare, is one of the loveliest little hamlets I have ever seen—we hooked up with an old logging road, and headed north, towards the Rio Conchos.

It is very pleasant to dayhike with no plan and no particular place to go—just to cruise at a mellow pace with little weight on our backs wherever this particular trail happens to go. There we were, sashaying through the cool pines hand-in-hand like we were sweethearts, rather than husband-and-wife. (Wait a minute. Did that come out right?)

After about two hours, we topped out on the Continental Divide, stopped for lunch—raisins, crackers, Mennonite cheese—and dozed in the sun. We hiked back via Cochipachi, which, again, was so primitively quaint that I felt I could live there the rest of my life.

This is high sierra country, with small, cold, meandering creeks weaving their way through rock-walled pastures. Like a more arid version of Vermont. The rock formations in the Cusarare Creek valley are icing on the visual cake.

We walked back via the dirt road connecting Cusarare with Norogachi. This road, which I talk more about in Chapter 19, is used fairly heavily by logging trucks, but it still makes for a nice walk. All told, about four hours worth of relaxing walking through some of the gentlest and most postcard-like terrain in Tarahumara-land.

Whenever you're hiking near a mission, you need to check the place out. The missions in Tarahumara-land are cool, whether you are religious or not. I got my chance to rub elbows with the interior of Cusarare Mission several weeks later, when I learned that an acquaintance, for reasons I didn't fully understand, possessed a key to the mission. This bit of information popped out about 11 PM to a bunch of crazed gringos who were, at the time, pounding down beers less than a mile away. We went.

Since there are no electric lights in the mission, all ten of us brought flashlights. Doors from the early 1700s slowly squeak open. The wooden floor creaks as we advance on the altar. There's a little roped-off museum to the left. There's a rickety-looking ladder to the choir loft. There's death to be had, for sure, for any gringos who try to make the climb this night. There are no pews. The Tarahumara congregation, during its monthly services, has to stand the whole time, which must be extremely pleasant, given the fact that Catholic services are well-known for their brevity. On the right, toward the front, is the pulpit, rickety and old and accessed by a dark flight of little stone stairs that pass through a musty corridor.

I head for those small stairs, pausing only long enough to gawk at the human skull on one of the little side altars. I had heard there was a skull on display in the mission, but it still

John leaving the Rio Urique, on the trail to Pamachi.
Divisadero is on opposite rim.

Copper Canyon Lodge in Cusarare.

*Tarahumara women weave baskets
at the train stop in Divisadero.*

*John gets directions to the Rio Urique
below Posada from a local resident.*

Burro at Rio Urique, near village of Urique.

Jay Scott at a swimming hole on the Rio Urique.

Bridge over Rio Batopilas near Satevo.

Tarahumara man carries a pack of straw on his back.

Ladder access to the canyon near Posada.

Sinforosa Canyon.

View on hike to the Rio Urique, near El Tejabán.

Tarahumara girl sells her wares along the trail to Cusarare Falls.

Cusarare Falls after a rainstorm.

Batopilas Plaza.

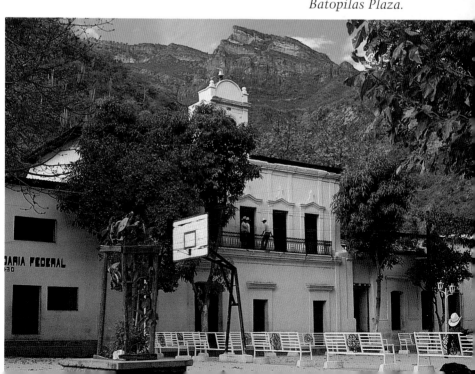

Señor and Señora Torres at Los Alisos.

surprised me as I caught a glimpse of it in my flashlight-lit peripheral vision. Nobody commented on the squeak that jumped wholeheartedly from my throat. They probably thought it was the floor creaking.

Now, why on earth would there be a dead person's head bone on an altar of a Catholic church? Got me. I mean it would be one thing if it had some practical use, like a pencil holder, but I believe this ancient bean was there purely for ceremonial reasons. Supposedly, this is the noggin of the original Cusarare preacher, though all agree that it is too small to have once been worn by an adult male.

The Jesuits, who got their foot in the door in Tarahumara-land minutes after Columbus' first visit to the New World, got ousted from Mexico by the Mexican government in the late 1700s because they were too active in temporal matters. They were only permitted to return about seventy years ago. While they were absent, the Tarahumaras started doing interesting things with Catholicism. Like mating it with their animist beliefs. Though any Tarahumara you ask will tell you that they are Catholic, some are more Catholic than others. They still use shamans, and they believe very seriously in all sorts of magic, both good and bad.

I had this plan to deliver a sermon that would have every-one there gathered thinking in terms of becoming nuns and monks and making donations to my spiritual cause. But, as soon as I stepped into that pulpit, the thing started rocking back and forth. It wasn't attached to the wall. It was perched there like a big wooden wine glass that you've just bumped and you're not sure yet if it's going to go over and mess up the white tablecloth.

I decided that it really wasn't all that important to me if everyone there went to hell in a handbasket. I abdicated the pulpit and returned to floor level, where I truly belong, just as our host, the keybearer, hurried us all out the door for fear that the scene was about to turn ugly in some way he could not quite conceive.

About a month later, on December 12, the feast day of the Virgin of Guadalupe, Mexico's patron saintess, Gay and I went to Cusarare Mission to watch the festivities. This day is a national holiday in Mexico and people flat-out party. As we approached Cusarare at night, the hills surrounding the mission sported dozens of campfires, owner-occupied by the scores of Tarahumaras who had come in from the outback for the celebration.

We entered the church during the middle of a Tarahumara ceremonial dance. During ceremonial times, the Tarahumaras wear bizarre, elaborate head-dressings and masks. I have no idea what this dance, performed by about twenty couples, was all about, but the moves were almost like the Virginia Reel—with one line of females and one line of males facing each other from ten feet away, while each couple took turns boogeying down in between the lines.

The jams were provided by a trio of Tarahumara men. One of the guys was picking a guitar, one was playing a drum, and the other a concertina. All the songs we heard consisted of the same couple of bars being played over and over ad infinitum. Each of these songs had a distinctly three-beat, almost polka-like rhythm, which I think is the most prevalent rhythm in the world, for reasons that escape me.

Several times a minute, all the dancers and the musicians would let out hoots and hollers. There was a choreographer who spent the whole time running around with a fanged rattle of some sort. Every once in a while he would shake it wildly next to someone's head. And that someone would scarcely pay one iota of attention to the fact that some maniac was violently shaking a rattle with rattlesnake fangs attached to it next to their ears. Right psychedelic scene.

One thing's for sure, these dances aren't officially Pope-certified. This is from the Tarahumara deep past, back when they believed their own beliefs rather than someone else's. A time so long ago that most Tarahumaras probably don't know what the dances mean. I have heard it said that converters are always, ultimately, converted by their convertees. This may be true of the Jesuits. One man told me that, when he was camping by himself on the Conchos in the early eighties, he awoke in the middle of the night, after being told earlier by the local Jesuits that he should be on his way at first light. A Jesuit priest was jumping through a huge bonfire in some kind of creepy-looking ceremony that included a dozen traditionally dressed Tarahumaras. This man told me that he was, indeed, on the trail well before first light.

At Cusarare Mission, we could not help but feel like we were intruding. After about three dances, each of which lasted four years, Gay and I left. But, most of the other gringos stayed, so probably we were just being a little uptight. We wanted to tap into the Tarahumara scene like genuine insiders, but we couldn't figure out any way to go about it. There were all those fires out there with Tarahumaras sitting around drinking *tesguino*, and we wanted to be sitting there with them, chewing the fat, shooting the breeze. But, any gathering would become tense if we just walked up, said howdy, and helped ourselves to a drink. So, while Tarahumara-land partied, we went back to camp and sacked out, a little let down with ourselves.

Like many of the *ejidos* near Creel, Cusarare is now charging admission to its tourist attractions, the mission being one of those. It now costs one new peso to be admitted inside the mission. Also, on your way into Cusarare, you will notice a large greenhouse on the right. This facility, built in 1991, is used to grow tomatoes and chilies. It was partly funded by the collection of admission fees to tourist attractions. So, you can see that the *ejidos* are capable of using that cash for good purposes.

Particulars

The whole Cusarare area is smack in the middle of the 1:50,000 Creel topo. To reach Cusarare Mission from Copper Canyon Lodge (Chapter 4), just walk upstream along Cusarare Creek for 2.5 kilometers (about 1.5 miles). Or, walk up to the main road, and back towards Creel for a few hundred yards, before following the sign the last half-mile to the mission. I recommend following the creek. The walk, though not thunderstruck intense with scenery, will be one of the highlights of your visit to Tarahumara-land.

From Creel, if you don't want to hook up with a tour that includes a short stop at Cusarare Mission, of which there are several, just plan on hitching a ride. You should be able to do this easily. A good plan is to leave Creel early and hit the mission and environs in the morning before heading downstream to Cusarare Falls. Top the day off with a beer at the Copper Canyon Lodge before thumbing back to Creel before dark. Cusarare can also serve as the jump-off point for multi-day excursions to the Rio Conchos. Just down the creek from Cusarare Mission is the hamlet of Yahuirachi. Hike from there due north to the Conchos. Though you will cross the Continental Divide, the hiking will be very easy. I would allow a full day to reach the Conchos.

From the Conchos, you can hike over to Panalachi—which should take a day—from where you can hitchhike back to Creel. Or you can hike from Panalachi to Tehuirichi (Chapter 18). You can also hike up the Conchos until you reach a point where you can hike directly back to Creel. This will require orientation skills. Plan on hooking into the road that passes through San Ignacio (Chapter 3).

It is also possible to hike down the Conchos to Tehuirichi. From there, you can either cruise over to Panalachi, or return to the Cusarare side of the divide via Choguita, a Mexican town 20 miles or so east on the gravel/dirt road that takes you from the paved road to Cusarare. From there, you can hitch back to Cusarare. (There are two Choguitas in this area, the other being between Creel and San Juanito, on the main highway to Chihuahua City.)

Following the Conchos, though fatiguing because of the number of river crossings—marked *"vados"* on the maps—is not in the same league of difficulty as following the rivers on the western side of the divide. The Conchos valley is relatively gentle.

It is tempting to recommend hiring a guide out of Cusarare if you want to make it to the Conchos, but the Tarahumaras who live in Cusarare aren't very familiar with the eastern side of the divide. They may be able to wing it, but if you really want a guide, get to Choguita, which, by the way, is not on the 1:50,000 Creel map, and hire a Mexican guide.

If you really want to experience old Tarahumara culture, plan a four-day trip, from Cusarare north to the Conchos. From there, go to Panalachi. From there, to Tehuirichi. From there, to Choguita. (See Chapter 18 for more details about the Conchos.)

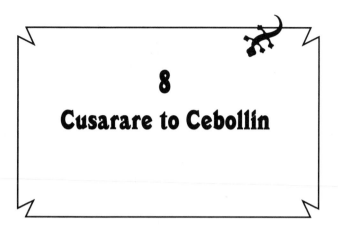

8
Cusarare to Cebollín

In all my years of hiking in and around Copper Canyon Country, I had never visited the one place that actually bears the name of, or, more accurately, has given its name to, the entire region: Barranca del Cobre, which is the name of a specific part of the canyon formed by the Rio Urique, as well as being the name of a little (and I do mean *little*) village at the very bottom of that canyon.

I set out in February 1990 with Lilliana Carruso, who, at the time, was the manager of Las Cabañas del Cobre in Cusarare, my friend Sahuaripa Gonzales, and another Cusarare resident, Nemecio something-or-another, to do just that. Actually, when I refer to Sahuaripa in this section as "my friend," that's not quite accurate. I didn't know him until this trip. I had already hired Nemecio as a guide, because he was born and raised in the village of Huacaybo, through which we would be passing. To say Nemecio knew the route from Cusarare to the small village of Cebollin was an understatement. Still, I put out the word in Cusarare that I needed second guide because Lilliana had said from the start that she had no interest whatsoever in carrying her own pack. Through the help of Jesus Olivas, who I have referred to in these pages as the "Mexican Gandalf" because of his dignified and magical demeanor, I made Sahuaripa's acquaintance.

The plan was to hike three hours the first day to a small spring near the ranchito of Bitorachi, where we would camp the first night. Then, we would hike to the canyon rim at

El Tejabán, before descending into Copper Canyon itself. The next day, we would hike through Huacaybo on our way to Cebollin, where Jesus would pick us up. All told, four days and three nights, which, when compared to some of the hare-brained itineraries I've found myself stumbling through in Copper Canyon Country, seemed like a mellow enough plan. Which is exactly what it ended up being. (For once.)

The hike to Bitorachi was uneventful to the point of actually being a little boring. We walked through ponderosa pine forests and gently rolling hills until we reached the spring, which was actually a mile or so short of Bitorachi. Although this is certainly not the most scenic stretch of trail in Tarahumara-land, it's always nice to kick a trip off with a relaxed day of hiking. It was also nice to be out in the woods with Lilliana, who I had known for several years, but had never hiked with. Generally, when I have hooked up with Lilliana, we have spent our social time in Creel consuming record quantities of Tecate, rather than wasting our time out in the fresh air.

Those first few hours also gave me a chance to get to know Sahuaripa a little. Sahuaripa is one truly special hombre. More than any other Tarahumara I have ever met, he seems to interface not only extrememly well, but also positively and productively with gringos, both on professional and social levels. While I'm certain he still harbors a certain amount of justifiable perplexedness towards those of us who choose to enjoy ourselves by going to Mexico and schlepping a pack up and down canyons all day, he seems to at least be willing to give gringos a cultural chance, which is more than I can say about a lot of Tarahumaras.

It was also interesting to visit with Nemecio, who I had met before, mainly because his wife, Rosa, used to work as a cook at Las Cabañas del Cobre. Nemecio hadn't been home to Huacaybo in three years, and he was very eager to visit with his two sisters and numerous nieces and nephews who still lived there. He told us in no uncertain terms that, because of his presence, we would probably receive a ticker-tape parade upon our arrival in Huacaybo.

Within the first hour on the trail, we knew we had committed an equipment *faux pas*. We had decided, since the weather had been so nice, to forego carrying tents, a decision that automatically attracted the attention of the Misadventure God, who, from that moment on, kept a keen eye on us. It began clouding up well before we reached Bitorachi, and, for the next four days, the threat of rain was near-bouts constant.

Our campsite was located on an old roadbed in the middle of thick woods. There was absolutely nothing in the way of views, which is, not surprisingly, a rarity in Copper Canyon Country. But, from the top of a little rise, about 200 yards from camp, there was what can only be described as a wonderful view of a view. Yeah, yeah, yeah, we could see Bitorachi, a lovely enough little ranchito nestled in a small, mist-shrouded, boulder-infested valley. But, further off, we could see the opposite rim of Copper Canyon itself. Though, from our far-away vantage point, that opposite rim looked like little more than a nondescript ridgeline, we knew full well that, once we got closer, our jaws would drop as streams of superlatives danced joyously from our mouths.

There was ample firewood around camp, and we had brought with us several bottles of recreational beverages, so it ended up being quite a jovial evening of around-the-fire fat-chewing. Despite the fact that Nemecio has almost Anglo-like blue eyes, he considers himself Tarahumara. So, he and Sahuaripa could hobnob in Tarahumara and/or Spanish. Lilliana, an American from Michigan who had Argentinean citizenship until she was twenty-three, speaks Spanish as well as she does English. And I am pretty conversant in Spanish, as well as being able to blunder my way through English. So, our conversations ended up sounding like crosses between pidginism, creole-ity, and bilingualism, all served up piping hot in one increasingly inebriated linguistic stew.

We had about eight hours of hiking the second day out. The first five of those hours, from Bitorachi to El Tejabán, were very easy. After about four hours, we passed the little dirt airstrip just outside El Tejabán. There are several interesting things about this airstrip. First, we couldn't help but notice that there were crashed-and-burned light aircraft at each end of the lone runway. Something to do with drug smuggling efforts gone awry, I'm sure.

There is one other thing about this airstrip. For many years, there has been talk about a hotel being built on the rim of Copper Canyon at El Tejabán. A few times, things like foundations have even been started, but, Mexico being Mexico, that's as far as it ever got. But, in October 1993, I was told by several people in-the-know that development efforts had begun anew. The current plan is to build a five-star golf course resort right at El Tejabán that would be serviced only by airplanes. Also, a tramway all the way from the rim to the Rio Urique was on the drawing board. Now, I'll bet, if you tried real hard, you could take a wild guess which Pacific island nation that is about the size of California and boasts a population of about 120 million the developers of this proposed project are from.

I fear that if it does take place, once more, the local Tarahumaras will find themselves on the doo-doo end of the economic stick. If they gain any employment opportunities whatsoever from such a development, those opportunities will, like just about every other development in Copper Canyon Country, with the exception of Skip McWilliams's two hotels, take the form of the most menial and underpaid positions. Same as it ever was.

We were all very excited about making it to El Tejabán. From the rim, Nemecio told us we would be able to view Huacaybo, located on a mesa overlooking an arroyo about a third of the way up the rim on the other side. For Nemecio, it would be his first view of home in a long time. For the rest of us, it would be a first-time visit to a place that is considered by many to offer up one of the best views in Tarahumara-land. No wonder that El Tejabán is one of the most consistently photographed areas in Tarahumara-land for things like promotional material and magazine articles.

When we finally reached the rim, we were dumbfounded by the beauty that spread out before us. Though the canyon here is "only" about 4,000 feet deep, the geological striations of both rims are some of the most awesome I have ever seen. The Rio Urique flowed bright turquoise far below. Picture-postcard-pretty Huacaybo looked so close it seemed like we could walk to it in an hour. And, all around us and below us, there were buildings and ruins as old as buildings and ruins get in Copper Canyon Country.

This was the part of Tarahumara-land that first caught the attention of the Spanish back in the 1600s, and, for generations, unimaginable quantities of copper, gold, silver, and lead were mined from the area right below us. The ore was carted via burro train to El Tejabán, where it was crushed and separated, before being burro-trained to Chihuahua.

We descended via that same, ancient burro trail. This is one of the few descents you can take into the bowels of a deep canyon in Tarahumara-land that is relatively mellow. The trail is nicely switchbacked, and, when you cut the nut, 4,000 feet of descent isn't all that much.

We stopped to check out some of the ruins in the area. One building especially caught our eyes. It was well off the trail, and perched right on the edge of a cliff, 1,000 or so feet below the rim. From our vantage point, it could well have been a residence back in days of yore. But, it was a residence with a backyard that dropped off to oblivion. That is one place that, if you had to step outside in the middle of night to relieve yourself, you had better be mighty careful.

We arrived at the Urique well before dark. Since there was a cave and a nice piece of beach on the El Tejabán side, we decided to camp without crossing the river. But, all was not well with our little expedition, despite the overwhelming beauty of our surroundings. On the way down, Nemecio had started telling Rio Urique stories. One in particular, which Nemecio obviously took for the gospel, caught Sahuaripa's undivided attention.

Nemecio related how the Urique was well known for its man-killing, maiming, and eating serpent population. These serpents, which Nemecio described as monstrously huge and snakelike in shape, apparently ventured forth from the depths of the river every now and again specifically for the purpose of nabbing an innocent human for din-din. Nemecio said he even had one uncle who, while fishing, found himself under attack from one of these serpents. He managed to fight the beast off and, as far as Nemecio knew, he was the only person in the history of Copper Canyon Country ever to survive a Rio Urique serpent attack.

Lilliana told me that she had read somewhere or another that Tarahumaras have been relating stories about Urique-dwelling serpents for generations. The ethnological studies she had read concluded that, probably, flash-flood-borne whirlpools were responsible for killing lots of people over the years, and those whirlpools probably formed the backbone of the serpent legends.

On our way down, Lilliana and I, both being captivated by the area's beauty, promptly forgot about the serpent discussion, right up to the point when Sahuaripa casually asked where we planned to camp that night. He cringed when I said we would be camping right alongside the Urique. He said something along the lines of, "Wouldn't we all be a little more comfortable if we went ahead and walked up to Huacaybo before dark?" His voice was more than a little strained. Then, it dawned on me that he had taken the serpent story to heart.

It was obvious that some fast talking was in order, if we were going to continue to have Sahuaripa as a guide, because we could tell from the look on his face that there was no way in hell he was going to offer himself up as Purina Serpent Chow by voluntarily rolling out his sleeping bag on the shores of the Rio Urique. So, I handled the situation the only way anybody hoping to salvage an expedition would, could, and should: I sort of stretched the truth. I told him that I would simply cast an anti-serpent spell, and all would be well.

This little white-person lie was not without foundation. The Tarahumaras, like many Native Americans, first of all, believe in magic and are practitioners of magic, and, secondly, they look at smoke as a substance with at least mild connections to the supernatural world. And, since I am a cigar smoker, I constantly am surrounded by thick smoke. I also play around with blowing smoke rings, and that has caught the attention of many Tarahumaras who have spent time with me. I have been called a "brujo"—witch—in varying tones of voice covering the gamut from "hee hee hee" to "oh, shit! hide the kids and run for your lives!"—by more than a few Tarahumaras. I even overheard Nemecio telling Sahuaripa before we left Cusarare to be careful around me, because he had heard I was a brujo. So, I just played on that theme and, a few minutes after we dropped our packs just inside the cave, I lit up not one, but two big ol' nasty, stinky cigars, walked down to the side of the river and performed a de-serpent ritual that, in retrospect, worked so damned well I have found myself using it often when I find myself in the presence of real estate developers, bureaucrats, and men of the cloth.

Now, what really caught Sahuaripa's and Nemecio's attention about all this was the fact that I did not incantate against any and all serpents that might be inclined to slither out of the water and consume whatever number of us that night, but, rather, I actively encouraged the serpents to attempt to do so. I told the serpents that, where I come from, there's nothing we enjoy more than the chance to kick a little serpent derriere. So, I let them know exactly where I would be sleeping and invited them, their cousins, and their amigos to pay me a visit at their earliest convenience.

You should have seen the look on Sahuaripa's face when I strolled back to the cave, hands in pockets, while trying hard to not choke to death right on the spot because I was still smoking two cigars simultaneously. He didn't know whether to laugh or to cry. And I think my green face actually enhanced my image as a *brujo* at a time when I could have used a quick puke.

While retaining a modicum of outward nervousness, Sahuaripa and Nemecio both seemed somewhat satisfied that they would not be consumed by serpents that night, mainly because they were convinced I would be the one the serpents came after en masse. Once I told them them I planned to sleep out on the sand next to the water, Sahuaripa and Nemecio both breathed significant sighs of relief because that meant I would be between them and the serpents.

The only problem with that plan was, just before dark, which, in the minds of my Tarahumara compadres, was about when the serpents were sharpening up their teeth, it started to pour rain. Which meant I had to sleep in the cave with Lilliana and the two Tarahumaras. Nemecio and Sahuaripa were distraught. To say that they were suddenly facing a wide-eyed, sleepless night is an accurate observation. They were both rigid with fear, as well as, I suspect, a certain degree of animosity towards me for inviting every serpent in the entire canyon to come and dine with us that very night. But, after an hour, the rain stopped and the sky cleared. Having a touch of claustrophobia, I left the cave and, as promised, moved my bedroll down to the beach. Sahuaripa and Nemecio finally exhaled, after a solid hour of holding their breath. The next morning, they were both surprised, and seemingly pleased, to find that I had not been killed. I was touched.

The crossing of the Urique was a little squirrelly, and it took us about an hour to de-boot, cross, and re-boot on the other side. We walked upriver to the last remaining occupied houses in this part of the canyon. From the outside, it didn't look like they would remain occupied for much longer. This neck of the woods was clearly in decline. The arroyo up which we walked to Huacaybo turned out to be the most interesting one I have ever visited in Copper Canyon Country. Almost immediately, we started passing ore-crushers—water-powered, circular-shaped devices used to pulverize gold and silver ore before it is sluiced and, finally, fine-panned. There ended up being literally dozens of these ore-crushers up Arroyo Hua- caybo, making this one of the most active mining areas in the region. We talked to several miners hard at work. They told us they get their ore from underground mines located up to sev- eral hours away. Then, they carry the ore down on their backs and put it into the crushers. Every year, we were told, half of the ore-crushers are destroyed by flash floods. As evidence, there were twisted and mangled ore-crushers spread through- out the arroyo.

A few minutes before we arrived in Huacaybo, we passed one of the most interesting little houses/ruins (well, actually it was more like ruins/houses) I have ever laid eyes on. It was about 8 AM, and, since the buildings were so intriguing, I decided to stop for a few pictures. Suddenly, the man of the house came out to chit-chat. He was about forty and looked like he had been drinking constantly since the moment he dropped out of the womb. This man was *drunk*. As it turned out, he had hosted a four-day *tesguinada* that had just ended about 15 minutes before our arrival. And—good news—this man told us there was still some four-day-old *tesguino* left, so why didn't we pop on in for a little post-breakfast fortification?

Great. We still had 4,000 feet to climb, and we had been informed by Nemecio that we would be invited for at least two meals in Huacaybo, and here we were, very shortly after consuming heapin' helpin's of instant oatmeal, being invited to partake of some *tesguino* that surely was on the verge of not only going bad, but, probably, of setting all sorts of world pathogen-growth records.

Of course, we accepted. We were promptly invited to step inside, which is not usual. This place was astounding. The man had no idea how old it was, but, he contended, it was built sometime back around when dirt was invented. The edifice contained three crumbly rooms, each occupied by a different family. Like Nemecio, these people looked, at a minimum, Mestizo, but they claimed to be full-blooded Tarahumara.

The man led us back to his family's room, which was home to the man, his wife, four children, and a cute, teenaged Tarahumara female "friend" (nudge-nudge, wink-wink). The room was about the size of my wife's Subaru. The *tesguino* was poured into four of the filthiest coffee cups I have seen this side of a Boy Scout campout. But, if there's one good thing you can say about *tesguino*, it's that it's dark-colored enough to hide any amount of filth.

It ended up that this *tesguino* was the best I had ever tasted, which is not saying a lot, but at least it's saying something. After one cup, though, we started saying our good-byes as fast as they could be said without giving offense. On the way out, the man asked if I had any stomach pills, which is a very common question to be asked in the boonies of Tarahumara-land. I laid a couple of Pepto Bismol tablets on them, took a quick family portrait, and we took our leave, wobbling slightly from the *tesguino*, which, it turned out (I'm just tickled pink to report) was very potent.

Just before entering Huacaybo, we passed the town cemetery. Nemecio told us his mother was buried there. From where we stood, maybe 100 yards away across the arroyo, he could see that the cemetery had been badly neglected in the three years he had been gone. He looked clearly disgusted. He told us how the cemetery was one of the oldest around, with headstones dating back to the 1700s. Several Americans were even buried there.

Finally, we entered Huacaybo, which is a pretty white-washed and fruit-tree-dominated hamlet of perhaps one hundred souls, not counting the pigs and the dogs, which, if counted, would swell the population to 300 million.

Almost immediately, the townspeople came steaming out to say howdy to Nemecio. There were cousins and friends and uncles and aunts and even a few people Nemecio had never met or even heard of who just seemed to be caught up in all the excitement, of which there probably isn't very much in Huacaybo. The town matron invited us in for a meal of beans, tortillas, and homemade fire, er, I mean, "salsa." We hung out for a while, before retiring outside for a smoke and to pass a bottle of our rum around, an event that evidently endeared us to the male population of Huacaybo forevermore.

Finally, we strolled up the hill to Nemecio's family homestead. It was obvious that Nemecio had suddenly come to dread this moment. He was still steaming about the state-of-the-cemetery situation, and the focus of that steam was his brother-in-law, who Nemecio considered the most slothful character he had ever known. He was convinced that the family spread would also be in a state of neglect. He was right. The house, which was built under a huge, overhanging boulder, was in shambles. The family orchard had not been tended to all year, and the trees, lovingly planted and nurtured by Nemecio's mother, were dying. Even though it was only February, there was little firewood left, and the family's food stocks clearly stood no chance of making it through the rest of the winter. Were it not for our presence, I'm certain Nemecio would have pummeled his brother-in-law to death.

We hung out for a few hours, had a meal, which consisted totally of backpacking food we had donated to the household, and prepared to move on. Nemecio was embarrassed to tears. On the way out of town, he indicated that he would have to cancel out on a guided trip I had scheduled for the next week. As soon as we returned to Cusarare, he was packing his bags and moving back to Huacaybo for a few months, to set his family's affairs in order. He said he had been gone too damned long.

Though fairly hot and steep, and despite our full bellies and alcohol hobbled heads, the hike up to the rim went smoothly. We camped at a small spring on the top and hiked out to Cebollin to meet Jesus early the next morning. Cebollin, which is located on the road to Guaguachique and Pamachi (it doesn't appear on any map I have seen), is a scuzzy-looking little place, populated by dour-looking folks who clearly would love to live somewhere else. But, it boasts a small store, so we were able to score a few softdrinks before embarking on the four-hour drive back to Cusarare.

Jesus had brought a teenage boy, named Chu, with him for company on the drive, and here you must forgive me for going off on a little tangent, while I tell you about Chu. Chu is a shortened version of Chunel, which, by the same kind of logic that makes Hank a nickname for Henry, is a nickname for Jesus. Chu was named after Jesus, and Chu's father, Reyes, has been Jesus' best friend for more than fifty years. Reyes was supposed to have come with us on our Cusarare-to-Cebollin trek, but had to cancel at the last minute because of a bad knee. He recommended that we hire Nemecio, who was a neighbor, instead. Cool.

On the way back to Cusarare, someone pulled out a bottle of tequila in the back of the truck while Lilliana and I were riding with Jesus up front. And Nemecio, Sahuaripa, and Chu commenced to drink the entire bottle in fairly short order. Nemecio and Sahuaripa were merely a little giggly and tipsy. Chu, on the other hand, had to be carried from the truck when we arrived back in Cusarare. His eyes were rolled back in his head and his tongue was dragging in the dirt behind him. I have literally never seen anyone as drunk. I was very concerned that he could die in his sleep from alcohol poisoning, but Jesus said he would keep an eye on him, and , once we all became convinced that Chu would make it through the night, we all got a good laugh out of his self-inflicted misfortune.

The next week, I was scheduled to guide a trip from Cusarare to Batopilas via Cebollin. Since Nemecio had to cancel out on this second trip and since Reyes still had a bad knee, I hired Chu as a guide/porter. The trip went pretty well. It ended up that Reyes was also from Huacaybo, and the matron of that town was Chu's great-aunt. Nemecio was in Huacaybo when we got there, and we also met Chu's grandfather on the trail.

Once again, we were treated like royalty, and we had a really good time. Chu's great-aunt fed us again, and she gave Chu a dress shirt so he would look his best in Batopilas. Chu, at seventeen, had never been to Batopilas, but he had heard that it was a town filled to the brim with available teenage girls. He was happy to have a dress shirt, and we were happy for him to have it.

We made it to Batopilas all right, and, in the intervening years, I came to hire Chu as my number-two guide, after Sahuaripa, every time I hit the trail in Tarahumara-land. I ended up getting fairly close to his family, and took several meals at their house in Cusarare.

Chu ended up being a damned nice kid, with the emphasis on the word, "kid." We joshed around and got into fake fist-fights, and I often ribbed him about his two alleged girlfriends, and we talked a lot about his future. All in all, as good a rela-tionship as a crotchety old fart such as myself is capable of having with a pimply faced, gangly teenager.

In 1991, I hired Chu and Sahuaripa to work with me as guides/porters on a mellow, three-day trip I was to lead from Batopilas to Munérachi and back. After we returned to Cusarare, I met up with my wife and two friends and we immediately returned to Batopilas and did the same three-day hike, without Sahuaripa or Chu. When we returned from that trip, I learned that, three days before, Chu, along with Reyes, had been killed. They had taken the money I had paid Chu for working with me on the Munerachi hike, gone to Creel, got drunk, and, on the way home, with Chu at the wheel, their truck went off the road, rolled, and exploded into flames.

When I found out about the accident, I was standing on the front porch of Las Cabañas del Cobre. The wind was kicked out of my body by the sheer, devastating weight of this most foul news. It had been a long time since someone I was close to had died. My wife told me later that she had felt the heavi-ness of my feelings from clear across the parking lot. She walked around the truck to see what was wrong, and she said she saw me stagger and almost fall.

Several of my Tarahumara friends at the lodge quickly jumped up and helped me to sit down. One of the dining room employees brought me a cold Coke. One of the nicest things about areas that are dominated by indigenous cultures is that silence is a big part of everyone's world. Americans are made uncomfortable by long silences, and, even to a blabbermouth such as myself, that is a shame. As I sat there, in the midst of six or eight people, but with quiet all around me, I remembered some weird vibes I got from Chu just a week before.

Usually, Chu was, like most seventeen-year-olds, vivacious and gregarious. If there was something going on, he wanted to be butt-deep in it. After every trip, I would always take Sahuaripa and Chu into Creel for dinner and drinks. This time, though, Chu begged off, saying that he wanted to get home to spend time with his family. As he was getting out of my truck, I said thanks for everything, and he turned around, grasped my hand, looked my square in the eye and said, earnestly, *"Egualmente."* Then he told me how much he enjoyed knowing me and how much my friendship meant to him and his family.

As Sahuaripa and I drove into Creel, I asked what the hell was up with Chu, who usually would part ways by saying something tender like, "Next time, I'm asking for a raise, old man!" Sahuaripa just shrugged and stared straight ahead. In retrospect, it seemed like Chu knew something catastrophic was going to happen to him. I have heard that such revelations visit people sometimes.

Chu was buried next to his dad in the small cemetery near the church in Cusarare. Though I have never had a religious bone in my body, I go by there whenever I get the chance just to sit and visit with Chu and Reyes. I often think of the time, after six days on the trail, when I treated a nasty blister on the top of his foot. He had kept his pain to himself, but, finally I noticed him limping and asked him what the hell his problem was. He tried very hard, as I was applying alcohol to what turned out to be a fairly grotesque blister, to act like it wasn't hurting. But, finally, he flinched, and I jokingly chided him for it. He laughed, and, with that laugh, he said his foot wasn't hurting anymore. He finished that hike with joy in his stride.

Chu had a good laugh. Guess he still does.

Particulars

You will need the 1:50,000 Creel, Samachique, and La Laja de San Alonso maps. All of this hike is also located on the 1:250,000 San Juanito map. Huacaybo, as far as I have been able to tell, is not located correctly on the 1:50,000 Samachique map. I recommend that you hire a guide for this hike, at least from Cusarare to El Tejabán and from Huacaybo to Cebollin. The route from Cusarare to the rim or Copper Canyon is tricky enough that, after having hiked it several times, I can't remember the damned thing. Try hiring Nemecio or Sahuaripa in Cusarare.

There is also a very rough dirt road all the way to El Tejabán, so you could hire someone to drive you. From El Tejabán, descend directly to the obvious ruins below on the river. The first part of the trail is actually a jeep track. The jeep track ends at a small tailings pile, then a very good burro trail takes over. You should be able to make this descent in a couple of hours.

You can camp on a small beach just upriver from the trail on the El Tejabán side of the river. There is a small cave adjacent the beach. Or, you can cross the river and camp on the other side, though the tentsites are few and far between. Either way, be very careful of rising water. The river once rose a foot during the night while I was camping on the Huacaybo side of the river, and, as a result, I very nearly lost a bunch of gear. This is serious flash flood area. The river crossing here is not the world's easiest, and it will take a half-hour or so to pull it off.

Just upriver from the crossing, on the Huacaybo side, there is a small, easily accessible cave well above high-water level. This was actually used as a jail cell back when the Spaniards were enslaving the Tarahumaras to work in their copper mines. The vibes are too bad for me, personally, but I have known people to sleep in that cave.

To get to Huacaybo, which you will have seen on your descent into the canyon, hike downriver a short distance to the cluster of small buildings, which may or may not be inhabited by the time you pass through.

Those buildings are located at the mouth of an arroyo. Follow the burro trail up that arroyo. You should make it to Huacaybo in less than an hour. From there, it's another three or four hours to the rim. This is another stretch where it wouldn't hurt to hire a guide, because, from the rim to Cebollin, there are many crisscrossing timber roads and trails. Also, there is a small spring in a side arroyo just below a prime campsite about an hour from Cebollin. This spring will be all but impossible to find without a guide, and it's the last water between the rim and Cebollin.

You will need to figure out a way to get out of Cebollin. You could hope to find a truck there to drive you out to the main road connecting Batopilas and Creel, from where you might be able to hitch. Or you could arrange to have someone pick you up there.

There is one potential interesting addition to this hike, which I have done. Instead of returning to Creel, you can hike all the way to Batopilas. A few miles from Cebollin, the road to Cieneguita breaks off. There is actually a shortcut from Cebollin to this road, through El Gallo, which, again, you will need to hire someone to show you. This shortcut, though only about two hours in length, consists mainly of fairly tough, steep up-and-down hiking. From this road, you can hook into the tail end of the route I describe in Chapter 17, Cusarare to Batopilas. It will take you at least three more days from Cebollin to Batopilas. And, remember the road to Cieneguita is long, hot, and dry.

9

Canyon Crossing
Cusarare to Divísadero

This five-day trip was unlike any I had ever done in several
ways, the least of which being that it is guided—by Skip
McWilliams, co-owner of the Copper Canyon Lodge—and that
we have a Tarahumara entourage. Seven gringos, counting
Skip, and as many as 15 Tarahumaras, including two teenage
sisters, Marta and Maria, who served as—get this—our tortilla
makers. Can't say as I've ever had a pair of tortilla makers along
on a hiking trip. *Can* say as I like fresh tortillas.

The fact that this was a guided trip had certain implications. Gay and I were offered a complimentary trip, if we would
promise not to give the exact route away. It is important to
understand the reasoning behind this. Certainly, there's some
capitalism involved on Skip's part. He went out and found the
route over the course of several years and he makes part of his
living by leading paying customers on it. But, that's only a
small part of the deal.

Because his "Canyon Crossing" route cuts very close to a
few Tarahumara homesteads that are way far away from anything and everything even remotely civilized, Skip feels a need
to limit the number of excursions through those areas. He,
through talking with the Tarahumaras in question, has picked
up on how many gringos they can live with tromping through
their neighborhood and how many are too many. Skip has limited his trips accordingly.

Though I understand and sympathize with that argument,
I still considered not going along because, I figured, I needed to

be able to tell folks, insofar as I mention the trip at all in this book, how to make their way along the same route. I chewed my mental cud over it for a few days and decided to go ahead and include this chapter anyway for two reasons.

First, by writing in very general terms where we went, you should be able to make your way from Cusarare to Divisadero.

At the same time, by giving only very generalized directions, even if you tried to follow directly in our footsteps, the chances of you succeeding are very slim—even if you hired a Tarahumara guide.

It's not that the route is overly hard, it's just that there are simply too many ways to get between the points we traversed. This is good. You will likely discover places we did not; yet, at the same time, you will view many of the same large-scale scenes, without impacting those aforementioned Tarahumara homesteads.

And, second, including one professionally guided trip in this book is a good idea because many of you might be considering employing the services of a guide for your Copper Canyon Country visit.

The seven gringos on our trip were: Skip, a female nurse from California, a male commercial real estate broker from Michigan, a female tour operator from California, a female karate instructor/triathlete from Florida—there's one serious human in every bunch, it seems—and Gay and I. We headed out from Las Cabañas del Cobre about the crack of noon, a civilized time to commence a multi-day trip. Gives one time to let one's breakfast omelette digest properly.

With the gringos, ten or twelve Tarahumaras (more would join us later), five burros, a couple of horses, a couple of dogs, and five live chickens, we looked like some exploratory expedition from British Colonial days.

The burros were along, not surprisingly, as pack animals, there being no other reason I can think of for that particular species to have evolved. I had only put my pack on a quadruped once before and, while I was tending to the repairs several days later, I decided to never do so again. But, since everybody else was doing it, we would have to also. We were told there would be "no problems" with our brand-new, multi-hundred-dollar packs.

We headed out from the lodge towards Basirecota, which is actually right on Cusarare Creek, the same as the lodge. We were going the long way as the crow flies, but the short way as the crow walks with five burros and a bunch of awkward gringos.

I have always had bad preconceptions about what a guided trip would be like. I had no idea whether the perfect strangers who I would be living in tight quarters with for the next five days—who seemed perfectly normal before the trip began— would all become crazy people with bad drooling habits or something equally disgusting after we'd been on the trail for a few minutes. Worse, I had no idea whether my otherwise extremely stable disposition would come unraveled when faced with the reality that someone else was responsible for route-finding, food preparation, and maintaining general group harmony. By and large, when I hit the woods with a group, it's me who, for better or for worse, fills those roles.

The walk to Basirecota takes only about three hours via the mountain route. There are a couple steep uphills, but nothing serious. This was the stretch where we all got to know each other a little bit. We were very relieved to learn that only the triathlete from Florida was in anything approaching good shape. Gay and I had only been in Mexico for a week or so, and, as usual, we hadn't exactly killed ourselves getting physically prepared for the trip. We were not enthusiastic about the possibility of finding ourselves in a group of gung-ho Outward Bound types on speed.

Our pace hovered somewhere around two miles an hour, with minimal weight. We rested frequently, because we were in no hurry. Though I have adopted this mellow sort of hiking strategy myself on more than one occasion, I felt a little weird about it here and now. For one thing, it seemed like I was "cheating" by having a pack animal carry my pack.

My wife, on the other hand, within about two steps of the lodge, was already talking in terms of never carrying a pack again in her entire life. She thought the concept of beasts-of-burden as backpacking compadres was splendid. So did our gringo companions.

Skip, who, we learned immediately, is not a guide cut from the traditional guide mold, could hardly see it any other way. He is perplexed and amused by many of the back country attitudes that typical American backpackers possess in the extreme.

Skip has been hiking in Tarahumara-land for twenty-five years. Yet, he has only recently started carrying a pack, and that is only about 1,000 cubic inches—designed more for dayhiking than five-day trips. Though he has been out for as long as a month at a time, the most Skip carries is a blanket, some pinole—a Tarahumara staple that is nothing more than ground corn, mixed for consumption with cold water—a knife and some basic personal hygiene items. This sounds as though Skip is a bad-assed, backcountry Muir-clone. Probably sports a beard. Talks little. Rather gruff.

None of these stereotypes even comes close.

Skip McWilliams lives in a Detroit, Michigan, suburb, where he runs an educational film company. He is clean-shaven, out-of-shape, and one of the few people I have ever met in my life who likes to hear himself talk as much as I·like to hear myself talk.

When we left the lodge, he was wearing some peepee-looking street shoes, with a piece of cardboard stuck in one of the heels because he had worn a blister on his last trip. He brought no extra clothing, no sleeping bag, no pad. And, he asked everyone to limit their gear to much the same degree. Before we left, everyone pulled everything out of their packs. I have never seen gear honed-down that much. By the time we pulled out, I had three people's gear stuffed into my pack—with plenty of room to spare. When I am on a backpacking trip, my pack is usually filled to brimming—just with my stuff.

The reason Skip was so insistent about cutting our gear was that, halfway through the trip, we would reach a stretch of trail that the burros would not be able to traverse. From that point on, we would be relying totally on Tarahumara porters. The less stuff we had, the less extra porters Skip would have to hire in Sitagochi, where the burros would be sent back to Cusarare.

Skip, unlike my preconceptions of wilderness guides, knows relatively little about the plant and animal life in Copper Canyon Country. For that information, Skip has a long-time pal, Jesus Olivas, who I have dubbed the "Mexican Gandalf," because, first, he looks like what I believe Gandalf would look like if Gandalf were Mexican and wore a cowboy hat, and, second, because he is as intimate with every aspect of Copper Canyon Country—from people to plantlife to the fauna to the local cultural dynamics—as Gandalf was with Middle Earth.

Jesus is one of the most wonderful people I have ever met. He grew up in Copper Canyon Country. His dad was a trader who ran burro trains all over Tarahumara-land. Jesus, from the time he was nine, followed his dad on his rounds.

Consequently, he probably knows the area as well as anyone.

Skip, on the other hand, is more interested in Mexican history than natural history.

He is completely fluent in Spanish—as opposed to being merely conversant like your humble narrator. He reads Spanish as well as I read English and has spent many years studying Mexican history, especially the Mexican Revolution.

Passing through the thick pines on our way to Basirecota, we learned a lot about Pancho Villa and his *tropa*—troop—the guys who effectively amount to Mexico's Founding Fathers.

Especially interesting was Skip's telling of the "Villa on the Cross" story, which is the name of a chapter in the book, *The Eagle and the Serpent*, by Martin Luis Guzman, who was the clerk of the *tropa*.

For most of the early years of the Mexican Revolution, Villa had the nasty habit of taking large numbers of prisoners and executing them—even those who were willing to change sides.

At some point, one of his underlings convinced Villa that he should mend his ways, for two reasons. First, people who know they are going to be killed if they are captured are likely to fight like the dickens to make certain they are not captured, and, second, when his enemies offered to change sides, it was tantamount to them admitting Villa was philosophically right.

So, Villa got on the telegraph and frantically wired someplace down the line where several hundred prisoners were scheduled to be shot that the executions should be stopped. For hours, Villa paced back and forth, figuratively "on the cross," until he got word that his message had made it through.

I don't remember whether it made it through on time.

We reached a high mesa above Cusarare Canyon. This is Chuyachi, our first view of the deep canyon country. We descended a steep side arroyo to the Cusarare River in the gathering dusk. Most of the Tarahumaras were already in camp. They were gathering wood, tending to the animals and shooting the breeze. To them, this trip was a laid-back vacation.

Camp was a small abandoned Tarahumara bean field just above the rocky flood plain of the Cusarare. About 20 feet from the fire ring were two small hot pools, each the size of a kitchen sink.

Downriver a few dozen yards are a couple larger hot spring pools.

Across the river and up a hill are a couple caves. Skip speculated that they were burial caves, but this is not as formal as it sounds.

Apparently, the Tarahumaras do not revere their dead. They operate on a day-to-day basis with the belief that nothing happens by chance, that a person wills all that transpires in his or her life—including death. Therefore, the Tarahumaras look at their deceased compadres as people who made the choice, for whatever reason or combination of reasons, to leave their loved ones behind in the material world. This, quite often, does not endear the dearly departed to those still operating in the mortal dimension.

Skip told one story about a Tarahumara man who chained his dead mother up and dragged her stiff carcass up into a cave, where she was kept for over a year, until the Tarahumara man was convinced she was too decomposed to re-enter the world of the living. The Tarahumara man was upset with his mom because she was supposedly an opium poppy farmer.

After a year, this man invited Skip and Jesus to join him on a journey to the cave, where he planned on retrieving the chains, with an eye toward selling them. Skip and Jesus were both, surprisingly, too busy that day to tag along.

The nurse and the triathlete went up to investigate the caves—before this story was told. It ended up that the caves were used for nothing more macabre than penning goats, although I learned later from my buddy, Sahuaripa Gonzales, that there is, indeed, a U.S. Grade-A burial cave in that immediate vicinity.

Our two tortilla makers were sitting down by the river when the gringos arrived at camp. I wandered down to see what they were up to, thinking, perhaps, I could pick up on some sort of Tarahumara tortilla-making tidbit. Before they noticed my approach, they had been jabbering away with enthusiasm. When I arrived, they shut up tight. I was looking down at their feet—which is where they seemed to be looking—hoping to see what they were up to. Then this little light bulb goes on over my putty-brained gringo self. Marta and Maria had been washing up in the river in a most private manner, which should have been obvious to anyone, save the world's most stupid piece of lizard dung—me.

These poor girls thought that I was sneaking down to the creek with the idea of getting a prurient peak before dindin. We hadn't even shared our first meal as a group and, already, the Tarahumaras were thinking they had a pervert in their midst.

The Tarahumaras looked amused as the gringos went about setting up camp. Gay and the tour operator shared our tent. The nurse and the triathlete each brought one-human tents, and they were busy setting them up. The real estate broker and I planned on sleeping under the stars, but, even then, it still takes gringos at least twenty minutes to get organized.

Dinner consisted mainly of pig meat, cheese, and tortillas— good eats for one who's used to freeze-dried beans and such on the trail.

During supper, the Tarahumaras pretty much stayed on one side of the fire, the gringos on the other. There were enthusiastic conversations on both sides, but not much in the way of cross-cultural interaction. This is not too surprising, since, besides Skip, I was the closest thing to a bilingual gringo on the scene. The Tarahumaras were all bilingual, but none of their linguals was English. So, of course, I decided to break the ice. I walked over to the other side of the fire and began asking everyone's name, with the intent of introducing everybody to everybody else. The instant I passed the line of demarcation, the Tarahumaras started looking nervous. I ask them each, one-by-one, what their name is. They answer so softly that I have to ask every one of them to repeat their whisper.

Then I begin the gringo intros with myself. John is difficult to pronounce for Spanish-speakers, so I am "Juan." Then I turn to start introducing the others. None are paying attention. By the time I turn back to the Tarahumaras, they have inched away. They face the other direction.

I consider, briefly, that I once thought I was perfect material for a diplomatic corps career. I even met with the State Department recruiter in college. Had I gone through with it, I suspect we would now be at war with whoever I was trying to be diplomatic with.

The scene around the fire soon evolved into relaxed tequila-sipping and soft-spoken story telling. There were two bottles of tequila and everyone, except the triathlete, partook whenever the bottles were passed their way. With me, we're just talking about a shift in alcoholic venue. With some of the other gringos, we're talking about a major transformation of evening beverage.

There are coughs and sputters. The Tarahumaras giggle. Then the Tarahumara tortilla makers each take small sips, droplets gleaming down their necks in the firelight. The gringos giggle. Cigars are torched.

A pot of coffee is boiled. Jokes are told in three languages, with everyone laughing at the punchline, whether it was understood or not. The creek babbles. The burros, hobbled away in the darkness, bray.

As my buddy Bame would say, "Handle it, handle it."

Tomorrow morning, we head straight back up to the sierra. Tomorrow night, after eight hours on the trail, we will sleep within sight of Sitagochi—the pueblo primeval.

One of our members has zero experience in the backcountry.

Everyone else at least has some experience, though no one is a world-class wilderness jock. Skip, who prefers customers with little or no backcountry experience, sets the groups' pace based on the person with no experience. He feels that it is best to maintain a pace that you can keep up all day, no matter how slow it is. Though this is somewhat hard on those who would feel more comfortable walking a little faster, it is a good plan for the group.

The gringos are off by 10 AM, heading a couple thousand feet straight up. The Tarahumaras are in no hurry to break camp. They have no fear of being left behind. We will follow the ridge that separates Cusarare Canyon from Tararecua Canyon until we reach Sitagochi.

As we slowly ascend out of Cusarare Canyon, we can hear the Tarahumaras below laughing at us. Sometimes I don't like Tarahumaras very much.

On the one hand, I am amused by the fact that we amuse them. I mean, we must seem like a population of materially affluent evolutionary miscues. We have no endurance. We are pudgy and soft. We can't start fires worth a damn. We bring too much stuff. So, they sit and laugh as we huff and puff.

I transfer the scene. How would it look if I sat there and laughed at a Tarahumara who was suddenly plopped into the middle of a large mall? I could send him into a Fashion Bar with a personal deficit enlargement tool—a credit card—and instructions to buy a set of sexy undies for his sister. Then I could sit back and have a good chuckle myself. But, of course, I wouldn't.

The worst single thing about backpacking is when you have to do a long, steep uphill first thing in the morning. We are moving stiff-legged and slow, though, man oh man, this is a lot better without backpacks. Though I am "one with" many of the aspects of life on the trail—the crappy food, the wet and cold, the frequent lack of frosty mugs of beer—the one thing that I could most easily live without is the backpack part of backpacking.

But, I still feel very strange knowing that our Tarahumara compadres think that the gringos *need* help with their gear, that we would be unable to make it without them and their burros.

Shortly after we reach the ridge top, we enter a Tarahumara ranchito.

Skip goes over and sits outside one of the fences. A few minutes later, a Tarahumara man comes over and commences to shoot the breeze with him. The man runs back into his abode, then returns. They both come over to where we are sitting, and Skip introduces the man. We shake hands all the way around.

The man is vending some little pine-needle sombreros that his wife has made. Each of us buys one—for 40 cents. Tarahumaras are astounding craftspeople, especially when it comes to weaving stuff out of pine needles and yucca leaves.

When we split, Skip tells us that the man will join us tomorrow morning. He will replace one of the burros. Meaning he will become a bearer and toter.

We look for, and find, a spring. Sometimes springs in Tarahumara-land can be hard to locate, because they are covered with flat rocks to keep livestock snouts away from the water. These covered water sources blend right into the local terrain.

By noon, the Tarahumaras catch up and lunch is prepared—tuna salad, biscuits, and fresh fruit. Shortly after stuffing our faces, we're back on the trail. We pass by an edifice that looks like one of those tacky scientific buildings down in Antarctica—the kind you see pictures of on TV specials about how the last continent is going to the dogs.

This building is not, its architectural countenance notwithstanding, the fault of scientists. No, this is worse. This building belongs to the Jesuits. It is a storage facility. No windows, one door, heavily locked. There's no telling what is in the building, but a good guess would be clothing. I had often wondered how the Tarahumaras—whose traditional dress is, for women, colorful, dignified skirts and blouses, and, for men, pure white, dignified dress-looking things—came to wear, on the whole, ill-fitting, polyester, pastel-colored, mismatched, leisure-suit remnants from Kmart bargain racks of fifteen years ago.

The answer, come to find out, is simple. The Jesuits, as well as many other groups with missionary bents, have succeeded in convincing the Tarahumaras that their traditional dress is un-hip. So, many Tarahumaras now wear gringo duds, which, of course, they need to get from the outside world. The Jesuits, being good business types, run clothing drives in the States for the poor unfortunate, naked heathens south of the border. I've heard reports that they then sell these dweeby-looking rags to the Tarahumaras.

The storage shed was accessed by a well-maintained dirt road that was built by the Tarahumaras. I have heard reports that, the Jesuits, when they need some work done—like road building—will simply scour the area for all able-bodied males. They will, essentially, draft them for as long as it takes to complete the task at hand. The Jesuits want nice roads like this built because they prefer traveling through Tarahumara-land in vans. It ain't my territory. I've got nothing to say.

We arrived at camp just before dusk and just after passing by a Tarahumara cave that was decorated by stone-age-looking wall art. This campsite was one of my all-time favorites. The fire was built inside a crumbling rock house formation just big enough for everyone to squeeze in. Tents were pitched in a small field with a view of Cusarare Canyon off in the distance.

Gay and I run off for the 20-minute walk to a point where we can view both Tararecua Canyon and Copper Canyon. Though the light is not good for photo-taking, suffice to say that this one view, one of the best in all of Tarahumara-land, is worth two full days of walking.

From the top of the small ridge above camp, we can see Sitagochi, which, I guess, is technically a butte, rather than a mesa, because it is eroded from, rather than to, or something like that. Either way, this looks like something out of a Conan the Barbarian film. Just this flat, treeless, wind-swept butte perched above the depths of Copper Canyon. It is from Sitagochi that the rest of our Tarahumara burro-replacement units will be procured.

The water source, a spring, I am told, is about a 10-minute walk downhill from camp. I am also told "I can't miss it"—my least-favorite words in the backcountry user's lexicon.

I head down, and, of course, I miss it. I do find a spring, seemingly 17 or 18 miles later, but it's definitely not the one everybody else managed to find. On the way back, I pass close by the tortilla makers—once again—taking a bath. If there was any doubt whatsoever in their minds about me the first time, there is none now. I can't believe it.

When I get back to camp, I take a big swig of my hard-won agua. The water tastes like dishwater, which, come to find out, is exactly what it is.

Often times, when there are several springs in one area, the Tarahumaras will use one for drinking, one for washing, and one for animals. I left in search of water, sweet water. I returned with three liters of Lux on the rocks.

Because this is our last night with the burros, once more, Skip asks us to pare down our gear. Anything we haven't used yet, we are asked to send back to Cusarare on the burros. By morning, eight more Tarahumaras have joined our group. With the exception of the guy we bought the little sombreros from, all the new recruits are under seventeen. Some have walked all night to get here in time.

This is good luck. In times past, Skip has had to wait until late afternoon before getting enough Tarahumara Sherpas.

By this time, I've got four people's stuff in my Lowe pack. I hope it holds together because two of its main support straps have been rubbing on the burro's saddle frame. They are frayed and, if they break, my pack becomes separated from its high-tech ABS-plastic frame. Never again will I put my pack on anything with more than three legs. This time, I mean it.

Even though none of us has much gear left, my pack is still heavy, because near-bouts every gringo for 50 miles has their stuff in it. It is given to Corpus, a surly little Tarahumara who stands about 5'1" and weighs maybe 110. I am hardly a tall man, but when my pack settles onto this poor bugger's back, I feel like "Wilt the Stilt." The hip strap is almost down to the guy's knees. He could use the chest strap as an athletic supporter.

All the other Tarahumaras end up carrying, like, small bags of fruit. So, Corpus has seemingly gotten the shaft. The seeds of dissension have been sown. Our very own labor dispute is about to begin.

Today is a big day. We have before us a multi-hour, multi-thousand-foot descent into Tararecua Canyon, at a point only a few miles upriver from the great bend of the Urique. For me, it's the first time I will enter the depths of Tararecua since Jay Scott and I spent six days down there three years before dancing a cheek-to-cheek slow dance with the angel of death (see Chapter 5).

The descent into Tararecua canyon was slow and hot. This was the time of year, late November, when every seed with a propensity to latch itself onto a passerby was ready for action. By mid-day, we were all walking flora reproduction aids.

Impossible as it seems, I remember passing, three years before, by the exact stretch of river above which Skip now chooses to camp. There's a little waterfall just upriver. Jay and I stopped by it to eat lunch. Minutes before, I had had my first experience with quicksand, which is a pulse-rate-increasing sort of way to spend a few tense seconds. I had jumped from the riverbank down onto some solid-looking dirt. Next thing I know, I'm thinking in terms of needing a fresh change of underwear. I was up to my waist instantly. But, that's as far as I sunk.

Jay and I had not even noticed the place where the Canyon Crossing crew camped. We had stayed on river level and blew right by it. Camp was an old Tarahumara homestead on a small rise above the river. The gringos slept in a very aromatic goat pen. The Tarahumaras slept on very rocky ground around the fire. It wasn't the best campsite I have ever checked out in the comfort sense, but it was very interesting in all other regards.

There were several swimming/bathing holes close by, as well as a hot spring pool that I had not noticed when I hiked through with Jay. From what I gathered, Skip had permission from the owner of the shack we were camped by to use the place.

There's a wonderful old *metate*—a big carved stone used for grinding corn—next to the shack. Since Skip's last Canyon Crossing trip, a couple of weeks before, this *metate* has been broken. Skip is near distraught, wondering if somehow he is responsible, wondering if his trips into the deepest recesses of Tarahumara-land aren't already resulting in negative impact. *Metates* are important to Tarahumara life. They are hard to make, hard to come by, and hard to live without. They are also, it would seem, hard to break, because these things are usually near-bouts 75-pound pieces of solid rock.

Our plan was to be on the trail before first light the next day because, not only did we have to climb all the way out of Tararecua Canyon—an elevation gain near-equal to climbing out of Copper Canyon itself—before lunch, but we would have to climb back down into a major side canyon of the Urique in the late afternoon.

We hurriedly breakfasted on day-old tortillas and fruit. This did not set so well with several of the Tarahumaras, who wanted eggs and cheese, like yesterday's breakfast. Skip came over and warned me that we might be facing a strike.

The trail out of Tararecua started directly across the river from camp. It was badly overgrown and the going was slow—

too slow for many of the Tarahumara porters who went up and around us.

By mid-morning, we had reached a level several hundred feet below the rim, at the top of the arroyo. This is where Skip ascertains how his group is doing. If folks are getting a tad tuckered from their time on the trail, he will bug out at this point— heading directly up to the rim. From there, he will hike out towards San Luis (see Chapter 10), meaning there are no more ascents or descents.

We decided unanimously not to bug out. Everyone was feeling pretty good, even those members of the group who were not accustomed to desert travel.

We passed two springs, one of which was a carved log placed strategically below a dripping cave ceiling. This place was almost jungle-like lush.

The trail, which, by this time, was wide and well graded, stayed level for the next few miles as we skirted around a few ridge fingers extending down from the rim. We stopped for lunch at a point with a wonderful view of the deepest part of Copper Canyon. We could see miles up the Urique, just above where it makes its great bend.

Lunch consisted of one piece of battered fruit each, which didn't bother the gringos one bit, as in our eyes, we had been gorging ourselves to this point. But, several of the Tarahumaras, especially Corpus, who was still stuck with my community-utilized pack, decided they had had enough. Skip had to do some heavy politicking to keep them from dropping our gear and heading back to Sitagochi. Even after he mollified them with promises of near-future feasts, there was concern that they might, at any point, simply drop their loads in the middle of the trail and head home. This considered, we tried to keep the entire entourage in sight. That way, if our stuff was indeed dumped, we would at least know it.

This stretch of trail is among the most beautiful in all of Copper Canyon Country. The whole time, we maintained views of three of the best canyons around—Copper, Tararecua, and Urique. As well, by mid-afternoon, the huge side canyon into which we would descend came into view. It was almost sensory overload.

Our goal was a small homestead that sported such a fine orchard, it was known as the "Place of the Orange Trees." The descent was steep and hot. As we cruised down, I recognized this side canyon as Arroyo Rurahuachi, the one just upriver from the arroyo I use to get from Divisadero to the Urique. I had twice been to the place where Arroyo Rurahuachi enters the Urique.

Only a trickle of water flows into the Urique from Arroyo Rurahuachi, but our camp was several miles up, where a nice little creek was flowing through a tight, multi-thousand-foot notch of a canyon. Great place.

The triathlete and the real estate agent each picked sleeping places down near the creek. Most of the group opted to sleep in the thick, seed-bearing weeds near our fire ring. Gay and I hopped over a stone fence into an orange grove. We laid out our groundcloth next to a small, hand-dug irrigation ditch. We strolled down to the creek for a bath. On the way, we passed well-tended rows of chiles, squashes, corn, beans, and lemon and orange trees. The Tarahumara owner of this spread, who was not at home, has himself a nice spot.

Dinner was indeed a feast. Since this was our last night, everything not yet on the road to digestion was fair game for consumption. We had oranges, tuna salad, eggs, tortillas, cheese, and guacamole.

The five chickens, which had been carried all the way from Cusarare, made their way to meet the poultry Buddha, though they weren't on the evening menu. They would be roasted slowly over the fire all night. Then, they would be distributed to all carnivores for breakfast.

Skip and I stayed up talking about the future of Tarahumaraland. Both of us agreed that there is, without near-drastic action, scant chance for the Tarahumaras to maintain their near-pure cultural integrity for much longer. The main culprit is the Mexican logging industry. Since Tarahumaras tend to be laborers rather than entrepreneurs when they enter the money economy, they have prices set for them by outsiders—in this case, Mexicans. The Tarahumaras often end up working for less than minimum wage, while, essentially, giving their timber away.

Skip thinks that, in order for the Tarahumara culture to survive reasonably intact, it needs to get better control of its economic destiny. He believes that one way to usher that in is to establish a series of primitive backcountry lodging facilities, owned and operated by the Tarahumaras. The plan would be for Skip to help the Tarahumaras set these things up with financial, logistic, marketing, and training help. Then, the Tarahumaras would take over.

These lodging facilities would be little more than hand-hewn cabins with small, community eating areas. Tarahumaras would do the cooking. Gringo backpackers would pay money to stay at these places. In effect, the Tarahumaras would then be relying less on their timber resources and, consequently, less on Mexicans who are trying to screw them economically.

Skip considers himself important to the actualization of this plan because he has the interest and the drive to get the ball rolling. He has connections with the local political and economic power structures, he has experience in running lodging facilities in Tarahumara-land, and he has the fiscal means which with to stake the initial stages of the project.

It's even within the realm of possibility that one day gringos will only be allowed to hike on certain trails and to sleep at these small lodges. Though this sounds like another case of over-gentrification of a land that is being touted in this book as interesting mainly because of its primitiveness, we must remember that the main thing here is the preservation of the Tarahumara culture. Everything else is secondary, including our ability to recreate ourselves in the backcountry of the Sierra Madre.

This proposed hut system would be no different, on the operational level, than the hut systems in the White Mountains of New Hampshire. And, though hiking hut-to-hut is not most people's idea of a wilderness experience, there are no indigenous cultures with a stake in the matter up in New Hampshire.

Too often places are ruined by overuse before anything is done to stabilize the situation. Though I haven't yet decided whether I agree with all or part of Skip's vision (and I likely won't until I see a test project in action), I do respect the fact that someone is at least thinking proactively about protecting Tarahumara-land before it gets Vibram-soled to death.

Once again, we were up well before dawn. As Gay and I sat on our groundcloth packing our packs, she turned to me and called me several names for spilling the water that she was sitting in. I politely informed her that I had not recently possessed, much less spilled, any water.

Then why was she sitting in something wet? she asked.

I don't know, darling.

Look.

She did.

She was sitting in a pool of blood. She had parked her posterior dead-smack on a blood-sucking Mexican bedbug—a cousin of the assassin bug. This little hoser had apparently had a gringo feast because, though bedbugs are only about an inch long, Gay was sitting in the A-positive equivalent of the Red Sea.

She focused her scientifically oriented self on the scene and summed up her feelings dispassionately and succinctly: "Gross," I believe, was the word she used. Before we completed our packing, we killed two other blood-gorged bedbugs on our groundcloth.

The plan this day was to hump it straight up to Divisadero.

We would stop for a quick and light lunch only, because we wanted to catch the second-class train for Creel by 2 PM.

This marked the third time that I had hiked out of the deep canyons to Divisadero. The previous two were marked by degrees of fatigue that did not go away for some days. This time, I hardly felt like I'd been hiking—except for the fact that I'd been wearing the same underwear for almost a week. The fact that we hadn't carried packs smeared a whole different veneer on the trip.

Though I will never forget the weird feeling of photographing someone else with my pack on their back, it was, by and large, okay. I don't feel comfortable hiring bearers and probably never will. And I don't feel entirely comfortable with the concept of someone else pointing the way and saying when it's time to eat supper. But, all in all, it was a great experience. We followed a route that I would have otherwise known about. And we got to meet some good people.

I have even got to the point where I have started recommending to people, especially people who are short on time and/or experience, that they consider utilizing professional guides for their introductory trip through the heart of Tarahumara-land. An integral part of that recommendation stems from my hope that, should you decide to take a guided trip, you would return to Copper Canyon Country, the next time, on your own.

Updates: Skip McWilliams, though still extremely active in Copper Canyon Country, is semi-retired from the guiding business. He is now remarried and very busy in Michigan with his business and with raising his two children. He says he simply doesn't have time to get down to Mexico much any more.

That said, Skip spent an entire year, several years ago, living in Batopilas restoring an old hotel there. (Much more on this in Chapter 13.) As for his plan to help establish a series of backcountry huts, he still feels that is the direction Tarahumara-land should be heading. He is involved in helping the people of Cusarare *ejido* set up a small eatery at Cusarare Falls. He looks at that as a first logical step in his grand vision.

Marta and Maria, our two tortilla makers, still work at Las Cabañas del Cobre. They have grown to forgive me for my seemingly prurient transgressions. I have even visited them at their home, and they seemed only moderately nervous having me around their loved ones.

Particulars

If you intend to try this route without a guide, you will need the Creel and San Jose Guacayvo 1:50,000 topos.

Since I have agreed to not be specific about describing this route, you'll have to go with this.

(This is one of those routes that I would recommend hiring a Tarahumara guide. My buddy, Sahuaripa Gonzales, knows this route well.) Even if you want to go this alone, hire a guide for the first stretch, from Cusarare to Basirecota Hot Springs—only about three hours of hiking.

From there, climb the ridge that separates Cusarare Canyon from Tararecua Canyon. Follow this ridge down towards the Urique—a full day's easy, level hike from Basirecota.

Towards the last arroyo in Tararecua Canyon before it enters the Urique, start heading down to the Rio San Ignacio in the bottom of Tararecua Canyon. Cross the river and head up the arroyo to the opposite rim. Cross the ridge between Tararecua Canyon and the first downriver arroyo past the great bend of the Urique.

Descend into this arroyo. Ascend the other side and point it towards Divisadero.

Because these directions are so vague, it may seem like it would be impossible to follow this route in even a half-assed fashion. If you are in good shape and know how to use a map and compass, you can do this. Just remember, don't define "success" during your trip by whether or not you achieve your geographic goal. If you find you need to turn around, or bug out on some alternate route, do so without hesitation. It takes a long time to learn the ins and outs of backcountry route-finding in Tarahumara-land. But no more so than any other geophysically demanding area.

This route alternates between high country and deep canyon camping. Therefore, November to February are the best months.

Remember, though, it will be cold up high this time of year.

You may pass some Tarahumara orchards on this trip. Remember that a Tarahumara family is economically relying on that fruit for survival.

If you want oranges, the Tarahumaras will be happy to sell them to you.

10
San Luis (Magimachi) to Tararecua Canyon

So here we are—four of us crammed into the bucket-seats of my Toyota pick-up, after what was supposed to be a 90-minute drive, that has ended up being three-and-a-half gut-jostling hours—when, before I've even turned off the engine, up comes running this toothless Tarahumara man who seems to be on the verge of a stuttering rage.

We're parked about 50 yards from the mission at San Luis, about five miles south of the road connecting Creel with Divisadero and about halfway between the two, south of Pitorreal. There's a fiesta going full-tilt, and we've decided to check it out. There are literally hundreds of Tarahumaras hanging out near the mission, including several million children, 900,000 of whom immediately descend on us in hopes that we have several tons of candy in our possession, which is how much it would have taken to give each child even one piece.

We get the impression right off that San Luis is not exactly on the normal tourist circuit—despite its proximity to the Chihuahua-Pacific Railroad. People are looking at us like we must have taken a major-league wrong turn somewhere near Mazatlan.

The toothless Tarahumara man, who is not speaking any language I have ever heard, is jumping up and down shaking his head and pointing up a dirt jeep track—the extension of the one we have been following—then pointing to my truck, all the time jabbering on and on. Finally, Juan, our Tarahumara guide—yes, the same Juan who went with us from Divisadero to Pamachi (Chapter 6)—steps in and plays the part of translator, though he is speaking Spanish. Ends up the man, likewise, has been babbling in Spanish, though his dental problems prevented me from even slightly understanding what in the world he was talking about.

Juan said that the man, who was the mayor of San Luis, was happy to have us there, and he extends the greetings of the entire village, and maybe later in the day he could arrange to throw a parade for us and give us the key to the city, but, right-the-hell *now* would we be so kind as to move our truck a few feet? Seems we parked right in the middle of a *rarahipa* course. *Rarahipa* is the Tarahumara national game. And a bizarre game it is. It is usually played among four to eight teams, each of which can have from four to eight male members. These teams often represent particular villages and/or ranchitos, so there's a lot of local pride at stake. This pride is often manifested by side-betting.

The Tarahumaras are among the most notorious—though maybe that's too negative a word—gamblers in the world. They will bet everything they own—except their land and family—on not only *rarahipa*, but also on other, less formalized forms of competition, including quoits and stone throwing.

The Tarahumaras find recreation not so much in the betting itself, but from winning those bets. Therefore, even non-team members take an active roll in *rarahipas*. For two or three days before the event, they help in team preparation. Non-participants massage the contestants' legs, feed them corn beer and peyote, and give them pep talks. Of course, at the same time, these non-contestants are also drinking corn beer and eating peyote themselves.

But, this is not the most interesting aspect of pre-*rarahipa* preparations. Though the Tarahumaras profess to be Catholic, they also cling to many of their traditional animist beliefs. They believe in, and practice, magic. So, much time before and during *rarahipas* is spent laying curses on the other teams. Concurrently, much time is spent warding off the other team's curses. The non-victorious teams do not look upon themselves as losers in an athletic competition sense. They consider that they were simply out-hexed.

I jumped in the truck and moved it 50 feet. The mayor came over, shook my hand, and thanked me profusely. Several minutes later, the team that held the lead came running by. *Rarahipa* is a cross between kick-ball and a relay race played on a course that varies in length between 18 and 40 kilometers. Most fiesta-centered *rarahipas* go on for about three days, which is how long this one will last. We are on the scene about mid-way through the first day, meaning the runners—*corredores*—have been "playing" already for about 12 hours.

The balls—*bolas*, which you can buy at the Tarahumara Mission Store in Creel—are carved out of wood. They are about the size of a baseball. As each of the team members moves along the course, one runner will pass the ball ahead to the next. The ball is not actually kicked, because the Tarahumaras wear toe-less *guaraches* during *rarahipas*. Bare toes impacting solid wood for three straight days could have adverse physiological effects, even on tough-as-nails Tarahumara feet. So, they scoot the ball on top of their passing foot and fling it ahead.

At no time can the ball be carried. Each runner totes a stick, which he uses to displace the ball if it gets stuck under something—like a poorly parked gringo truck. We're not certain what *rarahipa* rules say about twentieth-century mechanical obstacles in the middle of the course, but, given the Tarahumaras' propensity for tossing random hexes around, we're glad we don't have the opportunity to find out. Referees are stationed all along the course, and officiating is tight. Participants are allowed to rest, but they must make up any laps they miss before they're allowed to touch the ball again.

Although the runners who pass by us have put in at least 20 miles in very tough terrain, they aren't so much as sweating or breathing hard. One stops for a swig of water, but that's the only concession to fatigue we see. The contestants are carrying on a conversation like they're sitting around a poker table rather than hoofing it for several days through Copper Canyon Country.

Our plan is to drive out to a point overlooking the Urique River tonight, before hiking to the west rim of Tararecua Canyon in the morning. Unfortunately, the only way we can get to that point is to drive down the middle of the *rarahipa* course, the manners equivalent to a bunch of Tarahumaras running onto the court in the middle of a high school basketball game. We justify this by saying that we will drive off the side of the jeep track if we see any *corredores* approaching.

Juan, Gay, Gary Michaels—the real estate broker who was with us on our canyon crossing trip—and I hope to intersect Skip McWilliams's route (Chapter 9) at his "bug-out" point. We would like to camp near the spring where the water seeps from a cave ceiling into a carved log trough. Juan assures us that he knows exactly how to get there. He says he knows the neighborhood well, because his brother lives near San Luis. We are thinking we've heard this one before.

At dawn, we drive back towards the road connecting Creel and Divisadero, which is very rough and only suitable for four-wheel-drive, high-clearance vehicles. Juan directs us to a small Tarahumara homestead about three miles south of the Chihuahua-Pacific train tracks, where we will leave the truck unattended next to a corn field—something I hate doing. When I ask Juan if there's any danger of thievery or vandalism, he acts insulted. "No!" he answers emphatically, as though I have not only insulted him, but his entire tribe as well.

There was a well-worn trail from where we parked that headed up and over a small ridge. On top, we ran into two Tarahumara men we had met the day before at the fiesta. They had been blatantly drunk then, and, apparently, they had not mended their ways in the interim. They were plowed, and they wanted to chat. We were eager to be on our way, so we took our leave, which seemed to strike them as ill-mannered. Which was okay, except that they were heading in the direction of the truck. Great.

We descended several hundred feet into a small valley, where we passed several Tarahumara homesteads, including that of Juan's brother. Juan asked us to wait while he ran over to give his regards. He returned a few minutes later, saying his sibling was not home.

Gary had been fighting a bad stomach, so we hiked very slowly. We estimated that it would take us about four or five hours to hike to the spring—maybe 15 kilometers distant. This was some of the nicest hiking I have experienced in

Copper Canyon Country. About two kilometers south of Juan's brother's, we started following an arroyo downhill. Though it was hot and sunny, there was plenty of shade. We passed several springs, but did not fill up because they looked too dirty. After two hours, the trail forked and we headed to the left, slightly uphill towards a ridge top. Again, the hiking was very easy, but something seemed, to me, directionally amiss. I had been trying to figure out exactly where we were in relation to Skip's canyon crossing route. This was atypically tough for Tarahumara-land because the woods were very dense the whole time. Usually, there will be plenty of visual opportunities to check out the surrounding terrain in Copper Canyon Country. When we were hiking with Skip, he had pointed this route out to us from a distance of about eight kilometers. Though I was unable to take good bearings, it just seemed that we were off-track.

When I mentioned this to Juan, he looked at me as if I was the dumbest gringo ever to hoist a pack. He tactfully said something along the lines of how this was his territory so, perhaps, we'd all be better off if I kept my mixed-bearings to myself. Ordinarily, I would have been more argumentative. But, when I stopped and thought about it, it really didn't matter where we were going. As long as we crossed paths with a water source by nightfall, everything was hunky-dory.

By the time the ridge broke out of the thick woods, I was positive Juan was taking us to the wrong spring. I had ascertained which of the adjoining arroyos were which and, as far as I could tell, we were at least two ridges too far west. Juan kept shaking his head. Gary and Gay had not even been trying to maintain their bearings because they figured Juan and I had matters well in-hand. Ha-ha.

After four hours on the trail, we passed a campsite that seemed to fit the description of the one Skip uses on his bug-out route. It was right next to the trail, spacious, perfectly flat, overlooking a deep arroyo, with a small spring nearby and plenty of wood. Had we any brains, we would have dropped our gear and ourselves right here. But, I had remembered a very nice campsite near the spring that was our goal. And, if Juan was leading us to a different spring, that was okay, too, because, he said, there was a nice place to camp there, as well.

About half an hour later, the ridge got real skinny and we stepped out onto a small saddle. Then it all fell together. Juan, of course, had been correct all along. The ridge we had been traversing continued south until it became the point where we had stopped for lunch with Skip on the second-to-the-last day of his canyon crossing. We dropped off the saddle to the east and began descending into the side canyon we had climbed out of Tararecua Canyon with Skip. At this point, the hike became less pleasant because there wasn't much of a trail. What trail there was sported prodigious amounts of loose rock. And it was very steep. We picked our way through the spiny brush and, an hour later, we intersected the canyon crossing route. Ten minutes after that, we were filling our water bottles at the trough spring. Some Tarahumara, who knows who, who knows when, got a fairly good-sized tree trunk, carved out its innards and set it in this small cave, where water slowly drips out of the ceiling and fills it.

Though we were exactly where I was hoping we would be, we had a problem. I have been told over the years that too much beer will eventually cause your memory to erode like mud down a river. I thought I remembered a nice, flat, dry camping spot close to the spring. I must've been thinking about some other time, some other place, because there was nothing that even remotely fit that bill here. Gay and Gary both decided then and there not to buy this guidebook. We walked a short ways down the trail, following the canyon crossing route, until we reached a small point that was "only" at about an 89-degree slope—the flattest spot for miles. We placed our packs on the edge of a cliff with the "idea" that they would prevent us from rolling off during the night.

We gathered some wood and built a fire right in the middle of the trail because it was the only non-vertical place around. This section of trail is well used, so we worried about the possibility of a burro train passing by in the night. If that happened, we would have had to extinguish the flames because there was no other way around.

The views more than made up for our discomfort, however. When we had hiked out of Tararecua Canyon the week before, the light had been midday harsh. Now, it was sunset gentle.

The shadows and tricks of canyon light were interplaying with one of the deepest abysses in Tarahumara-land. And the vegetation surrounding us was more like Costa Rica than the rest of Copper Canyon Country. It was lush, cool, and thick.

This was about the time we realized that the *rarahipa* spectators must have hexed us after all. One of them had said, under his breath, something like, "Why don't you stupid gringos go where the sun don't shine." Which is exactly where we were. Our campsite, to the best of my knowledge, is the only place in this part of Mexico that is permanently in the shade. This is a great thing for all those times of the year that are not the dead of winter. We were here in, you guessed it, the dead of winter. It started getting cold fast. I had just brought a light sleeping bag because . . . hell, I don't know why.

Gay and Gary each had warm bags. Juan had only a couple of thin blankets. By 10 PM, Juan and I were having a teeth-chattering contest. I was winning. I have never been so cold in my life. I moved over next to the fire. By midnight, my stylish bouffant was near-bouts one with the coals. Juan got up about 4 AM and stoked the fire to the degree that I awoke thinking I was an integral part of a holocaust, which didn't sound all that bad.

We were on the trail early—though we ascended towards the saddle by a different route. In most places in Tarahumara-land, you are usually rewarded if you spend a little extra time route-finding. Just uphill from the trough spring, a burro trail headed up. And it went all the way to the saddle. So, our hour-long near-miserable descent the day before was an exercise in stupidity.

Four hours later, we were eating Ritz crackers and peanut butter back at the truck. The owner of the field next to which we parked had returned home. He walked over to chat, holding the filthiest baby I have ever seen. I mean, bugs were stuck to this kid's snotty, grubby, and food-infested mug. But, the kid looked happy and well fed.

Three hours later, we dropped Juan off in Creel. Unlike our rim-to-rim trip, we felt he had earned a good tip, if for no other reason than for putting up with my questioning of his route-finding abilities. He immediately ran off to buy a new pair of shoes—the first he had ever owned. I ran into him in Creel several days later. He was back to wearing his *guaraches* and his feet were sporting some serious-looking blisters.

Despite beaucoup return trips to Tarahumara-land, I have never again run into Juan. Perhaps he made his break from his home turf and is now living happily in some urban slum. Or, perhaps, he's just been avoiding me, for fear of getting lassoed into guiding gringos through the canyons once more.

Particulars

You will need the 1:50,000 San Jose Guacayvo map, although the 1:250,000 San Juanito map might suffice. This is a hard route to find, but it is worth the effort whether you want to just hike in and out, like we did, or whether you want to intersect one of the other routes in the vicinity.

Take the train to Pitorreal, a small Mexican town about halfway between Creel and Divisadero. There, you will need to hire a vehicle, which should be pretty easy. Just ask around. Tell the driver you want to go to San Luis. There are actually two places with this name—one being where the mission school is located, marked on the San Jose Guacayvo map as "Internado San Luis," the other being the original ranchito, marked on the map only as "Magimachi"—which is the one you want. Sort of confusing, but easily dealt with. Tell the driver you want to go to Magimachi. He will not be able to drive you all the way, but he will drop you off at the trailhead.

Hike over a small ridge, southeast towards the ranchito of Colurabo. From there, it will be a gradual downhill to Magimachi. Just south of Magimachi, you will meet a small arroyo that, depending on the season, may or may not have water in it. This arroyo is the east fork of the east fork of Arroyo Rurahuachi. The trail at this point will be well traveled and easy to follow. Hike south for three kilometers (almost two miles). When you reach the obvious fork, bear left and stick to the west side of the ridge. This ridge heads south and you will stay with it for several more kilometers.

You pass a perfect campsite on your right. Just before it, there is a very small side canyon where you can find water by following it down towards the bottom of the arroyo.

Continue down the ridge until you reach a small saddle. Cross over to the east side of the ridge here and look for a small burro trail. This will parallel the top of the ridge for a mile or so, before switch-backing down into the arroyo on your left. Two kilometers more and you will run right into the trough spring. You can either camp a few hundred feet past the spring, or you can work your way down into Tararecua Canyon, which is east of you. There is a good campsite on the other side of the Rio San Ignacio. It should take two hours to reach the San Ignacio. From there, you can cross over to Cusarare, following in reverse the route described in Chapter 9. Or, from the small saddle, you can descend into Arroyo Rurahuachi and make your way over to Divisadero.

If you choose to explore in this area, be aware that there are plenty of cliffs. Don't force a route that is not there. Also, you could find yourself wandering close to Tarahumara houses. Please be on your best manners here because these are people who have chosen to live way off the beaten path. We may all infer that they have chosen to do so because they like their privacy.

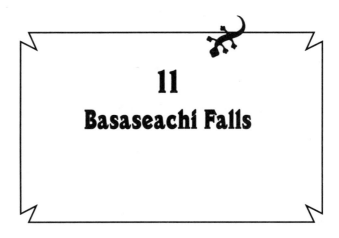

11
Basaseachi Falls

Here we take a short detour from Tarahumara-land proper. About a 140-kilometer (85-mile), four-hour, drive northwest of Creel is one of the highest waterfalls in North America—Basaseachi (bah-sah-SAY-ah-chee or bah-sah-say-AH-chee). While there is some disagreement as to exactly where 300-meter-high Basaseachi ranks—somewhere around the fourth-highest in North America—suffice it to say that this place is not to be missed, despite the fact that it is not conveniently located.

Like Cusarare Falls—indeed, like all waterfalls in the Sierra Madre—there is a big difference between rainy season and dry season water levels. Gay and I drove to Basaseachi from Creel on Thanksgiving Day 1988, understanding full well that we would not be witnessing Basaseachi at its most spectacular. But, since we had decided that we actually preferred Cusarare Falls at low water, perhaps such would be the case with Basaseachi, which is almost ten times as high as Cusarare.

The drive was interesting enough, in and of itself, to justify a 140-kilometer trip from the heart of Copper Canyon Country. And I'm not just talking about the splendid high-sierra scenery. Before we had been on the road an hour, we crossed a bridge at an unreasonable—in retrospect—rate of speed, maybe 80 kilometers per hour. This was no jeep track. We're talking about a fairly major dirt/gravel road that serves as the predominant transportation artery for several hundred square kilometers. Logging trucks by the dozen pass along it every day, as well as ordinary passenger cars.

So, I had 'er in fourth gear and was cruising along happily with a Tecate resting in my lap. Without warning, that Tecate became one with the atmosphere. We both found ourselves suspended in that uncomfortable nether region between the seats and the ceiling before, equally as suddenly, being replanted firmly back in our seats by at least nine "Gs."

A huge hole, about one-and-a-half meters deep, as wide as the entire road and 10 meters long had eroded on the north side of this bridge about 15 kilometers northwest of San Juanito. We felt like we were in one of those Nissan commercials filmed in the middle of the Baja 1000. The truck flew through the air with the greatest of ease, landed in the middle of the air some more, before resuming its appointed rounds. Thankfully, nothing in the oil pan or spring regions was damaged. The remainder of the drive was smooth as silk, at least partially because we drove the rest of the way in second gear.

We arrived at the entrance to Basaseachi close to sunset. Unlike the mythical Copper Canyon National Park that is marked on some maps, Basaseachi National Park actually exits. There's an entrance sign, but no other facilities within the park boundaries worth mentioning, which is the way a national park ought to be. There is also a small Mexican town named Basaseachi, but, it is a few kilometers further down the road as you are driving from Creel. We opted to stop for a quick look at the falls before dark.

It's about a five-kilometer (three-mile) drive from the main road to the overlook parking lot, which is an interesting place in its own right. There's no notice that you have indeed reached the point where you shouldn't drive further. Neither are there guardrails. A miscue here would be attention grabbing because from that parking lot, you can spit directly into the beautiful river valley into which Basaseachi Falls plunges.

You may notice several meters of locked-brake tire marks ending about 15 centimeters from said drop-off into said deep valley. (Guess who?)

We walked the few hundred meters to one of the over-looks—*divisaderos*. Although we had seen dozens of photos of Basaseachi, we were unprepared for its actual astounding geophysical grandeur. The falls themselves are on the opposite side of the valley. The late afternoon light was playing off the delicate ribbon of tumbling water, making rainbows that filled half the chasm beneath our feet. But the falls were just one—albeit the most significant one—of the things that make this place so beauteous. The whole valley, with some of the most sheer cliffs in northern Mexico, is wonderful. The trees at the bottom were at the height of fall colors.

We wanted to stay at the overlook for hours, but since it was getting dark, we drove into the village of Basaseachi. There are several ways you can make quick judgments of small Mexican towns. One of the best is to find out if it is wet or dry—that is, is it legal to sell alcohol or not? If it is wet, you can pretty much assume that the town is reasonably mellow. If it is dry, there is a reason and, unlike some places in the American Deep South that are dry, that reason has nothing to do with religion. The Mexican government outlaws the sale of alcohol only if a town or region is particularly rough.

Basaseachi feels particularly rough, which is not surprising considering that it is the center of the logging industry in the northern Sierra Madre. Nothing against loggers, you understand. We pulled into the parking lot of the local pool hall to ask a few questions about the town. The six gentlemen who were standing out in front looked like some of the nastier characters from the movie "Papillon." We drove on at the first opportune moment. I really wished that I had not asked them about camping in the national park. They were all smiling as we drove away.

We considered getting a room for the night. On the west side of town is a little four-room hotel named the Alma Rosa. Since we were here during the off-season, the proprietor almost started jumping up and down when we pulled up. Unfortunately, for both of us, his rates were a little on the high side—about $15 U.S. a night. There was an American family of four staying there because their rental car had developed a crack in the oil pan on the road between Basaseachi and La Junta. They were stuck without wheels until the rental car folks sent a new vehicle from Chihuahua City, an event that was supposed to happen "soon." I wouldn't be surprised if they are there still.

There's another entrance to the park heading south from the middle of town. We drove down that road in he dark, hoping to run across a good field to camp in. Just past the park entrance, we passed a sign proclaiming a "Zona de Acampar"—campsites. Sweet. We pulled in just as it started snowing. We celebrated Thanksgiving with spaghetti and tomato sauce—a nice change from our usual dried backpacking fare.

During the night, the wind started blowing heavy-duty. The temperature dropped into the teens. By morning, the skies were steel gray and it was sleeting. We opted to drive back to the Alma Rosa for breakfast, where we had some of the best cheese enchiladas we have ever eaten, washed down by about thirty cups of hot coffee each.

It was nearing noon when we returned to the park. From the trailhead near the "Zona de Acampar," it's two kilometers to the closest overlook. Signs point the way. The trail, which has got to be one of the most heavily traveled in Mexico—though we were the only ones there this day—follows Basaseachi Creek, which sports some wild rock formations along its banks. After 30 minutes of very easy walking, we found ourselves staring over the edge of the falls. The overlook we had stopped at last night was several kilometers distant—giving the long-view perspective. Though breathtaking and all, we preferred this view because we could peer over the edge.

I climbed down to the lip of the falls, where the creek passes under a small rock arch before plummeting down to the valley below. It was awesome. If it had been the rainy season, the creek would have been too high for this kind of tomfoolery.

From the top of the falls, the trail crosses the creek, before heading up and over a small ridge to the east. Then it goes DOWN, 300 meters in two kilometers. This is an aerobic experience to say the least—even on the downhill. Some poor soul actually carried enough sacks of concrete down here to make several hundred steps. A nice thought, but not very convenient because they lock you into a pre-measured step length.

Ten minutes from the bottom, there's a *ventana*—a figurative "window." This is the place where many of the published photos of Basaseachi are taken. For good reason. Because it was well past rainy season and because it was so windy, the tiny stream of water that comprised this superlative natural phenomenon was whipping back and forth across the cliff face like a cat flicking its tail. When the wind really kicked up, there was no water at all, only cold mist, most of which evaporated before hitting the valley floor.

At the bottom of the falls is another of those lovely pools that, were it not for the cold weather, would have made for some wonderful swimming. A trail leads from the pool downriver into the heart of Basaseachi Canyon. We wanted to follow it down a few kilometers, but the weather was getting even worse. So, we humped back up to the top, which took quite a while. Although this is a short hike, it is very strenuous.

We climbed around on the rocks upriver from the falls for a few hours and were as captivated as by these rock formations as with the falls themselves.

On the way back to Creel, we passed an old beater of a Toyota truck that was broken down on the side of the road. There were four people, standing around the open hood looking very bummed. The fan belt was broken and, though I always carry a spare, it was the wrong size for this corroded relic.

The owner of the truck was a physician named Victorio. We gave Victorio a ride into the small village of Yoquivo. He told us that he took care of three public clinics in this region, each of which was 75 kilometers from the next health care facility. All graduates of Mexican medical schools are required by law to spend one year working in the boondocks. He told us that the government paid him barely enough money to survive. As well, his budget for supplies and medicine was almost non-existent. Yet, he had become so attached to this part of Mexico that he was considering signing up for another year. He knew he could make more money elsewhere, but, he said, there was no place else where he could do as much social good.

We dropped Victorio off at the clinic/home of another public health doctor, who heartily loaded us with tostadas, tequila, and thanks. We were told that Americans don't have the reputation for stopping to lend assistance. Though I don't agree with that observation, it's always good to know that you've played a small part in remedying a misconception about one's people.

Particulars

I haven't had any luck obtaining a topo of this area, though you really shouldn't need one. Dr. Robert Schmidt's map, available at the Tarahumara Mission Store in Creel, covers Basaseachi sufficiently.

Because it is about 140 kilometers from Creel, Basaseachi is somewhat difficult to get to, although you don't want to visit Tarahumara-land without checking it out. There are three roads to Basaseachi, with direct bus service from Chihuahua City and Cuauhtemoc. The road from La Junta—one of the train stops between Chihuahua City and Creel—is paved just about the entire 80-kilometer distance. The 100-kilometer road from San Juanito is not paved, but it is in very good shape. Each of these roads see enough traffic that you could try hitching. There is also a paved road from the western city of Ciudad Obregon.

Both Margarita's Guest House and the Parador in Creel offer tours to Basaseachi, but they can be expensive. You would want to get together with as many people as possible to offset the cost. The problem with these tours is that they last but one day. So, you're looking at eight hours on the road in order to experience Basaseachi for only about four hours. The driver will be glad to stay over for a night, but that means you will be paying for an extra day's use of the vehicle, as well as the driver's meals and lodging.

If you are driving, gas is available in the town of Basaseachi. There are also several small stores there, but don't count on being able to buy very much in the way of food. Don't forget to try the enchiladas at the Alma Rosa, and beware of the poison oak along the trail from the top of the falls to the valley.

12

Umira Bridge to the Incised Meanders of the Urique River

By Robert Gedekoh

Not far from the tiny village of Umira—just as often spelled "Humira"—the Urique River flows through a deep, serpentine cleft in the Sierra Madre. Commonly referred to as the "Incised Meanders," this magnificent portion of Mexico's Barranca del Cobre provides a unique backpacking opportunity.

The canyon is visually stunning. Sheer cliffs plummet 2,500 meters to the very edge of the river. Towering pines cling to the rock walls, their size dwarfed by the scale of the canyon. The emerald Urique flows over, under, and through gigantic boulder fields and topples over falls. The river has sculpted its bed, leaving behind what must surely be some of the most inviting swimming holes in the world.

Such a magnificent area does not, of course, come without a steep price of admission. Access to the canyon is difficult, to say the least. The Samachique topo map does not show any trails into the Incised Meanders, and we spent most of our four days in the canyon bushwhacking, bouldering along the riverbed, wading in waist-deep, cold water, and scaling cliffs. Only on rare occasions did we stumble across any semblance of a path. The canyon is extremely remote. We encountered no one during our exploration and there was little evidence that the canyon is visited often, either by locals or by other backpackers.

When we entered the canyon, we knew we were on our own. There would be no rangers or mountain rescue teams ready to extricate us in the event of catastrophe. That sense of adventure is an integral part of the allure of backpacking in this part of Mexico, and those unwilling or unable to accept responsibility for themselves would do well to choose another destination. The risks of exploring this canyon are real. One of our party had a close encounter with a rattlesnake. We traversed several narrow ledges hundreds of meters in the air. Many of the boulders along the river were extremely slippery, providing countless opportunities for devastating orthopedic injuries.

We identified three ways to descend to the Incised Meanders. One could park at the bridge, about two miles south of Umira, and follow the riverbed. We did not choose this route because we were unable to locate anyone there to watch our pick-up truck while we were gone. We also noted that the riverbed downstream from the bridge was narrow with steep walls. Passage would have been possible, but difficult.

A better point of access lies about two kilometers up the road toward Umira. The road is cut into the mountainside here, and it is possible to look down into the canyon at the walls of the Incised Meanders. To reach the river, one must traverse or skirt a long talus slide into a dry arroyo. Beware of the loose rock on the initial steep slope. It would be easy to trigger a small rock slide. From the floor of the arroyo, there is a primitive path to the Urique. We used this route to exit the canyon. This point of access brings the explorer to the river about two kilometers upstream of the first major meander. It is easy walking downriver to the heart of the Meanders.

A more difficult, but decidedly more interesting way to enter the canyon is down the Arroyo Umira. We parked our truck at one of the ranchitos in Umira, the family graciously agreeing to protect our vehicle during our trek for 10 new pesos.

Then we hiked along the stream that flows from the village through a large apple orchard and several corn fields. A number of Tarahumara families live in primitive houses along the hillside and they laughed exuberantly as we strolled by, no doubt speculating on the misadventures likely to befall the gringos in the wild canyon below.

Eventually, the stream entered a forested area and the gradient increased dramatically, cutting into the plateau. Precipitous slopes and walls appeared on both sides of the stream, and it was necessary to boulder from side to side in order to continue. At some locations the stream became so congested by rockfall that it was advantageous to trek 30 or so meters above the level of the water.

Finally, after we had covered about five kilometers, the stream tumbled precipitously down a massive rock jumble. From our vantage point atop a seven-meter fall, we could see that the stream was about to make a plunge of at least 175 meters to the main canyon below. The streambed was clearly impassable without ropes and rock climbing expertise, and the cliffs on either side suggested that we had reached a dead end.

We set up camp on a tiny sand bar just above the falls, convinced that we would have to make the rigorous climb back up the arroyo the next day. Our surroundings were exquisite, but we were frustrated by our impasse.

My friend, Mike Bush, decided to climb the cliff on the right side of the arroyo, facing downstream, to take photographs in the evening light. It was there that he found himself seated less than a foot from a two-meter coiled rattlesnake, which, fortunately, seemed more nonplussed than alarmed by the intruder.

I spotted a ledge on the cliff across the stream which looked like it also offered a promising view, so I scaled the wall, knees trembling a bit more with each step. When I reached the sanctuary of a ledge about 60 feet above the streambed, I was surprised to discover the hint of a path that cut across the canyon wall to the main canyon. I followed this "trail" warily, hanging onto trees and vegetation for support and traversing one 10-centimeter-wide ledge above a 10-meter drop.

The path continued onto the very brink of a sheer rock wall, 200 meters above the Urique. And so, in the midst of an attack of vertigo, I got my first breathtaking look into the bowels of Copper Canyon. The last rays of the evening sun cast eerie shadows and several maples, far below along the river, blazed orange and yellow and red in response to the changing season.

After several minutes, I made a second startling discovery: a ledge cornered the angled-face of the cliff, giving way to a direct, albeit hair-raising, descent to the river. I returned to camp ecstatic that we would be spared the need to backtrack to the road.

The next morning, my compadres followed me into the canyon. Mike, who used to hang utility lines for a living, had no problems with the route, but Dean Fairburn and I, neither of us very fond of heights, found crossing the ledges with 30 pounds on our backs more than a little unnerving. Some climber's webbing, a 20-meter piece of rope and a few carabiners, and the knowledge of how to use them, would have come in handy.

We made our next camp at the base of the arroyo on a large sandy beach. Then we bouldered our way about six kilometers downstream to a point beyond which the riverbed seemed impassable without climbing gear. We returned to camp about dusk, built a campfire and settled in for the night. A full moon rose above the canyon walls. It was so bright, we didn't need flashlights. We watched the bats fly out of the caves carved into a cliff across the river and listened to the Urique gurgle past the rocks upstream.

The following day, we donned our packs and headed upriver. The going was tough for several kilometers. We bouldered across the river several times to circumvent rock walls. Other times we crawled through tunnels under the gigantic rocks that had tumbled into the canyon. Thick clumps of bamboo grow along the river and cactus seem to take root in profusion where handholds are needed most.

Being ardent kayakers, we evaluated the Urique as a potential run. All agreed that it would be a technical nightmare. The river flows under rocks as much as around them. At high water, the river would be ripe with undercuts and siphons. Portaging would be a logistical horror show.

After six kilometers, we approached the Incised Meanders and the river assumed a serpentine course. Fortunately, the boulder fields became less intimidating and we started to make better time. But it was necessary to wade the river six times because of the canyon walls. We hoisted our packs above our heads as we passed through chest-deep water.

We made camp that night in the middle of the Meanders, about a half-kilometer above river-wide, five-meter falls. We spotted large cat tracks along the river and concluded that they had probably been left by a bobcat, which are indigenous to the area. We slept again under the full moon.

The next morning, we continued upriver—about three more kilometers—until we reached the dry arroyo mentioned previously as an alternate point of access. Within an hour, we arrived at the road and I quickly hiked to Umira and retrieved the truck.

The Incised Meanders offer a spectacular wilderness experience to those adequately prepared to meet the challenge. This is clearly no place for carelessness. Rescue from the canyon would be difficult, if not impossible. Some climbing gear and experience might prove useful. Clumsy individuals prone to falls and those inadequately outfitted should not attempt this trek, especially the descent down Arroyo Umira, which is particularly perilous.

As always, low-impact camping must be the rule. The canyon is free of debris, fire rings, etc. It deserves to stay that way.

Robert Gedekoh, M.D., is a regional editor for American Whitewater. *He has written for* River Runner, American Whitewater, *and the* Pittsburgh Press. *He lives in Elizabeth, Pennsylvania.*

Particulars

You will need the 1:50,000 Samachique topo. Access to Umira Bridge may be somewhat inconvenient. It is about halfway between Creel and Batopilas, which is a long way to hitchhike, although I talked to three people who did so and said they caught rides easily. You may want to hop the every-other-day bus from Creel to Batopilas or the daily bus from Creel to Guachochi. Just ask the driver to let you off at Umira.

If you have your own vehicle, the road to Umira is paved. The drive to Umira from Creel should take about two hours, depending on how often you stop to ogle at the scenery.

Note: Please see Chapter 19 for more pertinent skinny regarding the Incised Meanders.

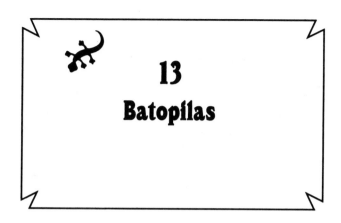

13
Batopilas

If there is one piece of civilization in Tarahumara-land worth visiting, it's the wonderfully weird town of Batopilas. Founded in 1632, Batopilas was once one of Mexico's richest towns, owing to the silver ore in the area. Until the late 1970s, there wasn't even a road to Batopilas. You could drive only as far as La Bufa, which, despite its prominence on some maps, consists of nothing more than a few houses built on and around a huge tailings pile. From there, it was five or six hours more on foot on the old Camino Real, a trail that follows the lovely Rio Batopilas. The town was electrified only in late 1988, after a failed attempt to do so in 1983. Many of the buildings there have had private generators for years, but that was it on the power front.

Batopilas is no ranchito. It is, rather, home to a couple thousand people. It has a large church, several hotels, several schools, and plenty of European-feeling curvy back alleys.

The road connecting Creel with Batopilas is a major-league engineering marvel. It is about 150 kilometers long, only the first 60 of which were paved as of late 1993. The trip from Creel, which takes a minimum of five hours, will be one of the highlights of your visit to Tarahumara-land, whether you drive it yourself or take the thrice-weekly bus. The road passes through high sierra topography, punctuated by spectacular rock formations and cliff faces. It goes through several towns, most notably—if that's the right word—Quirare. And it crosses the Rio Urique at Humira Bridge—the upper reaches of Copper Canyon itself.

But, all of that is small potatoes compared to the descent from the high country into Batopilas Canyon. A few miles south of Quirare, the view of the almost 1,850-meter abyss, which is one of the most breathtaking in all of Copper Canyon Country, opens up. And, what you see is what you get—the road heads right on down. In the next 16 kilometers there are over 200 curves and almost 20 hairpin-curve switchbacks. After that, the road crosses the Rio Batopilas.

Then, the *real* fun begins. The tendency, once you've completed the big descent, is to think that Batopilas is right around the next bend. Wrong. It's at least another hair-raising hour's drive downriver. This is my favorite part of the drive, though it is also the most dangerous because, every centimeter of the way, there's a major dropoff on the right-hand side as you're heading towards Batopilas. On the opposite side of the river, you can easily see the Camino Real, which is still used by locals—Tarahumaras and Mexicans—leading burro trains.

Batopilas is located on the west bank of the Rio Batopilas in one of the deepest and most arid canyons in Tarahumara-land. It was built between the river and the canyon walls. Thus, Batopilas is five kilometers long, but only a few blocks wide— at the most. In many places, it is only one block wide.

Batopilas is right in the middle of Copper Canyon Country's tropical fruit-producing region. Flowers bloom here year-round, lending a coastal, Central American feel to the town. But, this place is anything but coastal. Though the river runs a stone's throw from every building in town, Batopilas is in the middle of a cactus-adorned section of desert that makes Tucson seem mild by comparison. The highest temperature ever recorded in these parts—112 degrees F.; 44.5 degrees C.—was measured in Batopilas. Thus, I recommend visiting this area in the dead of winter. And not just because of the temperatures. Summertime insects here can be numerous and voracious. (I've been in Batopilas in the summer before, and, I tell you what, it is one seriously toasty place. It's really too hot to even move, much less hike through the hills.)

Batopilas is also one of the centers for drug cultivation and transportation in the Sierra Madre. This, combined with its isolation, gives Batopilas an air of the wild West, Sierra Madre style. You will see men walking around with pistols stuck in their belts and no-nonsense looks in their eyes. Surprisingly, or maybe not so surprisingly, Batopilas is a "dry" town—there are no saloons. If you want to wet your whistle here, you need to bring your own.

You will likely venture into Batopilas because it is the gateway to some of Tarahumara-land's most appealing backpacking. But you would be making a mistake if you did not spend at least a full day exploring the town.

Batopilas is an especially popular destination for picture-takers. Most of its buildings were built in the early twentieth century, but there are many ruins from the seventeenth and eighteenth centuries—to say nothing of the fact that even those "new" twentieth-century edifices look like they're as old as the hills. Especially interesting is the ruin of the Hacienda de San Miguel, located on the east side of the river just before the bridge, as you are coming into town. This building served as the residence of one of the area's first silver tycoons, Alexander Shepard. It also served as the office for the local mining company.

In 1992, another cool thing was added to the list of reasons to visit Batopilas. Skip McWilliams, who also owns the Copper Canyon Lodge in Cusarare, completed a four-year renovation project on a block-long hotel, Copper Canyon Lodge-Riverside, right in the middle of town. This is the most amazing hotel I have ever set foot in. For Skip, this project was a labor of love. He even moved to Batopilas with his two children for a year to oversee the initial stages of the renovation.

Skip tells a wonderful story of his first night in the hotel. The place hadn't been occupied in who knows how long. Skip and his *niños* were bunked down on the floor and, just before Skip blew the candle out, he noticed something glimmering in the light. It was an old silver coin from the Spanish era. He knew at that moment that his Karmic ducks were in a huddle *vis à vis* his new hotel project.

The only problem with the Copper Canyon Lodge-Riverside is that, in order to sleep there, you have to sign up for an eight-day tour, which starts and ends in Chihuahua City. Also, it's a little on the pricey side, but the place is so special, it's well worth it.

Another thing about Batopilas and its surroundings: This is one of the best places in all of Copper Canyon Country for seeing traditionally dressed Tarahumaras. This region boasts large numbers of Tarahumaras who were never converted to the Catholic faith. They are called "gentile Tarahumaras." Not only do they dress far more traditionally than most of their brethren (with the exception of the area around the upper reaches of the Rio Conchos), but they act differently. There is a dignified bearing to the Tarahumaras around Batopilas. They are taller, and they walk with a proud gait. They seem to revel in their Tarahumara-ness. And that is a wonderful thing to see.

One last thing: In Batopilas, despite the fact that it's legally a dry town, there are occasional, town-wide, street parties down on the plaza for which beer is allowed to be brought in. I've coincidentally been in Batopilas twice during street party days. One of those was in November, the other in February. I do not remember what the occasions were, but, in Mexico, it doesn't take much of an excuse to put on a fiesta.

If I can make a generic observation about Batopilas based upon two nights, I would say that, when Batopilas parties, hang onto your hat, because this place flat-out boogies down. There's live music and dancing till dawn and a community-wide ambience that can best be described as borderline debauch. In other words: fun.

The thing is, if you plan to get any sleep at all during a fiesta in Batopilas, you'd do well to lodge as far away from the plaza as humanly possible, because the revelry will continue, without even the slightest interruption, until dawn's early light. Then, at 6 AM, the local padre will make Batopilas pay for its indiscretions by ringing the church bell so loud and long that you think there must be an air raid or something coming on. You can tell from the instant the first chime shakes you out of bed that the padre obviously gets pissed off big-time during town parties, and, the next morning, he lets everyone understand that full well.

Batopilas is highly recommended for just hanging out and reading. It is a relaxing little town. The perfect place to put your feet up after your hiking trip into the backcountry of Tarahumara-land.

Particulars

There are buses connecting Creel with Batopilas, leaving from the plaza in Creel at 7 AM Tuesdays, Thursdays, and Saturdays. The trip can take as long as 10 hours. The buses make the return trip to Creel at 4 AM (yes, you read that right) on Mondays, Wednesdays, and Fridays. Fare is about $10 U.S. Be sure to verify times and schedules. You would be well advised to pack a lunch and water bottle for the drive. Also, a bucket of industrial-strength tranquilizers would be in order, just in case overt terror overcomes you while descending into Batopilas Canyon!

Also, Margarita's, the Parador, and the Hotel Nuevo in Creel all offer guided tours to Batopilas, as does the Copper Canyon Lodge in Cusarare.

If you are not on a tour, and the thought of getting on the bus from hell at 4 AM doesn't titillate you, ask around town to see if anyone is heading to Creel anytime soon. This is usually the way I make my way back to civilization from Batopilas. Start your quest for transport by visiting the local grocery stores. Since all supplies in Batopilas come from Creel, there is a surprising amount of traffic between the two towns. If you are successful in locating a ride out to Creel, you may be disappointed by the accommodations. I've ridden out sitting for five hours on a sea of empty Coke bottles, in the back of a flatbed that was predominantly occupied by a Volkswagen van that was tied in with bailing twine, and in a pick-up truck driven by a man who was clearly not only psychotic but, at the same time, had visions of Formula-1 grandeur. You will be charged about $7 U.S. for the ride, no matter how nasty it is.

There are four other lodging facilities in Batopilas. The Hotel Mary is located right across the street from the church. This is where I have stayed most often in Batopilas. It is open and airy, and boasts a decent enough (though slow-moving) restaurant. Private rooms cost about $10 U.S. a night. Room cost is the same for one or two people. There are three clean communal baths with hot water.

The Hotel Batopilas is located about three blocks north of the plaza. Rooms are rented for $5 U.S. per person, no matter how many people share a room. Sports one bathroom that is kept in a barely acceptable state of cleanliness. Monse Bustillo's is located right on the east side of the plaza. This place is run by an English-speaking woman—not surprisingly, Monse Bustillos—who also deals in Tarahumara artifacts. She sells some of the nicest pots in the area. Cost is $5 U.S. per person with communal bath. There is also a new hotel on the way into town that I have not visited. From the outside, it seems nice enough.

There can be nights when all hotel rooms in Batopilas are full, so you may have to hike outside of town a kilometer or so and camp. There should be no problems with this, though I would try to pitch camp in a place where passersby won't notice you or your gear. Also, I have heard that families are willing to put people up for a night or two. Ask around town.

There are numerous places to eat in Batopilas, most notably Michaela's, which is south of the plaza on a winding side street. You should ask directions. Doña Micha, as she is known, serves meals in her house at a cost of about $4–$5 per person for breakfast and about $6 per person for lunch or dinner. Prices include one soft drink. You pretty much get served whatever she has on hand, though the portions are always hearty. You should stop by her house several hours before mealtime to let her know you plan on eating there. For breakfast, cruise by the night before to make reservations.

The Hotel Batopilas also has a family-run restaurant, which is nothing more than okay. The tourism boom that is enveloping Copper Canyon Country has made its way to Batopilas. So, there are new restaurants opening up all the time. Since you'll likely be walking around town anyhow, keep your eyes peeled for off-the-beaten-path eateries.

There are several small grocery stores in town. All of them sell cheap fresh fruit, which Batopilas is famous for. You can also buy gas here most of the time.

Though it is tempting to explore the area surrounding Batopilas in great detail, you would be well advised to stick to the main tourist routes, several of which are detailed in the following four chapters. If there is any place in Copper Canyon Country where you can find yourself stumbling into a marijuana field, the Batopilas area is it. If you do not stray far from the beaten path, you have nothing to worry about. Despite its drug roots, Batopilas is a very laid-back place. You may, however, be approached to buy drugs. Just say "no!"

Also, be prepared for military check-points on the road between Creel and Batopilas.

Besides the hikes I describe in the following chapters, there are two others—neither of which I have taken—that are worth considering. Apparently, there's an old mine outside of town that makes for a good hour or so jaunt. Ask Martin, who manages the Copper Canyon Lodge-Riverside, about this. Also, if you're looking for something a little longer and more arduous, consider dayhiking to Camuchin, which is accessed by a trail that follows the arroyo that begins basically in front of Doña Micha's. This round-trip hike should take the better part of the day.

14
Batopilas to Satevo Mission

At any moment, I expect Alfred Hitchcock to walk around the corner, the look on his face betraying the fact that even he feels spooked. This place—Satevo Mission, two very easy walking hours downriver from Batopilas—puts the Bates Mansion to shame when it comes to potential horror quotient. If a bunch of your buddies got you so drunk that you passed out near-dead, then carted your inebriated carcass to Satevo and placed you on the altar on a moonlit night, your psyche would never recover. You would wake up and, once you checked out your surroundings, that would be that with regards to your sanity. You would run screaming into the dark Mexican night, badly bent forevermore.

The trail from Batopilas to Satevo, which is no longer a trail, but, rather a dirt road that was built in the early 1990s to service a mine that stayed open for about a month before closing down—meaning this road was built for nothing—and provides the best dayhike in Tarahumara-land. Not only is the hiking as easy as it gets, but the scenery is unparalleled. This is the heart of Batopilas Canyon, the walls of which rise almost 2,300 meters—7,400 feet—straight up to the high sierra, dotted the whole way by huge Organ Pipe cactuses. At the same time, the Rio Batopilas is making an argument for being the most attractive river in Copper Canyon Country.

But the walk takes a backseat to the destination—Satevo Mission. The history of this mission has been lost. No one knows for certain when it was built, or by whom. According to local sources, it is older than Batopilas, meaning it was built in the very early 1600s—about the same time as Jamestown, Virginia, was being founded. More intriguing than the "when?" or "by whom?" of Satevo Mission's history is the "why?"

Satevo Mission is a very large worship facility by local standards. The area has never had a population large enough to justify a hallowed edifice of these proportions. Thus, why on earth would anyone—almost certainly a Jesuit—feel a need to come into the wilderness to build such a monstrosity? It must have taken years to complete. And, the work must have required the services of scores of Tarahumaras. They dedicated what surely must have been years of their lives to make Satevo Mission a physical reality.

No matter the fabric of its history. Satevo Mission is a day-hiking destination to beat all dayhiking destinations. Located in a particularly arid, two-kilometer-wide stretch of floodplain along the Rio Batopilas, Satevo Mission is the centerpiece of a small Mexican community of the same name. The mission itself has three domes and a belltower several stories high. Like most backcountry missions in Tarahumara-land, it fell into a state of considerable disrepair. Locals were even using some of the side rooms as goat pens.

But, in 1991, a couple of locals cleaned the old church up, put a lock on the door, then started charging admission to get in. Which is cool. Then, in 1992, the church was painted and the Batopilas padre started hosting regular services in Satevo. The mission seemed like it had made its way back from the dead, though many people think the new paint job makes the mission stand out too much, where before, it blended into the surrounding countryside most tastefully.

I have visited Satevo numerous times, and would not consider visiting Batopilas without simultaneously considering visiting Satevo. It's just too special of a place. The first time I visited the mission, there were four of us—a French-Canadian male, a French female, Gay, and I. We made the trip to Satevo one sunny scorcher of a December day. While the higher elevations of Copper Canyon Country were in the throes of winter, we were wearing shorts and smearing on sunscreen. There is no winter in Batopilas Canyon.

The trail-turned-road, which you can drive down very easily, by the way (okay, I'll admit to having cheated on this once or twice), is an extension of the old Camino Real. Meaning the grades were designed for pack train use. Meaning it's a piece of cake to hike on.

We pulled out of Batopilas in the early afternoon, so we would be able to hike back in the photogenic early evening. The walk was uneventfully wonderful, though we were filled with a modicum of apprehension because we were all so seriously psyched about visiting Satevo, which you can first see after the trail rounds a bend about two kilometers upriver from the mission.

The instant we arrived at the mission, a dozen or so children ran up, imploring us to purchase soft drinks from them. We had no idea there were stores in Satevo. Come to find out, there are two—each of which was represented by half the children. We ordered two soft drinks from one of the stores, and two more from the other. A few minutes later, the warm beverages were delivered, but the children refused to bring them to the mission steps, where we were sitting. They set them down outside the fence surrounding the mission. Okay, okay, we've probably got a couple of black check marks next to our names in the heavenly register for drinking in church. At least it wasn't beer, which, of course, is exactly what we wished it was.

As we were sucking the drinks down, a couple of local baby-toting women came over. They asked if we wanted to take pictures of their offspring, certainly with the idea of charging us for each photo taken. It's hard to tell someone that you have no desire whatsoever to photograph their snotty-nosed little *niño*. But that's what we did. They walked away rejected.

This photo solicitation stuff is getting out of hand in some places in Copper Canyon Country. And it's really a tough thing to deal with, because, when you refuse, you implicitly lay out the vibes that whoever is doing the solicitation is not worthy of being photographed—which, for the most part, is exactly what you're thinking. Yet, you can't just come out and say anything like, "Lady, that is the ugliest child I have ever laid eyes on, and, thus, I wouldn't consider wasting even one frame of film on him unless *you* paid *me*, and, even then,

I would do so only because this kid's so homely, people back home won't believe me when I tell them about him, so I'd need some photographic evidence." That sort of thing just doesn't go over real well.

I usually just end up telling people when they approach me that, since this area is so beautiful and the people so charming and handsome, I've used up all my film. Of course, then you put yourself in a position where you can't then suddenly pull out your camera and photograph the lovely flower you noticed point-two seconds after you lied through your teeth.

When we entered the gloom of Satevo Mission, our pupils went on red alert. It was impossible, for the first few minutes, to see anything. So, do we stand there until our eyes adjust? No. That would be too smart. We immediately started poking around in some of the little side rooms. The first one, on the left as you walk in, is especially dank and dark. Stuck in one corner was a carved, wooden Tarahumara ceremonial mask. In the darkness, the French-Canadian and I both thought it was a human head. We jumped about five meters in the air and both whacked our heads on the ceiling. Then, of course, being sensitive sorts of guys, we sent the females in without any warning.

There's a rickety ladder going up to the choir loft, which is about 10 meters above the main mission floor. We climbed up, as the ladder was shaking back and forth like a metronome. From the choir loft, you can, if you are stupid, ascend the bell tower. In addition to the fact that the bell tower looks like it could come separated from the mission at any moment with no external stimuli whatsoever, the ladder is a flimsy piece of kindling that is missing several steps. Then, to make matters even more interesting, if you fall, which you surely would, there's nothing to catch you until you reach ground level. We passed.

We hit the trail back to Batopilas about two hours before dark. On the way back, we stopped to take pictures on a rock outcropping above the river that affords a great view of the mission and a small suspension bridge. The evening colors lent a softness to the scene that, when you get right down to it, is anything but soft. Just about every plant in the area sports some manner of thorn. And the local fauna consists as much of rattlers and scorpions as it does Bambi and Thumper. But, this evening, the intense desert of the Batopilas Canyon seemed to mask its harshness well.

Come summer, certainly, such would not be the case. The temperatures this time of day would exceed 100 degrees F. The river would be in flood stage. The biting flies would be, well, biting. But right now, this is a little piece of heaven. The best dayhike in Tarahumara-land.

In 1991, Gay, Mark Fox, a photographer from my home town in Colorado, and Larry White, who I met while hiking the Colorado Trail in 1990, strolled on down to Satevo. While we were there, a group of about fifteen good old boys were out in front of one of the stores swilling beer and taking turns target practicing with a fully automatic Uzi. It made for sort of a tense scene.

When we passed on the way into and out of Satevo, these guys were giving Gay the serious hairy eyeball, which was a little nerve-wracking, particularly since they had a fully automatic Uzi, while I had a fully manual Swiss Army Knife. Nothing came of the situation, but it was uncomfortable.

While we were there, Larry talked me into going with him up on the roof of the mission, via the same flimsy ladder. It was definitely a sphincter-puckering experience. At any moment, I expected to go straight through the roof, landing on top of Gay's head, some 20 meters below. Before that trip, I had heard a rumor that there was a series of basements and catacombs under the mission that perhaps could be explored. Centuries ago, so the rumor goes, the Jesuit priests, being mortal males, would sometimes deep-six their celibacy vows and practice a little *l'amour* with the local female population. Occasionally, I was told, one of the members of the local female population would get knocked up by a priest, upon which case the unfortunate young lady would be put to death to avoid scandal, as if having someone put to death is not at least borderline scandalous. I was told that those alleged catacombs beneath Satevo were littered with the skeletal remains of those ladies who were killed.

Larry, Gay, Mark, and I looked all around the outside of the mission for any signs of basement access. We could find none. Then we looked inside, and, sho' nuff, right there on the altar is a small hole in the floor that clearly descends into the bowels of terra firma. I climbed down in it a short ways and decided, in no uncertain terms, to venture no further. I mean, under the best of circumstances, I am not attracted to places subterranean. I've visited both Mammoth Cave and Carlsbad Caverns national parks, and thoroughly enjoyed the experiences. But, those were huge ol' caverns with things like floodlights and underground restaurants. This was different. This was a small underground corridor that would spell instant psychic doom for someone like me who hip-hops through life with a modicum of claustrophobia. And, besides, if I found myself in a musty, dusty, spider-webby catacomb with a small backpacking flashlight and I came nose-to-nose with a human skeleton, the only thing that would happen before I died of fright would be for all my excretion functions to jump into action simultaneously. And we don't even want to talk about what would happen if my flashlight went out. . . .

Particulars

You can easily make this trip without a map. It is almost impossible to get lost. If you would like to see where you are going on paper, get the 1:50,000 Batopilas topo. Satevo Mission is a little off that map, but not far. If you want to see the whole tamale, try to get a copy of the 1:50,000 Rio Batopilas topo. You may not have any luck.

Satevo Mission is two hours—about eight kilometers—south of Batopilas. Just walk downriver from the town. If you stick to the riverbank, you will find yourself on the correct dirt road. Stay on the same side of the river as Batopilas all the way to Satevo.

Don't come here except in the dead of winter. Even then, you will be exposed to much direct sunlight. There are two very small stores in Satevo, and plenty of campsites near the mission.

If you were of a mind to make this cakewalk into an intense backcountry experience, you could follow the Rio Batopilas south until it intersects with the Rio San Miguel, which is an extension of the Rio Verde. I am told it is about 13 hours to the San Miguel.

15
Batopilas to Munérachi

When I first heard about Munérachi it was from Lalo Valdez, the ex-assistant manager of Las Cabañas del Cobre in Cusarare, who grew up in Batopilas. Lalo, who has since returned to his home in Madeira, is one of the most wonderful people I have ever met, at least partially because he has the gift of being able to make his Spanish understandable to the Anglo ear. And he comprehends gringo babble. Meaning, when you talk to Lalo, you actually feel like you're making progress with your Español. He would make a great teacher.

Lalo told me that, in his opinion, the weirdest little mission town in Tarahumara-land is Munérachi (moo-NAIR-ah-chee). Lalo and I had talked long into the night several times, in varying states of sobriety, about religion. We basically share the same non-beliefs, although I think Lalo is the more confirmed theological skeptic. His favorite quote is from one of the recent Mexican presidents, who once said something like, "Mexico's problem is that it's too close to the United States and too far from God." Lalo takes it one step further. He thinks Mexico's problem is that it's too close to both the United States and God.

Lalo said that during the time that the Jesuits were ousted from Mexico, the Tarahumaras started modifying Catholicism. He added that in no other place in Tarahumara-land was that modification more evident than in Munérachi, which struck me as slightly strange because Munérachi is actually one of the most accessible Tarahumara settlements in the Batopilas region. I would have thought that the weirdest aspects of

Tarahumara-land would be found in the most boondock little corner of the most remote canyon.

Munérachi is only about five or six nose-to-the-grindstone hiking hours from Batopilas. The hiking is very easy, however, along a trail that's as good as any I have ever hiked on in Copper Canyon Country. There are several Mexican villages along the way, but Munérachi is the first purely Tarahumara turf you run into on this route. Lalo didn't really specify what manner of weirdness we might witness in the name of religion while visiting Munérachi, but one thing was for certain—I was not going to visit the Batopilas area without checking this place out. Strangeness in all its manifestations—good, bad, and indifferent—is something that always merits investigation.

Lalo told me one other interesting thing about Munérachi. Apparently, there is a world-famous Tarahumara musical group from there. Lalo said they're on the road nine months of the year, and he didn't know if they would be home during our mid-December visit. From what I had heard in the way of indigenous Tarahumara jams, at the very least I couldn't imagine a local combo traveling around the world giving concerts. I don't mean to put the Tarahumaras down on this. It's just that each culture has its positive and negative aspects and, somewhere along the line, some artistic social evolution headed toward Tarahumara-land, while others headed to Vienna, the Andes, and Nashville.

There is also an American musician, Somebody-or-other Wheller, who lives six months out of the year in Munérachi. I have heard one of his tapes, and it's great stuff. He really focuses on incorporating Tarahumara rhythms into his music, and it is unlike any other music I have ever heard.

My first trip to Munérachi (I have returned, from several different directions numerous other times) was in December 1988. We were six on this three-day, two-night Batopilas to Munérachi round-trip: Andre, the same Canadian who accompanied us to Satevo Mission, Bob Gedekoh, an M.D. from Pittsburgh who wrote the Humira Bridge chapter, Mike Bush, an electrician from Ohio, Dean Fairburn, a student of the teaching arts from Knoxville, and Gay and I.

Bob, Mike, and Dean, who had driven down from the States together, left their vehicle parked in Batopilas and simply began walking on the trail that starts right where the bridge crosses the river above town. The trail is on the same side of the river as Batopilas.

Andre, Gay, and I drove back towards La Bufa, until we reached the turnoff for the ranchito of Casas Coloradas, about four kilometers from Batopilas. We asked one of the residents if we could park in his yard for a few days and, upon returning, paid him $3. This saved us about an hour of walking— although, of course, Bob, Dean, and Mike made us feel guilty about being the lazy pieces of vermin we are.

We hiked from Casas Coloradas down to the Rio Batopilas, pulled our boots off, crossed, sat down, put our boots back on, hiked a few hundred meters, realized we still had to cross the stream coming out of Arroyo Cerro Colorado, the side canyon we would be hiking up, removed our boots, crossed, and put our boots back on again. That, right there, was the hardest part of this hike.

There are two trails heading up Arroyo Cerro Colorado towards Munérachi—one on each side of the arroyo. The best one is on the left-hand side as you're hiking upstream all the way. It stays within 30 meters of the river all the way to the village of Cerro Colorado—about two-thirds of the way to Munérachi. Now, what I'm going to say is that the riverbed trail up Arroyo Cerro Colorado is a "can't-miss" trail. But, understand before I do so, that, on that first trip, the six of us managed to miss it on several occasions on the hike up. We'd be walking along a path so ragged a goat would be embarrassed to be seen on it, all the while looking over at this four-lane highway on the other side. We would scramble through the brush, down to the floodplain, cross the river at a place with no good crossings, scramble up the other side, only to realize several hundred meters later that, somewhere during all our scrambling, the good trail had crossed over to the side we had just come from. This was more funny than bothersome, and I have no excuses.

But, during one of these seemingly premeditated efforts to avoid walking on the trail, we passed through a small Mexican village that we would not have passed through otherwise, named "Australia." I kid you not, even though the woman who told me that's what the village was named might very well have been kidding me. There's a giant foundation of some ancient edifice, which likely had something to do with the local mining industry during its heyday two hundred years back. We asked several locals about the building, but none seemed to know its history.

We returned to the trail by passing underneath an old water viaduct, which is still being used for irrigation. It was so antiquated that it could have passed for something out of Roman days. When we got down to the river, we surprised eight or ten females, who all looked related. They were doing laundry and taking baths. One of the females, who looked about sixteen, was in a partial state of undress. And she was very easy to look at. Until, that is, the nuclear explosion of a spousal elbow impacted my rib cage.

When this underwear-attired nymph's grandmother—I guess it was her grandmother—realized there was a wife on the scene, the frightened look she sported when we first approached evaporated into a sly smile that spoke to the fact that all was well with the world.

Bob, Mike, and Dean told us that they were planning to camp at Cerro Colorado, where, they had heard, we would be able to buy soft drinks. Sounded like a good enough reason to camp there, and we decided to join them. Cerro Colorado—literally "red hill"—was located at the base of, you guessed it, a red hill, where active underground gold mining still takes place. It is about three hours hiking from Casas Coloradas, where we had parked our truck.

Placer mining also takes place on a small, though industrious scale, all along Arroyo Cerro Colorado. The ore is crushed in rounded, water-powered cisterns. Crude sluicing takes place after the ore is ground down. Because of all the mining activity, the little creek flowing through Arroyo Cerro Colorado was bright red. In some places, it literally looks like a river of blood. The locals told us in no uncertain terms that the red water was not only fit for drinking, but it was good water. I stuck with bottled mineral water sold at the little store in Cerro Colorado whenever I could.

Cerro Colorado is a real nice place. It has a main drag that almost feels like a little downtown. Of course, the main drag is also the only drag, but that just adds to the charm. The village has a decidedly tropical ambience. This is not surprising. It gets really hot in Cerro Colorado. Though it was getting close to Christmas, the daytime temperatures during our hike hovered in the low-90s F. When we mentioned to some Cerro Coloradans that it was hot, they laughed. When we mentioned that the flies were bothersome, they laughed even harder. They bade us return sometime in the dead of summer to check out real heat and insect misery.

Several parties of gringos had passed through in the last three weeks, the store's proprietor, a reed-thin woman who had seen at least two hundred summers, told us. She was tickled pink that business was booming. When she learned I was writing a book about the area, she all but signed on to be my local agent. She had visions of many, many soft drinks being sold in the future.

We camped right below town in a little field above the river. Within a few minutes, we were entertaining visitors. Both the mayor and the sheriff of Cerro Colorado dropped by for a chat. Then some of the town's less-young, young ladies showed up. The señoras at the store had noticed that there was only one female among us, and they commented on it. Being the only member of the group able to utter so much as one syllable of Spanish, I told them that our four comrades were all bachelors and that they should pass the word that there were eligible gringo menfolk at-hand.

I walked down to camp, did a few chores and promptly forgot all that babble about my compadres' bachelorhood problems. Then, we started getting visits from clusters of gussied-up thirteen- and fourteen-year-olds. I couldn't figure it out at first. Suddenly, it dawned on me that this was the local version of the parade of available female material. This is not as sexist as it sounds. Well, yes, now that I think about it, it is as sexist as it sounds. Regardless, it is a fairly common occurrence in Mexico. Gay and I have witnessed it on a reasonably large scale, in Santiago Ixcuintla, near Tepic. Every post-pubescent unmarried female in town was being led around by an older female while all the men in town stood on the sidelines with lecherous looks in their eyes. I mean, it was more innocent than this sounds. But, it amounts to the same thing.

The only problem was, all these young ladies were *young*. Which is not to say that several of them weren't very attractive. It's just that, in Mexico, especially those parts like this one, where there are plenty of firearms for everyone, even an extended conversation with a señorita could get you "invited" to join the family, which maybe wouldn't be so bad.

Around dusk, all our visitors left. We all "snuck" down to the river to take a bath. There is a suspension bridge across the river, above flood level, connecting Cerro Colorado with the trail to the mine a thousand meters up the opposite side of the canyon. (It also connects to the main trail to Munérachi.) The locals must have been mighty curious for a goodly number of years as to gringo bathing techniques. The instant we hit the river sans garments, the town hustled out en masse onto the bridge, as well as the path above—to check out our soaping and rinsing procedures. At first, we tried to remain mostly underwater while we scrubbed. But this was December. The water was freezing. So, after a while the townsfolk were able to add to the local trove of knowledge concerning goose bump patterns on extremely white posteriors.

The next morning, we dropped our gear off at the store for safekeeping and headed out to Munérachi, about two hours away. We decided to stick to the river bottom, and the hiking was very easy, with the exception of one place where we had to do a little simple scrambling.

We reached suburban Munérachi about noon. It is located in an idyllic spot at the confluence of two major arroyos. The mission is right next to a schoolhouse. There are a dozen or so Tarahumara houses in the near vicinity. School was not in session, and the only adult near the mission was a Tarahumara woman kneeling in the sunshine weaving a basket. A couple of her young children ran around playing. One, a little boy, about two, took one look at us and started screaming and crying.

The mission itself, this supposed bastion of Tarahumara-modified Catholicism, was unoccupied. The six of us walked around in it for a while and were generally unimpressed, probably because only two days before, we had been in Satevo Mission, which is the best church in Tarahumara-land. The floor of Munérachi Mission was besmirched with several centuries worth of various types of animal droppings, covering the gamut from chicken to cow to homo sapiens. Several ceiling beams in a side room were falling inward. The place had seen better days. But there was no indication that any bizarre variety of Catholicism was practiced hereabouts. We were hoping at least for evidence of a sacrifice. Human skulls, corpses of virgins, something. . . .

The only aspect of Munérachi that seemed out of the ordinary came in the form of two solar panels outside the school. I tried asking the woman weaving the basket if there was any live music to be had in the area, figuring that if there was a world-famous group headquartered here, everyone in town would know all about it. The woman looked at me like I was from Mars. She shook her head, then went back to her work. Oh well.

Since we had a multi-hour hike back to Cerro Colorado ahead of us, we didn't hang out too long. On the way back, the rest of the group made the mistake of actually thinking I knew where I was going. I decided to check out the trail that was on the left-hand side as we were going downstream. One meter from the river, it started heading intensely upward for about half a mile. I thought I heard the rest of the group say, as I was humping it up this incline, to hell with this, they were all going to return to Cerro Colorado the same way we had come—along the river.

I guessed correctly that the trail I was now on was going to pass by Cerro Colorado. (It ends up that this is the main trail connecting Munérachi and Cerro Colorado.) I decided to hike very rapidly to get ahead of the group, so I could photograph them down on the river with Munérachi Canyon in the background. This trail was a breeze. Once it topped out, about 150 vertical meters above the river, it was level to slightly downhill all the way to the point where it began switchbacking down to the river just above Cerro Colorado.

After about an hour, I stopped in the shadow of a spindly tree and rested. It was about 100 degrees F. Suddenly, I saw Andre rounding a corner about half a kilometer back. Then, one by one, came the rest of the gang. Though I was really enjoying the trail, I was afraid that everyone else would be displeased that I had led them away from the tranquility of the river. Quite the contrary. Everyone agreed that this stretch of trail was a nice change of pace. Though it was certainly more exposed to direct sunshine than the river trail, it provided more spectacular vistas.

We arrived back in Cerro Colorado in late afternoon. Everyone was ready for a cool dip and a cold beer. But, since there was no beer in town, we settled for nineteen or twenty soft drinks each. We were all sunburned and seriously sweaty. Andre made arrangements to eat breakfast with the store's proprietors the next morning. They told us that for a small price they would be glad to feed us all, but the rest of us had plenty of food. Andre ended up with pinole, eggs, and beans, which he enjoyed.

We set camp up, again, right below the store and hit the sack early. The night was very warm. I had carried neither a tent nor a winter bag and, for once, I didn't freeze my tail off. The next morning on the way back out to Casas Coloradas, we passed a Tarahumara man with a tumpline carrying a load of corn husks, which would be sold for goat food in Batopilas. This load extended about eight feet over the Tarahumara man's head. It had to weigh at least 80 kilograms. The man said he had been walking all night. When we passed him, he looked tired, but he was still keeping up a fast pace.

A few minutes later, we passed a threesome of Mexican women, all wearing plastic sandals and sporting bright pink lipstick. They said good day to us. They ignored the Tarahumara carrying the corn husks. And he ignored them. The peculiar harmony of Tarahumara-land. The cultural ballet of Copper Canyon Country.

Particulars

This whole route is located on the 1:50,000 Batopilas map. Arroyo Cerro Colorado can be accessed by walking or driving out of Batopilas. It is the first major side canyon on the left as you are heading towards La Bufa on the road to Creel. A trail leaves town on the same side of the river as Batopilas. It begins at the bridge across the Rio Batopilas. This is a major burro train trail. In about four easy kilometers, about an hour on the trail, you will fork to the left, heading up the left-hand side of a major side canyon—Arroyo Cerro Colorado. Just across the Rio Batopilas is a cluster of houses. This is Casas Coloradas, the place you would park your vehicle.

If you are driving, head out of Batopilas towards La Bufa. Take the rugged-looking left four plus-or-minus kilometers from Batopilas. Head down the hill until you come to a group of houses. Ask if you can park there and offer to pay 5 new pesos a day. Cross the Rio Batopilas and cross the stream coming out of Arroyo Cerro Colorado. Walk up the hill on the left side of the arroyo and intersect the trail.

Simply follow the arroyo up for about three hours— about eight or nine kilometers—until you reach the village of Cerro Colorado. For much of this walk, you will be able to see Cerro Colorado, the hill. It is on the right (east) side of the Arroyo Cerro Colorado as you are walking upstream. The village of Cerro Colorado is on the left side. You will pass through several other small Mexican villages between Casas Coloradas and Cerro Colorado. Of particular interest is Australia because of the ruins thereabouts.

From Cerro Colorado, where there is a small store owned by the mother of the mayor, you cross the arroyo on a suspension bridge below the store. Switchback up the hill, then hook into the burro trail that continues up the arroyo. That trail will cross a small ridge finger that forms the corner on the Arroyo Cerro Colorado-Arroyo Munérachi intersection. From that ridge finger, it's downhill all the way to the bottom of Arroyo Munérachi. You'll have to cross the stream just before entering Munérachi.

The trail from Batopilas to Munérachi, especially that part between Cerro Colorado and Munérachi, is one of the hottest and sunniest in Copper Canyon Country. Try to hike it only in the winter and, even then, in the early morning or late afternoon. You can also hike to Munérachi via the bottom of the arroyo. Just follow Arroyo Cerro Colorado up until it splits. Take the right-hand split.

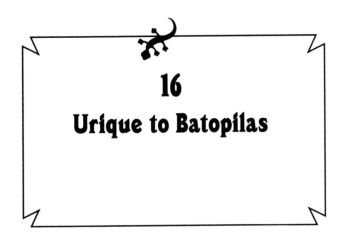

16
Urique to Batopilas

After ten years of hiking in and around Copper Canyon Country, it came as quite a surprise when it finally sank in that there was an entire section—well, actually, a full quarter—of Tarahumara-land that, except for passing by on the train once at night ten years ago after consuming all the beer in Mexico, I had not visited—that I had not even come close to visiting. The hike from the small town of Urique to Batopilas, which I took with my wife, Gay, my all-time best hiking buddy, Jay Scott, and fellow Colorado High Country dweller, Mark Fox, was our introduction to that section. And a fine introduction it was.

I had heard and read over the years that the Urique-to-Batopilas route was not the best hike in Copper Canyon Country, though I never understood why folks felt that way. After our three-day hike in October 1993, I understand even less what the problem with this route is. Even though we suffered through our usual number of directional discombobulations, we ended up having a wonderful experience which was chock-full of beautiful scenery, challenging hiking, and fairly positive cultural interaction.

As far as I am concerned, when you talk about a backpacking foray, every single aspect of the experience is part of the "hike." Getting to the place where you start hiking, the place you start hiking, the hike, the destination of that hike, and getting out of the place you hiked to are all part and parcel of the whole enchilada. In that regard, the trip from Urique to Batopilas has to rank as one of the top trips I have ever done.

We took the train from Posada de las Barrancas, about three kilometers west of Divisadero, to Bahuichivo, the jumping off point to Urique. Jay was supposed to meet us in Copper Canyon Country midway through one of my "let's see how much ground we can cover in thirty days" trips. It was one of those situations that only people who have been out in the sun too long too many times can even conceive, much less attempt to execute: "Okay, we'll meet you somewhere in Mexico sometime in October."

We had just finished a hike from Posada de las Barrancas to the Rio Urique and back, and we found ourselves a day behind schedule. This meant that we had to dunk a planned side trip to Los Mochis and head straight to Urique. I walked from Posada to the train station in Divisadero, figuring that Jay, or someone who would run into Jay somewhere along the line, would eventually stop by there. I put up a few notes around the train station filling Jay in on our new plans, which, true to form in this part of the world, consisted of a batch of highly detailed instructions: "Get to Urique somehow or another by tomorrow or die, gringo pig!" We had no earthly idea whether or not we would be laying eyes on Jay during this trip.

The train ride to Bahuichivo took three thousand years, for reasons I never quite figured out. It was simply one of those trips where we stopped often and long. Some of those stops were in villages, while others were in the middle of nowhere. We arrived at Bahuichivo two hours late. I had remembered Bahuichivo as a quaint little place, worthy of further exploration. Either it had gotten hit big time with the ugly stick since my last, and only, visit, or this was yet another example of how sinful living can have lasting effects on the information recall function of one's cranial mainframe. Based upon our 20-minute visit, I would have to say that Bahuichivo is one of the uglier little burgs I've seen in quite some time.

Our experience began with the kind of train station pandemonium that only Latin America can boast. We had arrived in Bahuichivo with no earthly idea how we were going to get to Urique. We knew for a fact that there was public transportation of one species or another as far as Cerocahui, about midway between Bahuichivo and Urique. So, we figured we would end up staying the night in Cerocahui and making our way by means unknown the next day to Urique.

It ended up that there were several variations on the public transportation theme, covering the gamut from seriously overloaded pick-ups to minibuses and flatbed trucks. About one hundred people, many of them tourists, got off the train at Bahuichivo, and every single one was yelling at the top of his or her lungs at the same time that everyone was bumping into each other and dropping their luggage in the mud. Even the Mexican tour guides were having trouble dealing with the scene. It was chaotic, and the three of us just stood in the middle of it with our jaws agape. It wouldn't have surprised me one iota if, an hour later, we were still standing there, alone in the parking lot, with our mandibles hanging down about knee-high.

Finally, a minibus driver yelled over and asked me where we were headed. I told him Cerocahui, and he said hop in. It ended up that this bus was going on to Urique after stopping in Cerocahui for five or so minutes. Very recently, daily bus service had been introduced between Bahuichivo and Urique, and it was our good fortune to have hooked up with it. Of course, typically for these parts, there were a few more people on the bus than there were bus seats. I ended up standing on the very last step leading out of the door, which wasn't all that bad, up until the point where I was staring down 700-meter vertical dropoffs.

Cerocahui is located in the high sierra, and it's a nice enough looking little town. It is also home to one of the area's best-known fancy hotels: the Hotel Mision. We were very tempted to spend the night in Cerocahui just so we could recreationally interface with the Hotel Mision, but we blew it off and headed directamundo to Urique.

The driver told us it was two hours to Urique, which did not seem possible, because the town is located at the bottom of one of the deepest canyons in Copper Canyon Country. When we left Cerocahui, we basically ascended for almost an hour, which meant, beyond the shadow of a reasonable doubt, that in very short order we were going to be facing one hour of eardrum-splitting, nosebleed-making downhill.

We began that descent just as the last tendrils of light illuminated Urique Canyon. Before the sun went completely down, though, we could make out in the distance several of the more captivating-looking sections of road that we would be traversing in total darkness. This road, which was only built in 1977, was a dead ringer for the road into Batopilas Canyon. It had at least twenty major switchbacks, and in several places, it was no wider than the bus. It could well have been named the "AAAAAHHHHH!!!! Highway."

Below, we could faintly make out the lights of Urique. I had thought it would have been a larger town, but, judging from the lights, or lack thereof, it looked like a medium-sized ranchito.

After a solid hour of brake-screeching, testicle-tingling downhill, we drove into Urique. The reason it had looked so small from above was that the electrical generator was on the fritz, a situation that was, from what we heard later, not exactly a first-time occurrence. The town actually boasts a population of several thousand.

The bus driver had told us we were lucky in that a town-wide festival was scheduled for the next day. People would be coming in by the hundreds. It was, we were told, going to be a raucously good time that we were sure to enjoy. Urique only had three small hotels, so there was some concern that we might not be able to get a room, what with all the people coming in from god-knows-where to partake of tomorrow's fiesta.

The driver dropped us off in front of the Hotel Urique, which he described to us as by far the nicest in town. And it wasn't bad. It wasn't good, either, but we've slept in far worse. Either way, they had one room left, and we took it without flinching. It was 8:30 PM when we arrived and, since we had not eaten since noon, we asked about the restaurant situation. The proprietor of the hotel ordered his eight-year-old son to escort us to a close-at-hand eatery.

The restaurant, which was illuminated by a 40-watt light bulb wired into a car battery, was also a butcher shop. The menu pretty much consisted of beef, beans, tortillas, and beef. Unfortunately, there was no curtain or door between the restaurant part of the business and the butcher shop part of the business. Gay and Mark spent the entire meal looking into a room that was decorated from floor to ceiling with animal parts. It looked like a bomb had gone off in a roomful of bovines. Very, very appetizing.

We walked down to the plaza for a few minutes before retiring. We might have stayed longer, but we couldn't see a damned thing in the depths of Urique's lack-o'-light. It was still about 80 degrees F. when we returned to the hotel, and our room was alive with all manner of insects. The cockroach contingent was especially impressive. But, we were all tired enough that we didn't really care if we were sharing our quarters with venomous sea snakes on amphetamines.

About half a second after we turned the light out (the hotel had its own generator), every cur for 200 kilometers came instantly awake. Word in the hyper-intelligent canine world had it that something important had happened, was happening, and would continue to happen. Consequently, they started barking—and we're talking about literally millions of dogs here—and they basically continued barking all night. Now, Gay and I have endured a few barking-dogs-dominated evenings in our extensive Latin America travels, but neither of us could remember a night that even came close to this night in Urique.

I have never been able to understand how Mexicans deal with their barking dog situation, which dominates the aural airwaves in every town in the entire country every single night. It would be easy to assume that Mexicans are simply much mellower than their hyper-tense American counterparts. That assumption implies that we should simply relax to the degree that entire legions of barking and howling mutts would not even register on the geiger counter of consciousness.

Every once in a while, the dogs in Urique would pipe down for a few minutes, during which time, I'm certain, they were planning their next vocal offensive. But, it wouldn't be long before a mosquito would fly headlong into a lamppost up in Seattle or something, and the Urique Metropolitan Canine Choir kicked off anew.

Finally, through sheer exhaustion, we all managed to doze off. But, in the middle of the night, we were awakened by the strangest noise I have ever heard in my entire life. Not only was it attention grabbing in the uniqueness sense, but, at the same time, it was as loud as a Guns 'n Roses concert combined with a 747 landing directly on my forehead. It sounded like a horse was giving birth right under our bedroom window. I got up to investigate and learned to my horror that whatever was making the hideous sound was not some quadruped lying prostrate in the street but, rather, it was a biped lying prostrate in the room next to ours.

Yes, it was human. And it was snoring like no snoring that has ever emanated from a *homo sapiens* mouth. A seagull could fly into your mouth and partially down your throat while you were sleeping and you would make not only less noise, but a more attractive noise, than this guy was making.

Though the silliest command in the English language—with the possible exception of "Charge!"—has to be, "Stop snoring," I had to give it a try. I mumbled through the window something along the lines of, "Hey, buddy, you're kickin' in eardrums two counties away." No response. So I repeated my message with incremental increases in volume maybe five times. Finally, I yelled at the top of my lungs, which didn't wake our neighbor, but it surely did wake up the dogs, who had been resting their vocal cords for a few minutes. I went back into my room and the three of us tried to return to the Land of Nod.

At 3 AM, a pick-up truck pulled up in front of the hotel and went through the process of waking up the owner to see about procuring lodging. This process took an hour, during which time much in the way of mirthful, beer-augmented conversation was made. Which, of course, woke up the few dogs that were not already up and barking.

The next morning we were wrecks. We were tripping over the bags under our eyes. We stumbled down to a restaurant for breakfast and 114 cups of coffee. We were going to have to just hang out in town until that evening's bus arrived, in the hope that Jay's butt would be on it. So, we didn't mind dilly-dallying. After chowing, we walked around town a bit. It ended up that Urique was not a bad little town—sort of a low-rent version of Batopilas. The plaza was nice enough, as was the church. And the people seemed, by and large, friendly. We were invited to shoot some hoops with the boys, but declined for fear that we would fall asleep during a pick and roll. Ordinarily, I love playing basketball in Mexico. When I play in the States, I'm always the point guard, because, at 5 feet 9 inches, that's really the only position available to me. But, in Mexico, I usually have the chance to play power forward. It's a gas playing low post.

We hoofed it through a couple of interesting back alleys and walked down to the river. Urique is located right where Urique Canyon opens up after about 30 kilometers of tightness. The setting is astoundingly beautiful. But, by 11, it was hot, which was okay because, by 10:59, we had just about exhausted all there was to exhaust in Urique on the sightseeing front.

Urique was all abuzz over the impending festivities. People who looked like they hadn't been to town since last year's party were strolling around in their Sunday finery. Though Urique is normally a dry town, by noon, every male over the age of about twelve had a Tecate in-hand. And—not that I know much about this sort of thing—judging from the serious-looking intent of the drinking, it seemed as though it would go on uninterrupted for about the next twenty-four hours. (That observation, by the way, proved to be correct.)

We spent most of the afternoon on the second-story deck of our hotel (we had changed to a room around back, in hopes of getting at least a minute or two of shut-eye that night), reading and trying to act inconspicuous. By 3 PM I ventured forth to see about buying a six-pack or three. Watching people drink has a way of getting me thirsty. I had no problem whatsoever locating a Tecate vendor. He was charging $10 a six-pack. I bought one, and instructed Gay and Mark to drink 'em in a slow, savoring sort of way.

The yard behind our hotel was fast becoming a gathering place for middle-aged pre-fiesta revelers. The fiesta proper was set to kick off in the plaza about 9 PM. I took advantage of this gathering to glean a couple of directions for our impending hike to Batopilas. Several people gave me their personal renditions of the route, and they basically agreed with each other, which is not always the case when Mexican men who are sucking down brewskis start giving gringos directions.

Soon thereafter, an American-looking guy came and visited with the people gathered in the yard. As he left, he invited us over to his house for a beer, and we gladly took him up on it. Ended up he was the local representative of whatever it is Mexico calls its national health service. His name was Tom, and he had lived in Urique since 1977. He was married to a lady from Chihuahua, although she spent most of her time in Chihuahua City, for reasons we never delved into.

Tom had a wonderful place about 10 minutes outside of town. He had built it, along with a long-time friend, Ken, who lived in Urique only part of the time. Ken was also married to a Chihuahua lady. In addition to having themselves a fine spread right on the Urique River, Tom and Ken had recently gotten into the tourism business. They built a guesthouse and several wonderful campsites. When we reflected how we could have slept here last night instead of listening to those damned dogs all night long, we almost puked. And, since we would have to make ourselves visible in town that evening in case Jay showed up, we would not be able to stay there that night, either.

By the time we got back into town, the fiesta was revving up. The fiesta was centered around the annual state-of-the-city address, which the mayor had made earlier in the day. This is an idea I truly want to take back to Colorado with me. The idea of the mayor having to give an annual address to the town I live in is not without considerable merit. I could see it now: The mayor's up there talking about the new sewage treatment plant or something, while the citizenry, which has been sucking beers all day long, is out there throwing things at him, calling him names and basically throwing things at each other while calling each other names. Now *that* would be a great manifestation of democracy.

As we were eating dinner on the hotel deck, Jay showed up. He said he had heard from one of the guests at Margarita's, who we had been camping with recently, that he'd better get his carcass over to Urique by the next night, or he would miss us. Jay hopped the train in Creel and basically got to Urique the same way we did—without the benefit of those notes I left at Divisadero. The bus driver told him on the way down from

Bahuichivo that he had just dropped off three gringos fitting our description the night before. And, *voila!*, we were in business. We went out and rubbed elbows with the fiesta, but we didn't last long, because we were all sleepy as sleepy gets, and we planned to hit the trail first thing in the morning.

The plan was to hit the trail early, because we didn't expect a cold front to make its way into Urique Canyon by dawn. Well, par for our organizational course, we left about 10 AM. It was already searingly toasty. The route to Batopilas commences with 11 kilometers of dirt road walking, through the village of Gualpaina, to the the ranchito of La Laja, where we would cross the Urique River by means of a *canasta*—a metal basket that connects the two banks by means of a steel cable. This was easy walking, but, by the time we reached La Laja, we were dragging rumpskis because of the heat.

We weren't certain in advance how the *canasta* worked, though it didn't take us long to find out when we strolled into La Laja. First of all, it didn't even have to work. The water level was pretty low, so we could easily have forded the river. But, as usual, we were looking for that extra molecule of "experience." And we got it in spades.

As soon as we passed into La Laja, we were approached by about ten youngsters, every single one of whom continuously yelled the word, *"dulces"* (candy) at the top of their lungs. We endured ten versions of *"Dulces! Dulces! Dulces!"* being shouted within one meter of our increasingly angry selves for at least fifteen straight minutes. It was the first time in all my travels in Mexico that I seriously considered killing children.

By the time we got to the *canasta*, several of the little tikes had disappeared, while the remaining ragamuffins offered to transport us to the other side via the *canasta* for a slight fiscal consideration. They seemed anxious, even furtive. They wanted to get moving immediately, and they wanted to get paid up front. We told them where to stick it regarding payment in advance.

They were only able to transport either one gringo or one gringo pack per trip, so this *canasta* thing was fast becoming time-consuming. At the end of each round-trip, whichever kid it was who had piloted the *canasta* (they took turns, because it was pretty exhausting work, and these kids were maybe eight or ten) demanded payment. We absolutely could not figure out why they were being so vehement about the money situation. I repeatedly informed them that we would pay them once we were all safely on the other side.

Suddenly, the meat of the story emerged, in the form of two teenagers whose family, they said, owned the *canasta*. Whether that was true or not, the kids who had just spent the better part of an hour laboriously transporting us and our packs to the other side were not only summarily relieved of their duties, but they were relieved of their duties by way of several smacks, kicks, and strong admonitions to never, ever try to move in on the lucrative *canasta* action again.

I felt a little bad for the kids, but, after they had made my head swim in the sweltering midway heat with their *"dulces"* crap, I considered the whole situation an exercise in near-instant Karma. Gay, Mark, Jay, and all our gear were already on the far side when this changing of the guard transpired, so, one of the teenagers took me across. I paid him a few new pesos and we hit the trail.

We had been told to start ascending into the sierra by way of the second arroyo we came to after crossing the river. It took us a few tries to find the trail, but, once we did, it was smooth, albeit cardiovascularly captivating, hiking. The trail followed Arroyo Los Alisos, which boasted a small flow of water most of the way up. It was hot as blazes, and Jay, Mark, and Gay were fading fast. It was one of the few times I have been the one who was hiking the strongest.

During one of our 2,000 water breaks, we were passed by an old man on horseback. He introduced himself as something-or-another Torres. He lived in the ranchito of Los Alisos, which he said was about another hour up the trail. He invited us to stay on his property, and, since we were planning to hike only another hour or so, we gladly accepted. He rode on ahead.

Thirty minutes later, the trail forked. Although it was fairly apparent that the right-hand fork was the more-traveled route, just in case, I dropped my pack and hiked ahead. It took me about 20 minutes of full-blast humping to find out that, sure enough, the right-hand trail was the right trail. There was

Señor Torres sitting on his front porch wondering what in the hell had become of us. I ran back to inform everyone that, for once, I had not chosen the wrong path. Since they had had a long rest in the shade, everyone was feeling better, and we made it to Los Alisos without anything bad happening, like, for instance, death.

Los Alisos, which means "the alder trees," had clearly seen better days. Señor Torres, who had lived every one of his eighty-five years in the house he shared with his wife of seventy years, said they were the last two people left in what once had been a thriving little hamlet. (The Torreses had had three children, but they all died "long ago.")

Señor Torres directed us to the old schoolhouse below his spread, which, he said, used to house as many as thirty kids. It closed for lack of enrollment in 1978. The schoolhouse, which boasted a covered porch, had a yard large enough for two tents. It also had a faucet and garden hose, which Señor Torres had hooked up to water his garden. It ended up being a nice place to camp.

After we had washed up and changed clothes, Señor Torres came down to bathe his horse with the hose. Soon after, his wife joined us. She was also in her eighties. They made for literally the cutest couple (and I know that's a weird description for a twosome that ancient, but it's a perfect description) I had ever seen. Their body language towards each other was so comfortable it was obvious they could communicate in detail without ever speaking. And, when they did speak to each other, they did so with tones of mutual respect and devotion that were so overpowering Gay and I almost wept. Suddenly, the notion of growing old together—perhaps growing *very* old together—seemed to take on a new meaning.

As the Torreses leaned close to each other, Gay and I met eyes, and it was quite apparent, though this was something we have only talked about briefly in our eleven-plus years together, that we, too, can communicate quite adequately without speaking. Through our eye contact, she said, romantically, lovingly, "It's your turn to pitch the tent," while I responded, with all the tenderness I could muster, "No, goddammit, it's *your* turn to put the tent up!"

Just before dusk, a pretty young lady came down, along with her two-year-old daughter, to water the garden. I asked Señor Torres who she was. He responded by saying that she lived just up the hill from him. I responded by saying that I thought he had said he and his wife were the only remaining residents of Los Alisos. He said they were, that his neighbors were Tarahumaras. Which, we inferred, meant that, in his mind, they really didn't count in the local population head-count. It was tempting to think poorly of Señor Torres at that moment, but, part of traveling in foreign lands is trying hard to not be judgmental about cultural matters. Sometimes, sad to say, that is mighty tough.

Señor Torres mentioned to us that the route to Batopilas was not exactly easy to find. He told us that, just last week, two Europeans had gotten lost for two days looking for the trail up from Los Alisos. He offered his services as a guide, and said that, if we hired him, he would carry Gay's pack on his horse. Just as I was about to say something along the lines of, "Gee, Señor Torres, I'm pretty good at finding trails and Gay would not feel comfortable having her pack carried up a 1,000-meter ascent by a horse," I got another of those non-verbal messages from the woman I love. We agreed that Señor Torres would meet us with his horse at 7 AM. He said he would guide us all the way to the point where it would be impossible, even for gringos, to get lost. That point, he said, was about three hours of hiking from Los Alisos.

Jay handled the renumeration negotiations. No matter how hard he tried to pin Señor Torres down on a specific amount, all the old man would say was that, when we parted ways tomorrow, we would decide how much his services were worth.

Just before dark, the Torreses took their leave, but not before we laid a bag of candy on Señora Torres. Her husband had noticed that we had some candy, and he mentioned that the missus had one well-developed sweet tooth, which, from what we could see, was about the only tooth she had left. As the sun set, we could see them sitting on their front porch, listening to the radio, eating candy. It was an idyllic scene.

Mark had a tent, as did Gay and I. Jay was going to sleep under the stars. But, just before bedding down, I went over to fill a water bottle from my water bag, which was hanging from a nail sticking out of a support beam on the front porch of the schoolhouse. From 10 meters away, in near-total darkness, I could see that the water bag was 100-percent covered with cockroaches. We pulled out our flashlights and checked the rest of our gear. Ditto on the roach situation. It took us at least 15 minutes to rid our packs, food bags, and stuff sacks of the roaches, and, even then, we knew full well that many of the little bastards had likely escaped our extermination efforts.

I did not realize until all this was going on that Jay would rather sleep naked on hot coals than sleep anywhere near roaches. He hates roaches the way Indiana Jones hates snakes. He begged for entrance into Mark's tent. I could not believe that Mark acceded to Jay's whimpering without extorting some sort of agreement that Jay would, at the very minimum, carry the tent the next day.

Señor Torres arrived, fully loaded, and ready to hit the trail, at 7 AM. It took us until almost 7:40 to get ready, and Señor Torres was clearly becoming impatient. He loaded Gay's pack, as well as both our tents, onto his horse. The exact nanosecond we hoisted our packs, he hit the trail. I had assumed he would be riding, but—negatory—this old fart was planning to walk. And walk he did. Like the proverbial wind.

From the get-go, the trail went uppity-up-up. Señor Torres had pointed out the night before where we would top out on the rim, and it looked like we had about 1,000 more meters of ascent before us. I felt as good as I have felt hiking in years. I determined that, no matter what, I was going to keep up with Señor Torres, which proved no small feat. This man could flat out fly, and it was obvious that he wanted to make the best time possible, so he could get home before dark.

Jay was hiking pretty well, but Gay and Mark were dragging a bit, so we had to stop and wait for them numerous times. Señor Torres looked nonplussed at how slowly we were progressing. We reached Pandito, about halfway between Los Alisos and the rim, at about 10 AM. All there was to Pandito, and I kid you not, was one abandoned *casita* and a few crumbling rock walls. The place had been sans occupants for years. I asked Señor Torres why they continued to refer to it by name when it had a population of zero. He said it reminded them of the old days, when the area was well populated and alive with human industry.

By midday, we crested the rim. We stopped for lunch instantly. For the gringos, lunch was Carnation Breakfast Bars and honey-coated peanuts. For Señor Torres, it was cold, greasy, flour tortillas and uncooked hot dogs, which he offered to share with us, but, sad to say, we were simply too full from our breakfast bars, which are not the tastiest food items I have ever bought. But, I would have eaten the droppings that were falling from Señor Torres' horse long before I would have eaten those hot dogs and tortillas.

Señor Torres asked if we wanted him to go with us farther. We said, per our conversation the night before, that we wanted him to stay with us until it was impossible to get lost. He said that point was only about an hour farther. Right after we passed the ranchito of Yesca, we parted ways with Señor Torres. He pointed out a canyon a few miles distant and told us it was Arroyo Cerro Colorado, which I was familiar with. He gave us a few basic directions, and told us there was no way in the world we could lose the trail, because it was so obvious.

Between us, we decided to pay him 50 new pesos, which was about $16. That, we agreed, was a little much, but he seemed like a nice enough old guy, and, with a pocketful of cash, maybe he could take the old lady out for a night on the town. When we handed him the cash, he continued to stand there with his hand out. We asked how much more he wanted. He said another hundred. As we started to balk, we remembered that, one, he had a gun, two, we didn't, and three, he still had a bunch of our gear tied to his horse.

We paid him the other 100, and he bid us a good day, telling us to come back by to visit him anytime. We felt, justifiably, like we had just spent the last hour or so bent over a log. But, we couldn't help but laugh, which is exactly what we suspected Señor Torres was doing all the way home.

We immediately hoisted our packs and hit the trail, because we wanted to sleep that night in Cerro Colorado. Señor Torres had told us it would take us until dark to reach Cerro Colorado if we hiked non-stop. We were walking through a gently rolling, high sierra pine and oak forest. It was shady and bird-tweetingly pleasant. Every once in a while, you will run into pockets of cool, virgin forest in Copper Canyon Country, and, when you do, you feel like you've died and gone to heaven, especially when you know that the temperature a few thousand meters below, down where the cacti dwell in blissful abundance, is around 100 degrees F.

After about an hour, we flat-out lost the goldanged trail, which, to this point, had been a bonafide burro trail. All of a sudden, we were hiking on bonafide goat trail. But, at least we were going in the right direction, so we continued merrily on our way. Jay and I even recognized a distant mesa from a hike we had done several years ago from Cusarare to Batopilas (see Chapter 17). In our heart of hearts, we knew all was well. In our brain of brains, we had a sinking feeling that we were on the trail of tears.

After another hour, what little trail there was simply vanished. We spent yet another hour combing the woods for the burro trail, with no luck. We had no choice but to return to the spot where we lost the burro trail in the first place. We were despondent. During the previous several weeks, I had felt rather studly about how easy it was becoming for me to find trails in Tarahumara-land. And, here, after being informed in no uncertain terms that one would have to be dumb as a clam to lose this particular trail, not only had I lost this particular trail, but I had lost this particular trail in the company of Jay Scott, who, like me, is fairly adept at making his way through the woods. We should have known better the instant we suddenly found ourselves on the goat trail, because burro trails simply do not end in the middle of nowhere. Rather, they end in towns.

As soon as we got back to the point where we lost the burro trail, we found the burro trail. It was embarrassing, because it was *right there*, 10 meters on the other side of an arroyo we had been standing in three hours before. I cannot believe it escaped our attention. Gay said later that she had known for a fact that the goat trail we followed could not have been the right trail, but she was too timid to offer up her opinion, which, of course, made me feel like crud, because the only thing that could have made her too timid to express what ended up being a correct observation was the fact that she is espoused to a hard-headed, egotistical hombre.

At that point, we had a decision to make. We had hiked a total of six hours already. Mark and Gay were exhausted, and it was, from what we had heard, another four hours to Cerro Colorado, which is another three or four hours from Batopilas. The next night, we had reservations at the Copper Canyon Lodge-Riverside in Batopilas, and we did not want to miss out on a night in that wonderful lodging facility.

We figured we could handle eight trail hours tomorrow, so we camped right where we stood. The arroyo boasted several nice bathing pools, and the pine and oak forest made for pleasant camping. As the sun was going down, a couple of Mexicans on horseback passed by, and, with their help, we fine-tuned our directions. They agreed it was about four hours to Cerro Colorado, and they told us it would be impossible to lose the trail. Great. Just what we needed to hear.

By 7:30 the next morning, we were hiking in a fairly serious fashion. It was uphill for about an hour, then we leveled off at the beautiful ranchito of El Manzano. This was a seriously attractive little hamlet, and we immediately regretted not having hiked here the night before. The corn had just been harvested and several dozen *casitas* were obviously ready for winter, with pumpkins and chiles hanging outside from rafters.

Children frolicked in the yards while their mothers did chores, smoke was rising from the chimneys, and the views were stupendous.

At the same time there were trails, trails everywhere. We took an educated guess regarding which was the right one and, of course, once more, we proved to the cosmos that our educated guesses aren't worth their weight in bat guano. A woman came running out and pointed us in the right direction. She said it was about two more hours to Cerro Colorado. It took us four. The trail was badly eroded, making the 1,300-meter descent a exercise in constant sloppy footing.

Mark and I arrived in Cerro Colorado about 3 PM, at most, we thought, about a minute ahead of Gay and Jay. I immediately bought and gulped a mineral water from the little store there and headed back, water bottle in-hand, to meet Gay, who I was certain was near death. She handles a lot of things well, but, sad to report, heat, which we had in abundance that afternoon, is not one of them.

I hiked about 15 minutes back up (and I do mean "up") the trail, and Gay was nowhere to be seen. I was starting to get worried. Then, about a million kilometers above me, I heard Gay yell. I was too far away to understand what she was saying, but, in my mind, it was, "I have been bitten on the neck by a huge rattler and I've been hit on the head by a falling satellite."

I sprinted up the steep grade as fast as I have ever sprinted in my life. Just as my heart was about to start melting down through my aorta, I heard Gay, who was suddenly standing about 10 meters above me, say something along the lines of, "Oh, never mind." I was happy.

It ended up that what she was yelling down to me was a directions-based interrogative. She had simply lost the trail, and wanted to know where the hell it was. When she hiked down to me, she wanted to know what the hell my problem was and why I was running around the canyons at a dead sprint on a day as hot as this.

We hiked back down to Cerro Colorado, where, much to my seriously perplexed dismay, Jay was not on the scene. We simply assumed he had paused somewhere for some picture-taking and would be there when we returned. After 30 minutes, I started getting anxious. I backtracked once again and, way up on a ridge line, I saw him. He was waving his arms and yelling something unintelligible. Those words, I was certain, were: "I have fallen and broken my leg. Please run up here and rescue me, because I am about to be killed by drunk banditos." Mark and I started, you guessed it, sprinting up the trail.

After a while, we stopped and made another attempt at something resembling communication with Jay. We were close enough that we could faintly make out words to the effect of, "Where's Gay?" We yelled back that she was sitting in the shade in Cerro Colorado enjoying a cool beverage. He responded that, if such was the case, all was well, and he would see us in a few minutes.

It ended up that Jay, who had been keeping an eye on Gay while I was up ahead looking for the trail down into Cerro Colorado, had lost track of my bride. So, he had, himself, backtracked to look for her. Somehow or another, Gay had descended via a different route than Jay, and they had simply missed each other. Jay, being a concerned sort, assumed Gay had been kidnapped and was, at that very moment, being sold into a prostitution ring. Jay told me later that he would have thought even more poorly of me than he does already if I had been sitting in Cerro Colorado, Gay-less, drinking Cokes while he scoured the entire Sierra Madre looking for my lost wife.

After catching our breath in Cerro Colorado, we took off for Batopilas, where we arrived at 8:30, well after dark, and 13 hours after we hit the trail that morning. I don't know how Gay made it. We had put in at least 30 kilometers in searing heat, and yet she had barely complained. Of course, she did not exactly spend the day singing tunes from "The Sound of Music," either. But, all in all, she handled it very well. Needless to say, I was one obsequious husband that night, but, hell, that's just the kind of guy I am anyhow. It's my nature to wait on my wife hand and foot after 13 hours of hiking.

The next day, we hung out at the Copper Canyon Lodge-Riverside, which is by far the nicest hotel I have ever stayed in. And, the next morning, we caught a ride out to Creel in the back of a flatbed truck. Easy as pie.

Particulars

You will need the 1:50,000 Batopilas map, which covers the whole route. Take the train to the village of Bahuichivo, which is about an hour west of Divisadero and about five hours east of Los Mochis, depending on the whims of those kooky railroad gods. At Bahuichivo, you will be able to catch the bus to Urique. About halfway between Bahuichivo and Urique is the town of Cerocahui, which is worth a night or two if you've got the time. The Hotel Mision is one of the best (and most expensive) in Tarahumara-land, and the mission after which the hotel is named is, likewise, wonderful.

It is about three hours by bus from Bahuichivo to Urique, which is a big enough town that you could buy most of your supplies for this hike. (Don't expect anything fancy.) In Urique, stay either at the Hotel Urique or camp out at Tom and Ken's house, which is about 10-minute walk upriver from the plaza. Since Tom (Tomás to the locals) is a health care professional, everyone in town knows him, so just ask directions.

I definitely recommend hiring a guide for this hike. There are many crisscrossing trails, and this is a piece of paradise that is dominated by heat. Even in the dead of winter, you are talking about some seriously toasty turf. You don't want to find yourself wandering disoriented through the wilderness hereabouts when it's 110 degree F. So, hire a guide and, if possible, pack animals.

This hike begins by walking downriver from Urique for 11 kilometers, to the ranchito of La Laja. From there, either ford the river or, if the water is too high, or, if you just feel like a little extra adventure, use the *canasta*. You won't be in La Laja long before you are approached by people willing to take you across the river.

Once on the other side, head downriver again for two kilometers or so. Cross the little ridge finger that comes all the way down to the river. On the other wide of the ridge finger, you descend into a little field. Take a left up the arroyo you are now in, Arroyo Los Alisos. Follow the burro trail all the way to Los Alisos. Whenever you're in doubt about the trail, there's a little powerline-looking wire that goes all the way from the Urique to Los Alisos. Follow it.

If you do not have a guide, you can probably hire one in Los Alisos. His name will be Señor Torres. If he's not at home, or if he's dead by the time you take this trip (see, you should have gone last year), try to find someone who can point you in the right direction. You can actually see the point where you top out on the rim from Los Alisos. It's the point way up there, just below the moon's orbit.

Once you pass over the rim, start walking down another arroyo, with the burro trail staying on the left-hand side as you descend. This trail will, after a kilometer or two, cross the arroyo and begin climbing up to El Manzano, where there are numerous trails. Ask someone to show you the right one. From this point on, you will be descending into Cerro Colorado. From there, it's an easy four-hour jaunt to Batopilas (Chapter 15).

According to Tom and Ken, there are many other hiking options out of Urique, most notably to the village of Churo, from where you can access the train. Again, ask around Urique for directions and/or a guide and/or pack animals. Whatever you do, remember this area is very hot. Come here only in the dead of winter.

17
Cusarare to Batopilas

Somewhere during the process of putting together the first edition of this book, Skip McWilliams talked me into at least entertaining the notion of starting a guide service in Copper Canyon Country. He told me he would bankroll the operation, at least as far as start-up costs, like advertising and printing brochures and such, and I would provide things like a reasonable degree of expertise *vis-à-vis* the area in which we were talking about my leading trips, namely the boondocks of Tarahumara-land.

Though the thought of guiding had never really entered my head—at least partially because I have long had a rent-paying vocation: writing—I agreed to give it a whirl. After all, I reasoned to myself, I could always use some extra cash. And, besides, how hard could guiding gringos through the woods be?

The first thing I felt I needed was a really sexy route to guide. I already was more than familiar with many different cool hiking itineraries in Copper Canyon Country, but, in order to ask paying customers to shell out many hundreds of dollars for the honor of walking with me through the hills, I wanted to put together something special, near-bouts beyond belief. And, in my mind, such that it is, that meant somehow including Batopilas in the itinerary.

After chewing my mental cud over this for a while, it finally dawned on me: Why not offer a hike from Cusarare all the damned way to Batopilas? I could think of no real reason why not. All I had to do was actually partake in a little on-foot reconnoitering, and all would be well. And that reconnoitering would have to be relatively fast and smooth, because about nine seconds after Skip and I shook hands on this guiding deal, we had customers signed up and ready to go.

So, in November 1991, Patrick Brower and Aurel Burtis, both friends from the Colorado High Country, and Jay Scott (who else?) joined me for a reconnoiter that ended up being one of the most outrageous hikes I've ever been on: an eight-day, estimated 200-kilometer hike from the Copper Canyon Lodge in Cusarare to beautiful downtown Batopilas, by way of the Urique River.

Two days before Aurel and Pat arrived in Creel, the weather turned sour, as sometimes it does in November. The Sierra Madre, though a mighty mountain range, is not tall enough in those parts to block ornery Pacific weather fronts, which can be mighty bad between Baja and the mainland in the late fall. Usually, these fronts last no more than three days, but, by and large, that's exactly how long they last, and those can be some funky days. As soon as the first cloud moved in, I knew what we would be facing: at least one day of rain on the trail. (I was right.)

Jay and I had pretty much planned the trip out, at least as much as one can plan a trip on a map. Our plan seemed, while staring down at the map while downing beers in the Parador Bar in Creel, deceptively simple, which meant, somewhere along the trail, it would surely become not-so-deceptively complicated. That is the way of the world, and I am finally getting used to that reality as I near my fortieth year.

We had hired two guides out of Cusarare who would lead us from there to Sitagochi, following Skip McWilliams's canyon crossing route (Chapter 9). From there, we would hire the next set of guides, who, we hoped, would take us at least as far as Pamachi. From there, we would hire guides to Guaguachique, Cieneguita, and Munérachi. From Munérachi, I knew the route to Batopilas.

The day Pat and Aurel were set to arrive on the train from Chihuahua City, Jay and I walked over to re-confirm with our guides, Jose Felipe and Antonio. It was about 7 AM, and we could tell from a distance that something was sorely amiss. Maybe it was intuition, or maybe it was the fact that there were about fifteen people passed out face-down in Antonio's yard. Either way, we were right, something was amiss. Unbeknownst to us, there had been a small, informal *tesguinada* the night before, and both Antonio and Jose Felipe were as drunk as drunk gets. Which meant, the next day—the day we were scheduled to leave—they would be as hung over as hung over gets.

And, as if that wasn't bad enough, they insisted we join them for an early morning cup of *tesguino*, which is not usually my beverage of choice at 7 in the morning. But, being mannerly sorts, Jay and I each chugged down a filthy plastic cupful not only of *tesguino*, but bottom-of-the-barrel *tesguino*, a beverage which, even if it was served in Elle MacPherson's shoe, with Elle MacPherson's foot close-at-hand, would be more than a little lacking in the palpability arena.

We left disgruntled, worried that, when dawned cracked the next day, we would be guideless. Also, we found ourselves burping *tesguino* burps for the next 15 hours, during which time, if memory serves me correctly, very few beautiful women ran up and French kissed us. Pat and Aurel, who live in Grand County, near Rocky Mountain National Park, arrived on the right day and on the right train, which is always a good omen. Both of these folks are professional body nazis. They do things like run and nordic ski and hike and bike about a billion kilometers a week. I had warned Jay of this reality, but he did not care, as he keeps himself in great shape all the time as well. Then it hit me: I was the only member of our party who was in terrible shape. Drag.

Neither Pat nor Aurel had ever hiked in Mexico, and I had informed them well in advance that the trip we were about to embark upon had no concomitant guarantees. We might get lost for a day or two. The route itself might not be very attractive. The trails, or lack thereof, might suck. But, my warnings did not deter them; they seemed enthusiastic about the trip, as I knew they would be.

The night before we left, Pat and Aurel stayed in Cusarare while Jay and I stayed in Creel, which meant, needless to say, that we went out and got falling down drunk at the Parador. When our ride came by Margarita's to pick us up just after sunrise the next morning, we were, uh, not feeling very chipper.

But, not to worry, because we were only going to hike three hours to Basirecota Hot Springs that day.

As soon as we arrived in Cusarare, we ran to check on the status of Antonio and Jose Felipe. They were up and at 'em, feeling fine and dandy, and rarin' to go. They wanted to know why we looked so green around the gills.

At noon, we hit the trail. I thought I was going to die every step of the way. The Spanish word for hangover is *"cruda,"* which I have always considered near-bouts onomatopoeic. Whether you look at the applicable part of *cruda* as "crud" or as "crude," no single word could better describe my state-of-being as we walked towards Basirecota. My mouth tasted like I had been chewing on a dirty sock for the past twelve weeks, and my head felt like someone had spent the better part of the previous night beating on it with one of those big city library dictionaries.

But, we made it to Basirecota all right, despite the rain, which did nothing to improve my hungover disposition. Within a minute of arriving at Basirecota, I lurched toward the hot spring pools, where I dozed for the better part of the afternoon.

Antonio and Jose Felipe were having such a good time, they asked if they could guide us all the way to Batopilas. I reminded them that they did not know the way to Batopilas, which we considered a fairly important thing to know in this context. Aurel had taken a liking to them, though, and it wasn't long before they were invited to go along to Batopilas as porters, if not guides. The next day, we made it to metro Sitagochi, to the same spot where we camped the second night out with Skip on his Canyon Crossing trip. The rain had cleared out, and, this day, it was windy.

It started to get very cold. All night, we heard Antonio and Jose Felipe shivering. They each only had one blanket and not much in the way of warm clothes. They got up in the middle of the night and stoked the fire and remained within a half meter of it until morning. By the time I got up, they looked like victims of a failed cryogenics experiment, with icicles hanging off their noses and all, and they wanted to go home.

Of course, I was very mature in my response to their desire to dunk the hike to Batopilas, mirthfully reminding them that they were members of a tribe that was well known for being able to deal with all kinds of adversity without so much as batting an eye. I was trying to toss a levity salad there, to lighten up what was clearly an embarrassing moment for our amigos, but my efforts produced exactly the opposite effect. They still wanted to head back to Cusarare ASAP.

Jose Felipe ran off to Sitagochi proper, about two kilometers away, to round up another guide for us. He soon returned with Corpus, the same guy who had carried my pack on Skip's Canyon Crossing trip. He hadn't got any friendlier.

We bid adieu to Antonio and Jose Felipe, having no earthly idea that the real fun was about to begin. We walked over to Corpus's house, where his younger brother, Jamin, who was maybe fifteen, joined us. We began descending to the Urique River almost immediately. The trail was terrible. I asked Corpus if it was going to get any better, and, in his eloquent, helpful way, he said, "No." I was expecting some sort of additional information, like, "The trail used to see a lot more use, but no more." Or: "There never has been much traffic between Sitagochi and Pamachi, so, what do you expect, a four-lane highway?"

The descent, which lasted four solid hours, was miserable. The trail was covered with low-hanging tree branches, which Corpus and Jamin, being of traditional Tarahumara stature, had no problems with. We, on the other hand, had to walk down a steep, loose-rock-covered path while partially crouched over for half a day to avoid having tree branches ripping our lips right off our faces. But, it's only possible to crouch so much when you're hiking. The tops of all our packs were ripping branches and leaves off by the truckload. After only a few minutes, there was enough organic tree branch matter down the back of my shirt that you could have planted corn rows up my spine.

By the time we got to the Urique, there were four uncomfortable gringos on the scene. The river crossing was very easy, and we decided to camp on a nice beach on the other side. We all went our separate bathing directions within about point-two seconds of dropping our packs. Corpus and Jamin each found a good sitting rock, and there they perched, motionless, for hours on end. They didn't talk; they didn't smile. Laurel and Hardy they weren't.

By this point, everyone was beat. But I was setting the standard for beatness. I had done nothing in the way of pre-trip physical preparation, and, a mere three days into the hike, my butt was dragging big time. And, tomorrow, we would hike some 1,700 meters all the way up to the rim. I couldn't wait.

My physical condition, or lack thereof, was exacerbated by the fact that, in an attempt to cut into the weight on my back, I had decided to forego carrying camp shoes with me. I had blown off camp shoes a few times in my life, but never on an eight-day hike, and, already, my feet were killing me.

That night, sitting around the fire, I happened to glance at Jamin's well-worn feet. He was wearing guaraches, so it was easy to check things out. What I saw shocked me. One of his big toes had recently suffered some sort of fairly dramatic injury, to the point that some serious-looking infection had set in. I asked him what happened. He just shrugged, which, for Jamin, was the communications equivalent of a Senate filibuster. It was the closest he came to speaking in the three days we were with him. I told him that his toe looked very bad and that, before hitting the trail the next morning, I was going to have to treat it, or else he might be in for a life of big-toelessness, which, I told him, would not help his dancing any. This time, he didn't even shrug. He just stared into the fire. That Jamin; what a kook!

True to my word, the next morning, just before breaking camp, I pulled out my medical kit. I am a medical First Responder, licensed by the U.S. Department of Transportation to treat people, so I do know a little about first aid. Jamin's wound, which looked like the result of a severe burn or an axe accident, was filthy beyond belief. Now, I understood then as I understand now that backcountry-dwelling Tarahumaras are often not overly concerned about personal hygiene. Still, the state of Jamin's wounded digit was beyond comprehension. It was like Jamin, after doing whatever it was he did to injure himself, invited all of his buddies over for an evening of premeditated wound soiling.

I spent 30 minutes just cleaning it. By the time I was done, I was almost down to the bone. This was a very pleasant experience early in the morning right after eating a bucketful of instant oatmeal. There's no way what I was doing wasn't very painful, yet, to his credit, Jamin sat there stoically. His brother, on the other hand, was not buying into this treatment stuff one bit. He was demonstrating his impatience with the whole procedure in a most theatrical way, looking at his watch, then sighing loudly, then looking at Jamin like his sibling was a sissy of the first magnitude. I finally told Corpus to lighten the expletive expletive expletive up, lest he get fired, and maybe even beaten up, right on the spot.

Finally, I was done, but I told Jamin he would need treatment again that night and again the next morning. I had a bunch of amoxicillin with me, which I knew I wasn't allergic to, and the temptation was to lay some on Jamin. But, it would be far better for him to lose a toe than to die of shock from a negative reaction to antibiotics, so, I resisted the temptation to lay some pills on him.

The beginning of the trail from the Rio Urique to Pamachi was very pleasant indeed. It followed the bottom of an arroyo, where there were plenty of shade-making fruit trees. The oranges were prime, and we were sorely tempted to pick a couple, but, knowing how bad-mannered that would be, we decided to pass. But, suddenly, the owner of the orange grove appeared and agreed to sell us some. They were some easy eating oranges, I might add.

Less than an hour into the ascent, Jay found a nearly perfect Georgia O'Keefe-like cow skull and decided on the spot that he was taking it home to New Mexico with him. Now, this skull weighed three or so kilograms, and we were 1,700 meters down in Copper Canyon, with five more full days of hiking ahead of us. But Jay was adamant about taking the skull back to Silver City. Besides, what the hell did we care if Jay carried a bovine noggin with him all the way to Batopilas? No skin off our joint and several posteriors. No skin, that is, until Jay handed me his mammoth sleeping pad.

Jay carries one of those two-kilogram pads that has about forty different compartments that inflate to different thicknesses, so your shoulders have more padding than your knees, or vice-versa, or whatever the hell it is. When inflated, you could invite the whole Tarahumara tribe over for a slumber party and still have room for a couple cases of beer. Even deflated, it is terminally bulky.

And he was handing it to me. To carry. Because, with the pad tied onto his pack, he wouldn't have enough room to carry the skull. There is probably only one person in the world who can talk me into carrying a two-kilogram sleeping pad up 1,700 meters of vertical terrain for reasons that had nothing to do whatsoever with my sleeping comfort. And that damned person is Jay. I—growl, growl, growl—carried the pad.

The ascent soon became torturously steep and seemingly endless. It was one of those days where the only plan-of-action option was to keep on keepin' on. By mid-afternoon, we were standing right below the place where Gay and I camped with Juan several years before (Chapter 6). This is when and where we learned that the little bastard had not guided us all the way to Pamachi after all. When Corpus told us we still had at least an hour to hike to the village of Pamachi, I thought I was going to ralph right on the spot. I was so exhausted, I could well have taken up residence right then and there to avoid ever having to hike one more step in my entire life.

Yessirree, Bob, I was one hurtin' cowboy. While we were all standing there waiting for me to catch my breath, I made yet another Copper Canyon Country-inspired oath: Just send me a helicopter and I swear, oh Lord, I will never again let myself fall into such a hideous state of physiological disrepair! I will eat nothing but bran muffins and spinach forevermore, and I will take up marathon running immediately upon returning home and never again will so much as a molecule of beer pass these lips!

No helicopter came, so, naturally, I blew off the oath shortly after uttering it. But, the celestial Powers That Be did lay a consolation prize on me: a completely unexpected little creek. Once you start getting up high in the sierra country of Tarahumara-land, the creeks become shallower, muddier, more fouled by stock dung, slower-moving, and generally less appealing. (It's very much the opposite of the situation in Colorado, where the higher the stream is, generally the nicer it is.) But, this one was Tahiti-like turquoise and even boasted some little pools and cascades. It was gorgeous and, were we not basically in a hurry, we would have stayed there for the night, if for no other reason that my legs were suffering from some overwhelming lactic acid build-up.

I had been trying to hide my out-of-shapeness from my amigos, but it was becoming more apparent to them that I was the anchor dragging behind the stern of this little expedition. By and large—and even my wife will agree with this—I am remarkable when it comes to doing not very much in the way of exercise then embarking on a physically demanding trip and hanging with the physically demanding part of that trip very well. Mind over matter, that kind of thing. But, the older I get, the more I understand that there is a definite bell curve that's part and parcel of that little mind-over-matter graph, and, where the increasing age line intersects the "just how badly out-of-shape are we this time?" line, there can be trouble. There is no doubt that my ample hiking experience was trying to throw me a lifeline here, but, sad to say, the current in my personal river of pre-trip slothfulness was fast rising towards flood stage.

Just above the little creek was one tightly wrapped Tarahumara homestead. The rains had been good for two straight years, and many Tarahumaras were celebrating rare consecutive bountiful harvests. There was clearly a Karmic jolliness on the land that, in a basically subsistence-farming area, only comes when it's a sure bet that famine would not visit this year. The land feels happy that it has given its people ample sustenance. (Yes, I think the terra firma part of Tarahumaraland likes the Tarahumaras a lot.) And the people sure as hell are happy, because they know this will be not a winter of want, but, rather, a winter of scootin' a little closer to the fire while sitting back with yet another steamin' bowl of frijoles.

We soon made the acquaintance of the man of the house, Francisco. He asked if we wanted to buy some apples. He had plenty, he told us with a wide, mostly toothless grin. He took us over to his storehouse, which was overflowing with squash, corn, pumpkins, and apples. I commented on the prodigiousness of his larder, and he could do little more than observe to me that, yes indeed, it had been a very good year. He could scarcely keep from giggling. We bought some apples, which were not very good—Tarahumara apples rarely are—and he offered to walk with us to Pamachi. He said it was about 30 minutes away.

The first 15 of those minutes marked the grand finale of our ascent from the Rio Urique. It was very steep going and, once again, everyone had to wait for me at the top. And, once again, my tongue was dragging 42 meters behind me when I caught up with them.

Once we rimmed out, we started walking across the eerie specter of Mesa Ruhuerachi. I had seen Mesa Ruhuerachi from a distance many times. It is the large mesa a little to the right from being directly across the canyon from Divisadero. And I had heard about it. But, even given all that, I was still far from prepared for what we saw. Mesa Ruhuerachi was a wasteland. It literally could be used for the location of a post-holocaust movie. I kept half expecting to see the Road Warrior drive by at 150 kph with a pack of motorcyle-riding bad guys in hot pursuit.

The earth was gray and black, with blood-like streaks of red clay running through it. It was a textbook case of unimpeded erosion, and it made us cringe just to look at it, which we did because we walked across it for 15 minutes. I don't know whether Mesa Ruhuerachi was once soil-covered and productive and that some environmental calamity struck it, or whether there is some inherent geological reason for its starkness. Either way, there's no way any village located close to something this hideous was going to be a nice-place, vibes-wise.

And I was right. Pamachi ended up being a weird little town. It is as far in the middle of nowhere as a place with a church, a school, and a store can be in Tarahumara-land. There is a dirt road all the way to Pamachi (it takes off from the road from Creel to Batopilas). But, this is a town that does not feel like there is much of a connection to the outside world. It looked and felt like a place where in-breeding was probably the norm, and anyone born with a full set of chromosomes was likely considered the pick of the litter.

The first building we came to was the store. This was the end of the supply line, the last store before there were no more stores. There should have been a sign: "NEXT SERVICES, THE

OTHER SIDE OF THE CANYON." The owners were all lying around on sacks of grain getting drunk. It was obvious that the last thing they expected to see walking up were four gringos, accompanied by three Tarahumaras.

The store was a mess. Boxes and sacks of flour were lying all over the place haphazardly, and there was dirt an inch thick everywhere. We bought a couple of Cokes each—you have to run far into the woods in Mexico to escape the presence of Cokes—as well as a few boxes of cookies and crackers. Then we walked over to the church, which was nice enough from the outside, but locked, so we never did see the inside.

Francisco took his leave, but not until we had hired him to guide us to Guaguachique the next morning. Corpus and Jamin would be heading back to Sitagochi right after breakfast, so the guide relay race was continuing.

There was a nice lawn in front of the church, so we decided to just camp there. The school was close-at-hand, so, within minutes, we were completely surrounded by several dozen curious Tarahumara children. This was a boarding school, and served an area covering several hours walk in every direction. The boys stood a respectful 10 or so meters away from us at all times, and the girls never came closer than a stone's throw.

I asked where the water was, and one of the schoolboys meekly pointed up a small arroyo. I got my water sack and water bottles and headed out. It ended up being a small hose coming out of a diminutive spring about 15 minutes away. It didn't look very clean. But, I was so tired and dehydrated, I would have been perfectly happy with a water bagful of cow perspiration.

Before dinner, we each tasted a couple of the cookies we had bought. The only size boxes they had for sale at the store contained literally 100 cookies. They were terrible, which is not surprising, when you consider that it takes at least several weeks for any type of supply to make its way from the factory to a place like Pamachi. In such a case, making something taste fresh is not the prime consideration; keeping it from outright spoiling is. So, these things must contain about a dozen ingredients specifically designed to prevent total decomposition of the product before it is purchased and consumed.

At the same time, people living in places like Pamachi are probably not all that picky about their cookies. They probably don't hold it against a cookie just because it's not straight from the Pepperidge Farm bakery. We, on the other hand, being the gringo snobs we were and are, could not handle these alleged cookies. They were dry as a bone, had white and pink frosting, and were fundamentally awful. So, I walked over to the school's dining room and asked how many kids were going to eat there that night. The cook said something like thirty, so there were plenty of cookies for everyone. I handed the two boxes to her, and she smiled brightly.

Sooner or later, we knew that, in order to eat our supper, we were going to have to start cooking in front of several dozen hungry Tarahumara children, and we did not relish that fact. I've been butt-deep in that scene plenty of times before, and it's never comfortable. Even though we may bitch about backpacking fare, compared to most Tarahumara meals, we eat like kings on the trail. We decided to keep the meal simple, thus avoiding (at least we hoped) the possibility of being washed away by a flash flood of Tarahumara children drool.

We pulled out the stoves and cook kits and foodbags and started heating water. We decided to have instant soup and instant rice, which, we hoped, would not come across to the Tarahumara kids as anything even approximating a feast. Hopefully, they would look at our fixin's and feel that what we eat is not that much different from what they eat. But, as soon as we got to the point in the dinner-making process where the kids could start identifying individual food items, the dinner bell rang, and they all ran off at Warp Factor 9.5 towards the dining hall. Knowing the kids would be back as soon as they were done eating, we hurried to fix our meal. Just as we were about to pour the soup into the pot, we all noticed a disgusting thing: the boiling water looked like (and I have thought long and hard about a more delicate way to describe this, but, there is no other way) someone had poured a fair amount of nasal discharge into it. Our enthusiasm for dinner, which was not high to begin with, started to dwindle fast. We could not imagine what had happened to our water. So, we dumped it out and started again. Just as it was about to boil, the same thing happened. It was some sort of chemical reaction, brought on, we guessed, by the heat of the stove. We could not imagine what substance could cause such a reaction, and we purposefully avoided letting our imaginations run rampant. No matter the cause, once again, we found ourselves staring down into a vat of snot stew. We started regretting giving away those cookies.

We were getting so damned hungry we simply strained the water through a not-perfectly-sterile bandanna (figuring that one disgusting item can perhaps negate another) and went ahead and poured the soup mix and rice in. We ate the meal in stony silence, wondering what the Tarahumara kids were having, and wondering if maybe they had some extra.

The kids, as predicted, came back after dinner. One of them had obviously been volunteered by the cook to thank us profusely for the cookies. Since he was the first one of the tikes to speak to us, I decided to jump on the conversational bandwagon. I asked what they had had for supper.

"Beans," he said.

"Anything else?"

"No, just beans."

"Didn't you have any tortillas?"

"No, just beans. But tonight," he added, "we had cookies after our beans." And that was pretty much the extent of my conversation with the *niños*.

Pat, Aurel, and Jay chatted with them a little longer, but I had to step around the side of the church to relieve myself. That was probably the worst part of camping right in the middle of town; there were no restroom facilities. Poor Aurel had to walk about a quarter-mile to a rickety old outhouse that she described as being less than absolutely sanitary.

As I stepped around the church, I was almost knocked off my feet by one of the most gorgeous sunsets I have ever seen. It was almost over, and we had not even known it was going on, since the church was blocking it from our view. We all grabbed our cameras and fired off a few quick frames, but, basically, it was a sunset missed.

Finally, the end of a long day had come. The kids had been called off to bed and Corpus and Jamin had curled up around the fire, which was under a little overhang connected to the church. Pat and Aurel had set up a tent and had crawled into it. Jay and I slept under the stars. Not long after crashing, Aurel yelled over to me that someone was over giving Corpus and Jamin some grief about something or another. I got up to check it out, and sure enough, there was some drunk Mexican schmuck demanding that Corpus and Jamin pay him to sleep next to the church. Corpus and Jamin both just laid there without batting an eye, looking like they were members in good stead of a tribe that had received so much trouble from Mexicans over the years that a little verbal abuse scarcely even registered anymore. By the time I got over to the fire, Jay and Pat had got up, as well.

The drunk guy was a belligerent bastard. Pat and I ended up tossing him unceremoniously head-over-heels into the darkness, the same way drunks get "escorted" out of saloons in old Westerns. The vibes were going downhill fast. Seconds later, a large rock came whistling out of the darkness, care of our amigo, we suspected. It missed us, but we had no way of knowing if that was the last we were going to hear from him. We learned later that he had spit on Jamin's head before we got up. If we had known that, we would have pummeled the scumbag.

We did not sleep well that night, and, as soon as I finished cleaning Jamin's toe in the morning, we left. Francisco, true to his word, had arrived with his son, all set to do some guidin'. Since Guaguachique was only three hours away, Francisco and his son did not plan on spending the night. So, we had to send the blankets we had brought with us for our guides back to Sitagochi with Corpus and Jamin. Which meant, essentially, that we had just given the brothers a couple of blankets.

We walked along the dirt road all the way to Guaguachique, so we really didn't need guides for this stretch. But, once in Guaguachique, which is a fairly large settlement, we took advantage of Francisco's presence by asking him to round up a guide for us. He said he thought that would be impossible, because this was town meeting day. And, at town meeting day in Tarahumara-land, government officials discuss the disbursement of that year's social welfare payments to the local population. Therefore, you couldn't pry an adult male away from town unless you put a gun under his nose. There wasn't even an adult male of whom we could ask directions. They were all sitting in the schoolhouse, paying very close attention to the goings-on.

We were stuck. Finally, I spied an older gentleman strolling by, and cornered him for some input. He told me at least how to get started towards our next destination, Cieneguita. We restocked our provisions at the little store in Guaguachique and cruised. I reminded everyone of my warning that we may end up getting lost for a day or two, and I told them that the next day or two might very well be those days.

We hiked out of town and over a small pass. The trail was great and, just before dark, we descended into a small, heavily forested arroyo, where we decided to camp. This was the site of an abandoned old mine, and Pat and Aurel actually pitched their tent on a small tailings pile. As we ate dinner, the clouds rolled in and it started to thunder. Pat and Aurel, having a tent, didn't seem to mind. Jay and I, not having a tent, were less than pleased.

When the rain started, I crawled into my uncoated-nylon bivvy sack, in hopes that it would keep me at least a little dry. Jay opted to keep his gear packed away in his pack, hoping to wait out the storm. He just sat around the fire in his raincoat, smoking a cigar.

By midnight, it stopped raining. Jay left camp to go sleep under a close-at-hand overhang. His stuff was completely dry. My stuff, on the other hand, was completely saturated. I tried to dry my sleeping bad over the dwindling fire, to no avail. So, I sheepishly walked over and asked if I could join Pat and Aurel in their two-person tent. They were thrilled beyond words to see my stinky self entering their little lovenest.

It was apparent from the get-go the next morning that we had no earthly idea in which direction we should be walking. None of us had slept well, and we were all feeling funky. The arroyo we were following was idyllic, and the sun had broken out, so we decided to stop and bathe. This arroyo looked like something out of New England. The grass was verdant and deep, and the woods were thick and dark.

Unfortunately, the scene was tainted by the fact that we didn't have the slightest idea where we were. I don't mind being a little disoriented, but I hate not having a directional clue. A Tarahumara family soon walked by, and I asked them how to get to Cieneguita. The response was to point up the side of one of the ridges bordering the arroyo. So, we cinched our packs down and commenced to bushwhack up the ridge.

It wasn't a high ridge, but it was a gut-bustingly steep ascent. From the top, though, we could see for miles and miles in the direction I felt we wanted to go. Jay was skeptical. While I felt certain beyond the shadow of a reasonable doubt that, way, way off in the distance, we were looking at Batopilas Canyon, he felt it was Urique Canyon. He was right, but there was no way on earth I was going to be dissuaded until we had traipsed aimlessly over the entire visible landscape for the better part of the day. Which is exactly what we did.

At least partially in my own defense, we did see some splendid territory during that aimless traipsing, territory that is so far off the beaten path that I'll bet not too many gringos have ever traversed it. But, scenic beauty notwithstanding, by late afternoon, we were no closer to finding our way to Cieneguita than we were when we broke camp that morning.

We were also completely out of water. We decided to drop down into a small side arroyo. While looking for a way down, we came across the nicest Tarahumara house I have ever seen. Most times, Tarahumaras spend more time building their storage sheds than they do their houses, a reality that has always perplexed me, because Tarahumaras do not handle winter weather well at all. They hate cold, yet their houses always look like "forts" built by eight-year-olds out in the woods of rural America. This house, though, was tight. It had well-set windows, which was surprising because Tarahumara houses are usually windowless.

There was a trail down into the arroyo starting right in front of the house. On the way down, we passed a six-year-old Tarahumara boy on his way back up carrying two buckets of water. He froze in his tracks at the sight of me, but, almost instantly, he smiled. We asked if that was his house, and he answered in the affirmative.

I asked if his dad was around, and he, again, said yes. He asked me if I could hear some wood-chopping on the other side of the arroyo. He said that was his dad. He added that his dad would soon be coming home for the evening, by way of the very trail we were standing on. I asked if we were anywhere near Cieneguita, and the little boy said we were, indeed.

We descended into the arroyo, which boasted several seemingly abandoned Tarahumara casitas. It was a very nice little valley, with a trickle of water and an abundance of firewood. I am always careful of using firewood in populated areas, because I know the Tarahumaras rely on that wood. But, in this place, there seemed to be plenty for everybody, so we built a fire.

Finally, I decided to set out looking for the little boy's dad. So, as tired as I was, and as much as my feet were hurting, I laced my boots back on and headed up the other side of the arroyo. Within a few minutes, though, I crossed paths with the man-in-question, Miguel, who, along with his ten-year-old daughter, had been working all day taking in wood. The daughter saw me first, and I thought she was going to gulp her tongue right down her throat when I first walked up. She didn't exactly expect to be running into a scuzzy-looking gringo that day.

Miguel, on the other hand, looked like gringos passed through his back yard all the time, though he told us later that we were the first Americans he had ever seen in that neck of the woods. We walked back down together to our camp. After he shook hands all the way around (and made his daughter do the same), I asked if he would be interested in guiding us to Cieneguita. He said he would be unable to, because, with winter coming on, he needed to be spending his time chopping firewood. I offered him $7. He declined. $10. No thanks. $15. Too busy. $20. Well, okay. He said it was at least three or four hours to Cieneguita and that he would return at 7:30 the next morning.

That night, the temperatures plummeted well below freezing. We all awoke with thick frost on our everything, and we didn't have enough time to dry out everything before hitting the trail. So, we packed up wet gear, which probably added two kilograms to each of our packs. When Miguel arrived, we fixed him and his two kids some oatmeal and hot chocolate. Then we were off. His boy stayed behind, and the daughter walked with us as far as a neighbor's house. It was pure joy to watch this little girl in action. She skipped through the woods as much as she walked on the trail. She giggled and sang songs and basically stole our hearts.

After she took her leave, it was just the five of us walking through some of the sweetest territory I have ever seen. Numerous have been the times that I guessed I was hiking through plus-or-minus virgin forest in Copper Canyon Country. But, this time, I knew for a fact that this area had never suffered the indignity of the chainsaw. There were huge fir- and spruce-looking trees. It was almost like hiking in Colorado. There was moss and an amazing feeling of lushness.

After about two hours, we hooked into the dirt road to Cieneguita. Since even nimwits of our scale could not possibly lose a dirt road, we thanked Miguel for his help, and said he could go home.

It was about this time that I noticed my boots were on the verge of blowing out. The sole in the front of my left boot was loose and flopping around in a most depressing fashion. I pulled out everything I owned that contained even one iota of stickiness—duck tape, tent repair tape, and my Therm-a-Rest repair patches—and applied them to my boots. I knew this was not a field repair that was going to merit a write-up in *Popular Mechanics*, but it was the best I could do under the circumstances. I really most sincerely regretted not carrying camp shoes, and I vowed to never ever again be so terminally idiotic.

The walk to Cieneguita was interminable. We walked and walked and walked some more, all the time thinking that we were caught in a Star Trek-esque warp in the space/time continuum. I was having to walk in such a way as not to impact my rapidly decomposing boot with the road, which only added to a sense of deep-down fatigue that was beginning to dominate my psyche, as well as my physiology. Aurel, likewise, was starting to experience boot decomposition problems, although she had been intelligent enough to bring running shoes with her.

At long last, we arrived in Cieneguita, which is one seriously dumpy little town. Cieneguita is a lumber town populated by maybe two thousand people. It is basically dirty, unkempt, and not overly friendly. But, it has a few stores, and we took advantage of that situation by drinking several soft drinks right on the spot without so much as taking our packs off. Our supplies were fast dwindling, so we scored some crackers, cans of tuna, and candy bars for the last stretch into Batopilas. After gleaning a few directions, we hit the trail again. Since we had to be in Batopilas the next night, we hiked until dark, then dry-camped on top of a little hill. It was our seventh day on the trail, and we had yet to have an easy day. We all went to bed understanding full well that the next day would, by far, be the hardest.

We started hiking the second it was light enough see. So far, the directions we had received in Cieneguita had worked out very well. We were told to basically follow a dirt road all the way to a point where we were looking over a cliff down into Arroyo Munérachi. We were also told that, since this was a logging area, there were many primitive roads crisscrossing the vicinity, and, therefore, it might be hard to stick to the main dirt road, because, basically, it wasn't much better than the myriad of non-main logging roads we would be crossing. We were told that, at some point, the main dirt road would split, with the left-hand fork going into Huisuchi and the right-hand fork going to Rancheria Sorichique. We had been told to not sweat it either way, that, even if we missed the fork, everything would work out fine, although, if possible, it would be better to make our way directly to Sorichique.

We, of course, found ourselves in Huisuchi, rather than Sorichique, which was all right, because there was a little store there, and, since we hadn't waited around camp long enough to make coffee, a nice caffeine-laden Coke would go down right easy. The only problem was, because it was only 8 AM, the store was not yet open. A man who lived near the store sent his son to fetch the store owner, but, after 45 wasted minutes, she still had not arrived. So, after fine-tuning our directions, we hit the trail once more.

We were directed to a trail that went down into an arroyo, then back up the other side. At that point, we intersected with the road to Sorichique. We were clearly heading out onto a mesa that, before long, would drop off into Arroyo Munérachi. By 10 AM, we were on a promontory from which we could see Munérachi, 1,000 meters below. We had no time to waste if we wanted to make Batopilas that night.

The descent was fairly harrowing. My boot was getting worse, and I had what I thought was a blister, but ended up being a corn, on my left tootsie. It's amazing how one little sore spot on one little toe can have a full-grown man hobbling like he had just had his entire foot hacked off with a machete. Aurel was also starting to suffer mightily from blisters. Also, after almost eight hard days on the trail, Aurel was starting to get a tad stressed. She had handled the hike a lot better than me thus far, but it was evident that she was going to have to be nursed a little bit through the homestretch. Which was okay, because we had Pat, and, as the resident boyfriend-of-Aurel, it was his job to perform any necessary nursing.

I was enjoying this, the last day out, more than any other day so far, despite the fact that I had accepted the fact that, before long, I would have no boot on my left foot. After seven-and-a-half days, I was finally starting to get my trail legs. And that felt mighty good.

We made Munérachi by 2 PM. We had to stop and rest and moleskin Aurel's feet. Her blisters were so bad that, as Jay worked on them (Jay is the blister master of the known universe), she was having trouble keeping from crying.

We took the high route to Cerro Colorado, because it's a little faster than following the river. Unfortunately, it was late afternoon by the time we topped out and began our descent into Cerro Colorado. It was over 100 degrees F., and all the more intriguing signs of heat exhaustion made themselves evident in all our faces. At one point, Jay stopped in the desert sun for an Advil. He dropped the vial and the pills went everywhere. I watched him trying, and failing, to pick the pills up. The medic in me justifiably asked if he was feeling dizzy, and he snapped at me something along the lines of "you're damned right I'm dizzy, you putz; do you want to try to pick these pills up with all these little pebbles on the ground?"

Jay has snapped at me a total of about twice in seventeen years, so I knew something was wrong. And that something was the sun. We needed to get our asses to Cerro Colorado pronto. Which we did. And, after a couple of cool beverages and some chow, everyone was feeling better. Unfortunately, it was past 5 PM. At that time of year, darkness descends upon the land at about 7:30. In our state of exhaustion, it was clearly going to take us four solid hours to make Batopilas.

One of the things I like most about backpacking is the autopilot component. I am pleased to report that I have never been one to consider backpacking a "sport." I simply do not look at this, my favorite non-sexual activity, as an athletic endeavor. To me, it is pure recreation. But, I do concede that, as a very physically demanding form of recreation, it does have athletic-like components. One of those quasi-athletic components is the occasional necessity of separating the discomfort of the body from the conscious part of the brain. Though your feet may feel as though they are suffering irreparable harm, you simply stroll along at 5 kilometers per hour over rocky terrain like you're walking down to the convenience store for a pack of cigars. You put yourself on autopilot, or you take your pack off and stop hiking for the day, something we could not afford to do.

By the time we reached Batopilas Canyon, it was too dark to hike without flashlights. The main advantage of the darkness quotient was that I could not see my boot, which was hanging on by a thread. The walk from Arroyo Cerro Colorado to Batopilas takes only an hour, and it is very easy. At the risk of bringing in some more athletic terminology we almost looked at that stretch as a cool down.

Then, we were there, in Batopilas, happy as pigs in the proverbial slop. Unfortunately, Batopilas is about five kilometers long, and our hotel was at the far end. After walking for 13 hours, those last few kilometers along cobblestoned streets made for painful perambulation. When we reached the Hotel Mary, it was 8:30, probably too late to be bothering Doña Micha for a meal, although, since I know her pretty well, I thought I could maybe convince her to have mercy upon our poor starving gringo carcasses.

So, I limped as fast as what was left of my feet would carry me to Doña Micha's to beg her for dinner. She was just getting ready to go out for the evening (there was a street party that night), but, she took pity on me. She said that, if we could be back in twenty minutes and if we didn't mind being served whatever she had handy, then she would feed us. I crawled on all fours back to the hotel, laid the skinny on Jay, Pat, and

Aurel, and we were back at Doña Micha's in seventeen minutes. I don't even remember what she served us, but I'm sure it was plentiful and good.

After dinner, we walked slowly by the street party, which was just getting going in the plaza. I wouldn't have minded partying down a bit, but I was simply too tired. By 10 PM, we were all sawing logs while Batopilas boogied down until dawn.

In retrospect, I decided to forego offering this route as a guided itinerary. I would love to do the hike again, but I would rather take two weeks to do it. So, after eight days on the trail, I found myself right where I was before we left Cusarare: without a route upon which to guide those paying customers. Well, screw 'em. Something'll turn up. It always does when you're out there in the woods of Tarahumara-land.

Particulars

I'm going to keep this one simple, because I don't believe you should try this hike without guides. That said, you will need the 1:50,000 Creel, San Jose Guacayvo, San Rafael, and Batopilas maps. And I do mean "need." Unless you are very familiar with the topography of Copper Canyon Country or unless you have guides every foot of the way on this, you will likely stumble upon directional misfortune on this hike.

The thing is, you'll likely have trouble finding a guide who knows the entire route. So, like me, you will likely have to participate in a guide-hiring relay race. Also, although we did this hike in eight days, I would highly recommend that you take at least ten, and preferably twelve. That way, you can hang out a little in some of the cooler parts of this trip.

Okay, first you need to get to Basirecota and, from there to Sitagochi. You can hire guides in Cusarare who know the way that far. You will probably have to hire additional guides in Sitagochi. From Sitagochi, you will descend into Copper Canyon. Then, you will ascend to the village of Pamachi, where there is a small store. From Pamachi, follow the dirt road to Guaguachique, where there is another store. From Guaguachique, you *need* to hire a guide to Cieneguita, where there is also a store. From Cieneguita, get to Munérachi and, from there, go downriver to Cerro Colorado and Batopilas. (See Chapter 15 for additional skinny about this last stretch.)

You could easily bug out of this route at Guaguachique, where you could probably hitch a ride out to the Creel-Batopilas road. Also, you could bug out at Cieneguita, which is connected by dirt road to the road that connects the road from Guaguachique to the road that connects Creel and Batopilas. Understand? I knew you would.

18
Panalachi to Tehuirichi

At long last. After four visits to Tarahumara-land, I finally find myself with an invitation to a *tesguinada*—a Tarahumara corn beer bash. It's not much of an invitation, mind you. I mean, the head of the household where the festivities will be held did not send a runner to my residence bidding me join the fun—which is the way it's usually done. Rather, it came from someone I rather doubt, in retrospect, was formally invited himself. But we won't nit-pick.

Gay and I had driven from Creel to the town of Panalachi, on the east side of the Continental Divide, by way of Bocoyna and Sisoguichi. This two-hour drive is one of the most pleasant I have ever experienced. Bocoyna, which is a Chihuahua-Pacific Railroad stop on the road that connects Creel and San Juanito, is a Mexican town near the headwaters of the Rio Conchos. It sports one of the oldest missions in Tarahumara-land, built in 1702.

At this point, the Conchos, the largest tributary of the Rio Grande, is but a trickle. The roads crosses it without a bridge, but even a passenger car could make the crossing with no sweat. This is the last we will see of the Conchos, though, until we arrive at the mission ranchito of Tehuirichi (tay-wheer-EE-chee), the goal of this little excursion. By that time, it will be a fairly good-sized river.

We had been told by a Spaniard we met at Margarita's Guest House in Creel that the doctor in Panalachi would be happy to put us up for the night in his home, which also serves as the local hospital. Or, more accurately, the hospital also serves as his home. We remembered the health care facility we stopped at on our way back from Basaseachi Falls and decided, before the fact, that we would likely pass, even if we were offered a night's lodging.

Panalachi is an unusual town in that it is part Mexican and part Tarahumara. Usually, villages go one way or the other. It is also a fairly affluent looking place, dotted by numerous good-sized chalet-style dwellings.

We drank a couple of soft drinks in the morning sun in front of one of the town's several stores and asked about the doctor. The proprietor told us that we would be expected to stay at least one night at the hospital. We weren't planning on spending a night in town because it was early enough to hit the trail. But, we still needed a place to park the truck for the next few days. So, we drove up the hill to the doctor's residence.

We were at once surprised. This facility looked like a place where you could actually be treated and cured. The doctor greeted us before we were even out of the truck. He told us that we couldn't have come at a better time because this was a fiesta/*tesquinada* day at Chacarachi, one of the local Tarahumara ranchitos. And, since he was invited, we were invited. Though we were very eager to get to the Conchos, a *tesguinada*, the backbone of any Tarahumara fiesta worth its salt, was something we could not pass up. We asked several times if he was certain it would be okay for us to go to the fiesta. There was no doubt, the doctor responded.

The doctor had been the sole health care professional in Panalachi for twelve years, as of late 1988. Like all Mexican doctors, he was required by law to spend his first year after graduation from medical school in a rural setting not of his choice. He was sent to Sisoguichi, which is a wonderful little mission town halfway between Bocoyna and Panalachi. He decided to stay in the area, not only because he liked the small-town ambience (he was born and raised in Mexico City), but because he thought there was a capitalist opportunity at hand. The locals, he said, though appreciative of the newly graduated doctors who blew in and blew out of town every year, were desirous of a more permanent health-care situation.

So, the doctor decided to build his own hospital, though in Panalachi instead of Sisoguichi because of cheaper land. It was a pure business decision undertaken without government funds. It took a year to complete the hospital, which also houses living quarters for the doctor, his wife, and child, who were off visiting relatives in Chihuahua City when we arrived. The place was well stocked with equipment and medicines. We were offered use of the two-bed "ward" for the night.

The doctor was uncertain what time the *tesguinada* would begin, so we drove over to Chacarachi, only about three kilometers east of town, in early afternoon. Like most Tarahumara ranchitos, Chacarachi is nothing more than a cluster of small log-cabin-like dwellings. The residents were hard at it, getting ready for the *tesguinada*, which was being held because it was some local holiday, which I didn't even remember long enough to forget.

The females of the ranchito were busy cooking the *tesguino*—in a full 200-liter drum. This corn beer had been fermenting and cooking for a total of eight days. And it would have to be consumed within three days, because, after that, it would spoil, which, in retrospect, is clearly a relative term. They were also boiling up a vat of a dish that I am surprised has never become a mainstay of the American diet—cow blood. Ummmm . . . Gay and I could barely keep from drooling all over ourselves.

Several local males were busy cutting up the carcass from which this blood had been drained. There was a mound of cow parts several feet high. Families that put on *tesguinadas* not only supply the beer, but the food as well. *Tesguinadas* generally last until all the beverages and victuals are gone.

The doctor seemed on friendly terms with all the residents of Chacarachi. Indeed, within two minutes, he had placed a food order with one of the resident females, who sort of rolled her eyes, smiled, and went into one of the houses. Several minutes later, she came back out with a plate of cooked beef cubes and several blue corn tortillas.

The doctor ate the meal and then took us on a tour of *his* house, which came as something of a surprise. He was in the process of building a traditional Tarahumara dwelling about three meters from the rest of the houses in Chacarachi. He planned to use it as his weekend getaway, despite the fact that we were but 10 minutes from his main house. Since it is illegal to sell *ejido* land, which certainly this was, we couldn't figure out how the doctor managed to wangle a house on Tarahumara land. Perhaps he offered reduced-rate medical care to the residents of Chacarachi in exchange for them putting up with his non-Tarahumara self.

The *tesguinada* wouldn't commence until about sundown that night, so we went back to the hospital for lunch and a siesta. We returned to Chacarachi about 7 PM, finding our way through the dark by focusing on the four huge fires that were illuminating the ranchito. Wherever a group of Tarahumaras is gathered, there will always be more fires than it would seem necessary. It is important to understand that *tesguinadas*, though punctuated by vast amounts of alcohol consumption, are ceremonial occasions. Thus, they have little in common with, say, a backyard barbecue during which a bunch of the boys get plowed on Budweiser while playing horseshoes. When we arrived, the local shaman was blessing the drinking circle— about 10 meters in diameter—which was marked out by rocks. He was chanting, dancing, and waving a wand. The other eight or ten people gathered there were just sitting around staring into the huge bonfire, not paying much attention to the shaman.

We "shook" hands with everyone. The Tarahumara "handshake" differs quite a bit from the American/European handshake, although, often, Tarahumaras will use our technique when meeting a gringo. They seem pleased when we know how to do it their way. They gently touch, just for an instant, the tips of each others' fingers, from about the second knuckle down, using the right hand.

It became obvious that our presence was unexpected, if not unwelcome. For one thing, *tesguinadas* are strictly sexually segregated. The females hang out around one fire, the males another. The fact that Gay was standing around the men's fire, which was about 20 meters from the houses we had visited that afternoon, seemed unsettling. The Tarahumara men kept looking, not exactly viciously, but at least irritably, at her out of the corners of their eyes. So, we went with the doctor up to the women's fire, where the finishing touches were being put on the *tesguino*. The doctor joked around with the dozen or so women who were there—all of whom seemed a little flustered that there were two men and two Americans there. The doctor helped himself to some beef and popcorn. Then, he asked for a gourd, cut in half length-ways, out of which corn beer is always drunk. He dipped himself a gourdful out of a barrel, took a sip and passed it to us.

This is not the way it's usually done. One usually consumes *tesguino* while sitting around the officially designated drinking circle. The host starts things off by filling the gourd and handing it, first, to the eldest man there. After that, the gourd—and there's usually only one gourd per drinking circle (larger *tesguinadas* can have more than one circle)—is passed around. You are obligated to drink the entire gourdful, in one fell swoop, which is quite an accomplishment because these things hold at least a liter. When you're done, you stand up, walk over to the vat, refill the gourd and hand it to the next person. If you just hand the empty gourd back to whoever handed it to you, they will fill it back up and give it back to you.

It is not bad manners to leave the circle, but this is best done under the pretense of needing to relieve oneself, rather than, say, expressing a simple desire to split because you don't like the company. If you wish to drink no more midway through a gourdful of corn beer, there's a way out of it without losing too much face. All you need to do is spill the remaining *tesguino* all over your front and everyone there will laugh and think that you've just had a few too many. At this point, you will be relieved of your obligation to drink more when it's your turn again.

None of us had any desire to knock off that gourd of corn beer, especially the doctor, who had mentioned earlier how he dislikes *tesguino*. And a more foul beverage I had never tasted. I mean, mescal mixed with prune juice would be better than *tesguino*. I was disappointed. I guess I have this false image of myself as world-traveler that includes enthusiasm for all native alcoholic beverages.

We walked back to the men's fire with the now-half-empty gourd. The shaman was still doing his thing, meaning, in the eyes of tradition, the drinking lamp had not been lit. And, yet, there we were with a gourd of beer. We made banal chit-chat for an hour or so. Several of the men had wrapped themselves in their blankets and were dozing on the frozen ground. Since this party would last three days, maybe four, there was no hurry to get things moving. During that hour around the fire, I drank the rest of that gourd of corn beer. The more I drank, the better I liked it. I don't think I would ever order it in a bar, mind you, but it was better than I had first thought. At least, after a liter, that is. Gay, on the other hand, took a polite sip or two and vowed never to stray this far from Labatt's Blue again.

We headed back to the hospital before the party got going full-bore—seemingly much to the relief of our Tarahumara hosts. On the way, we stopped at the home of a local guide. The doctor had been telling us all day that it would be impossible to find our way to Tehuirichi without a guide. When we told him that we thought we could make it alone, he acted insulted. So, we went along with it. He made all the arrangements, except for negotiating the price, while we sat in his van. He arranged for us to meet the guide at ten the next morning.

This we did. The guide was a seventy-year-old Mexican man with the most rotten teeth I have ever seen. He had a horse, which was saddled and ready to go when we arrived. A lever-action rifle was stuck into the scabbard. We asked if there was a reason for the weapon. He just shrugged and smiled.

During the five-minute walk from the hospital to the guide's house, we met a Canadian, Edmond Faubert, who is one of the best-known experts on Tarahumara arts and crafts. He helped author *The Other Southwest* with Bernard Fontana and Barney Burns, and he obtained most of the items photographed in Fontana's book, *The Material Tarahumara*. In addition, he aided Fontana in his field work during the research phase of *Tarahumara: Where Night Is the Day of the Moon*.

Faubert was on his way to a small ranchito on the Conchos, where he hoped to buy a couple of pots. He offered us a ride to the top of the small ridge that lies between Panalachi and Tehuirichi, which is as far as the dirt road goes. We told the guide we would meet him on the other side. He hopped on his horse and rode out ahead of us, saying that he would be taking a different route.

Faubert and his two Mexican companions dropped us off eight kilometers later and we waited an hour for the guide. He never showed, so we began walking to Tehuirichi. We weren't exactly sad. Faubert had given us detailed directions and we had maps. This part of Tarahumara-land has little geographically in common with the rest. The Rio Conchos area has much gentler terrain. This is not to say it's like Iowa. It's just easier to pick your way from one point to another without running into any 1,000-meter-high cliffs.

We were told in Panalachi that it would take about three hours to hike to Tehuirichi. Faubert laughed. He said it would take us five hours from the place where he dropped us off. He warned us to always multiply by at least two the number of hours the Tarahumaras tell you it will take to walk someplace.

Our plan was simple, though not complete. We wanted to walk to Tehuirichi and then back to Panalachi via a different route, if possible. Though not spectacularly beautiful in the same way that the deep canyons of Tarahumara-land are, the Conchos Valley is one of the highlights of Copper Canyon Country. There are only a few places where the Tarahumaras still live basically the same way they did four hundred years ago. The Conchos is one of those places. You won't see many Tarahumaras dressed in Kmart reject clothing in these parts.

At least three old Copper Canyon Country hands had told us that Tehuirichi was their favorite part of Tarahumara-land. This area was all but unvisited by gringos as little as ten years ago. This is also the heart of Jesuit country. We were forewarned both by Skip McWilliams and Faubert that we would be made to feel very unwelcome by the priest and the two nuns who call Tehuirichi home. This is somewhat ironic because the Tarahumaras we ran into on this trip, both in Panalachi and on the trail to Tehuirichi, were the most friendly and outgoing we had ever met. They smiled easily and welcomed us to their territory. They seemed pleased that we were interested in visiting.

There are several trails from Panalachi to the Conchos, all of which are as good as any in Tarahumara-land. They are all designed for burro supply trains, so they are well graded and wide. From the point where Faubert dropped us off, we followed a trail that paralleled an arroyo that eventually intersects with the Conchos just south of the ranchito of Arroyo Hondo. (This is a different Arroyo Hondo than the one that intersects the Urique River near the village of Urique. "Hondo" simply means "deep.") At the site of an old abandoned mill, where there are several occupied Tarahumara dwellings, we followed the wide path that started up the side of a ridge. Though it was December, the afternoon sun was harsh and hot. When we topped out on the ridge three kilometers later, the view of the Conchos Valley opened up to the south. It was a wonderful scene.

It was here that we made a small directional mistake. We should have followed this ridge down towards the Conchos. But, the grand trail we had been following continued southeast into another arroyo. The trail that followed the ridge directly to Tehuirichi was faint as it exited from the trail we had been following. We didn't know this until our return trip two days later. This presented no real problem. Quite the contrary. Instead of following the same trail both directions, we ended up finding a nice little loop.

The trail we followed went straight down into the arroyo, which was, at this point, only about 100 meters deep. The rock formations we passed beneath were spectacular. About 10 or 12 kilometers later—three hours past the point where the trail topped the ridge—we found ourselves on a small bluff overlooking a trickle of a river that was the Conchos. We had expected something a little larger. This thing was much smaller than Cusarare Creek. But volume wasn't the only "problem." The river seemed to be flowing in the wrong direction. The Conchos flows directly east for several hundred kilometers until it joins the Rio Grande at Presidio, Texas. This section was flowing almost due west. We hiked down the bluff into one of the most beautiful floodplains I had ever seen. The tall grass was golden in the late afternoon sun. There were several abandoned Tarahumara homesteads on the hills near the river. We had been told that Tehuirichi, which we thought this cluster of houses was, was almost totally—albeit temporarily—abandoned, due to a very poor corn harvest the year before. The residents were mostly in Chihuahua City and Juarez—begging their way through the winter.

Gay wandered off to take pictures while I strolled down to the river with the water pump. Purifying water is, without a doubt, the worst camp chore there is. I own a Katadyn filter, which is the bee's knees of backpacking water pumps. It is still a drag to use, as are all other types and models. The few companies that manufacture backpacking water pumps all say stuff like ". . . purifies a liter of water in 90 seconds." My ass. I think they arrive at those figures by putting professional wrestlers in the middle of the Sahara for three waterless days and then promising them all the cold beer they can drink if they can pump a liter of water through one of these buggers in 90 seconds. And, even then, if they tried to pump second and third liters through in the same amount of time, they would fail. I estimate that it takes me about five or six minutes per liter, which is a drag when you find yourself going through ten liters a day per person.

But, slow pumping was the least of my worries this fine evening. I couldn't get over the fact that the damned river was flowing the wrong damned way. I pulled out my map and compass and oriented and re-oriented them. Nothing, including the possibility that we were in the middle of a huge yazoo-type bend, would explain the matter.

A couple of male Tarahumaras passed, dressed in their traditional white dress-looking garments. I ran over and asked them if this was the Conchos and if this was Tehuirichi. Yes, they said, this was the Conchos, but Tehuirichi proper was a few kilometers downriver.

Once again, due primarily to chronic laziness, I did not tote a tent. And, once again, we froze. Though I knew the Conchos Valley was nowhere near as deep as Copper Canyon, I was operating under the assumption that the temperatures would be warmer here than in Panalachi. We awoke to the heaviest frost I have ever seen—and I live in the Colorado mountains. Our bags were soaked through. It took until 11 in the morning to get them dry, which was no problem because we only planned on hiking as far as Tehuirichi.

The hike down the Conchos was a cakewalk. The trail was perfect, the sunshine warm, and the scenery splendid. The valley at this point was perhaps 500 meters deep, with rounded hills bounding it, punctuated by occasional cliff faces. Gay said later that this was her favorite stretch of trail in all of Tarahumara-land. We had to cross the river a few times, but, since the water was so shallow, those crossings were easy.

After an hour, we started passing a few more Tarahumara orchards and houses. I yelled up a hill to a couple of Tarahumaras who were building a chicken coop, asking them if this was Tehuirichi. They said it was. We rounded a bend and the mission came into sight. But that wasn't all. A big river, at least 20 meters wide, also came into sight. The Tarahumara men I had talked to last night must have misunderstood my question, or else I misunderstood their answer. The creek we had camped next to was not the Conchos after all, just a small tributary, which explained why it was flowing the wrong way with so little water.

There was a school near the mission. As we passed, dozens of Tarahumara children came pouring out to watch us. We waved. No response. We yelled *"cuira"* (koo-EE-rah)—Tarahumara for "hello." Again, no response. The friendliness we had experienced over the last few days was not in evidence in Tehuirichi. We plopped our packs right in the mission courtyard. One of the resident nuns walked around a corner just as we arrived. She tried to ignore us, but I would not let her. I asked where we could camp. We could tell from the look on her face that she did not relish the thought of having us for neighbors, even for one night. She pointed, in response, north, towards Panalachi. Actually, I was joshing with her. We had decided, since it was getting colder than we had expected, to head back towards Panalachi that night.

We went down to the river to fill our water bottles, and were joined by two young Tarahumara boys—about ten years old—who were, likewise, on water detail. I asked, in Spanish, if they spoke Spanish. They both shook their heads, meaning they understood at least a little. A few minutes later, one of them shyly asked if I had any *dulces*—Spanish for "candy." I responded that I thought they didn't speak any Spanish. They giggled at being found out. We chatted for a few minutes before they headed up towards the school with a full bucket of water.

Gay and I ate lunch next to the mission. The nun pointed to the arroyo behind the mission when we asked her what the most direct route back to Panalachi was. We left, hoping to camp at the abandoned sawmill near where Edmond Faubert had dropped us off the day before. A few minutes out of Tehuirichi, we passed a Tarahumara woman who was returning from the *tesguinada* we had been to. She was in bad shape, with dried *tesguino* all down her chin and the reddest eyes this side of Mardi Gras. She was staggering and looked like she had the worst hangover in the history of the world. She was friendly, though. She had heard about the gringos who had crashed the party, sort of chuckling as she said this.

The hike back was surprisingly difficult, at least partially because we lost the trail. This was frustrating because this is a well-traveled route. An hour north of Tehuirichi, we found ourselves looking down a small cliff. I think this is where the trail and us went separate directions. I climbed down a rickety wooden ladder. Gay went off in search of an easier way. This transpired at the edge of a Tarahumara ranchito and the whole clan came out to watch the gringos. They were laughing and pointing. Once again, we were the entertainment.

After following a goat path for several kilometers, we finally hooked back up with the main trail. This must have been the route that Faubert had described to us. He had mentioned that we would be passing some of the most interesting rock formations in the region, which we did—dark Precambrian-looking spires a hundred meters tall that seemed straight out of some old caveman movie. The trail followed a ridge that sported a fascinating butte that we had seen from a distance on our way down the day before. From higher up, you can see the flat top of this butte. It looks putting-green smooth. The trail skirted the cliffs that formed the base of this butte, which was about 30 meters higher than the ridge at this point. The top seemed inaccessible.

Once again, the late afternoon sunlight was lip-scorching hot. Much of this trail was shadeless, with short little ups and downs, the most tiring kind of hiking. We intersected with the trail we had followed the day before just as the sun was sinking over the Continental Divide. At this point, we were only about 15 minutes from the place we wanted to camp, so Gay stayed behind to take pictures while I went ahead to set up camp. I didn't want to camp right in the backyards of the Tarahumara shacks near the old mill site, so I walked about 30 meters up the arroyo and laid my pack right in the middle of the trail, which, at this point, was as wide as a road. It was also the only flat spot around. By the time Gay caught up with me, I had our little love nest set up with dinner—home-dried chile—bubbling on the stove.

It took us about three easy hours to hike back to Panalachi the next morning, via the same dirt road we had ridden over with Faubert. We stopped by the residence of our "guide." His wife came running out with tears in her eyes, thanking God that we were alive. The same thing for the guide. Apparently, the old man had misunderstood where he was supposed to meet us, which wouldn't have been hard because we, having never been there before, weren't exactly specific. He had spent almost 24 hours combing the woods looking for us, returning home only after he was convinced we were dead meat. He and his wife were trying to decide whether to call the army in to look for our corpses. We went ahead and paid him the same as if he had led us by the hand to Tehuirichi and back.

On our way out of town, we drove by Chacarachi. The *tesguinada* was still going strong. We considered stopping by again, but thought better of it. We could wait until we reached Bocoyna, the closest place where we could buy gringo beer. A little less romantic, perhaps, but much easier on the tongue and stomach.

Particulars

You will need the 1:250,000 San Juanito map, or a combination of the San Juanito, Creel, and Nararachi 1:50,000s. It is doubtful you will be able to buy the 1:50,000 Nararachi topo, which contains Tehuirichi, in Creel. Try at the Mission Store.

The most difficult part of this hike is access. There is no public transportation to Panalachi. You could hire a taxi in Creel, but this will prove expensive. If you can get to Bocoyna by train or by hitching from Creel, you should be able to hitch southeast to Panalachi. The dirt road, which is in pretty good shape, is traversed by many logging trucks. It could take you more than a day, however, if traffic is light. Halfway between Bocoyna and Panalachi is the town of Sisoguichi, which has a nice hotel and an old mission. I have seen advertisements for tours to Sisoguichi at Margarita's and the Parador in Creel. You could sign up for one of these and hitch the rest of the way. Or you could ask Margarita or the Parador to put together a custom tour for you all the way to Panalachi. To save money, this is better done with several people.

Panalachi can also be accessed by hiking from Cusarare, and Tehuirichi can be accessed from Choguita (Chapter 7). There are no hotels in Panalachi, though the local doctor rents out the traditional Tarahumara house he has built at Chacarachi, which is only a few minutes out of town. Anyone in Panalachi can point you to the hospital where the doctor lives. We were invited to stay in the hospital, but you shouldn't go to Panalachi expecting the same offer, especially if tourism picks up in this area.

The trail to Tehuirichi goes over the ridge east of town. You can see the trail from the hospital. Hike over that ridge, a distance of about eight kilometers, heading down the arroyo on the other side. This arroyo will take you all the way to the Rio Conchos, about eight more kilometers, via the ranchito of Arroyo Hondo. There is a good trail. You can hike downriver from there to Tehuirichi—again, about eight kilometers away.

Or, from the arroyo, you can hike up the ridge directly to the east. Before ascending, hike down the arroyo until you come to a cluster of Tarahumara houses, located at the site of an old abandoned sawmill. You will see a distinct trail switchbacking up the ridge. Follow this trail down the ridge to a saddle, about three kilometers from the houses. Here, you have two choices. You can continue on the east side of the ridge, skirting the beautiful butte you will see to the south. The trail will, at first, be a little hard to find, but it leads right to Tehuirichi.

Or, you can bypass the ridge trail and keep following the main trail down into the next arroyo to the east. This arroyo intersects a small creek after about eight kilometers. Follow this creek downstream—to the west—a couple of kilometers.

It will interest with the Rio Conchos at Tehuirichi. From there, you can follow the arroyo directly behind the mission back towards Panalachi. Or, you can head upriver for eight kilometers or so until you come to Arroyo Hondo. Follow this north until you meet the main trail to Panalachi.

Though the Conchos is not as tough as, say, the Urique, it will still be a rough slog if you decide to follow it any distance. You will have to cross it many times. And you will be walking on sand with wet boots the rest of the time. You would be well advised to dayhike around Panalachi. This little town is located in a beautiful high valley worthy of exploration. There are several small stores in Bocoyna, Sisoguichi, and Panalachi, but nothing in Tehuirichi.

19
The Sinforosa

Despite all my wanderings in Copper Canyon Country, one destinational gem still eluded me, and that gem bears the name "Sinforosa." Since the Sinforosa Canyon of the Rio Verde is well off the beaten path in Tarahumara-land, I had always put visiting it on the back burner, in order to pay more attention to those hiking and backpacking destinations a little closer to, well, the beaten path. But, from what I had heard and read, one really hasn't interfaced entirely with Copper Canyon Country until one has trod into and out of the Sinforosa, which is more than 2,000 meters deep.

To access Sinforosa Canyon, you head to the town of Guachochi, located about three hours by car and about two hundred years by bus south of Creel. In late 1993, Sahuaripa Gonzales and I loaded up Worf, my 1989 Jeep Wrangler, and drove to Guachochi, a town I had never set foot in before. I had heard Guachochi, which boasts a population of about fifteen thousand, described variously as "the way Creel used to be before it was discovered," "a real town," and "the next tourist hot spot in Copper Canyon Country."

Any and all of those descriptions pretty well sums up Guachochi. It is a muddy-streeted, wild west feeling, old logging town that very well might become a new center for gringo explorations of the area, as more and more people hear about the stunning grandeur of the Sinforosa.

I guess I should note here that it was with more than a little trepidation that we embarked on this trip. I had heard from several people, most notably my friend Russell Ray, who has spent a lot of time in this area, that the Sinforosa was a U.S. Grade-A professional hotbed for drug cultivation. Russell himself had stumbled into a pot field during a hiking trip down the Rio Verde, and he had come face-to-face with forty or fifty Mexican soldiers who were very interested to know what his white butt was doing down in a canyon notorious for its marijuana growing.

Now that I think about it, this is an opportune time to talk a little bit about Russell, who, along with his amigo Dean Bruemmer, is without a doubt the most serious canyoneer to tromp through the backcountry of Copper Canyon Country, maybe ever.

Russell, who lives in southwest New Mexico, first started traveling in Tarahumara-land in 1987. Like many people before him, myself included, his first trip to the area was a decidedly seat-of-his-pants kind of affair—mapless and sans specific itinerary. And, like many people before him, myself included, he found himself instantly hooked on Copper Canyon Country. He returned in 1990, when he hiked down from Divisadero to the Rio Urique. That trip really whetted his appetite for exploring Copper Canyon Country. Like, big time.

Russell had read somewhere that you couldn't hike down the Urique River from Humira Bridge because of the impossibility of passing through the Incised Meanders, described by my friend Bob Gedekoh in Chapter 12. Russell got that kind of stubborn gleam in his eye that only intrepid explorer-types can muster. He organized an expedition that included Bruemmer, Scott Steinberg, Gail Ray, and Jane Martin. The theme of that expedition was, basically, to prove wrong the person who wrote that it was impossible to cruise through the Incised Meanders. They put in at Humira Bridge and, 14 days later, emerged in the village of Urique, essentially, none the worse for wear. Ray even told me that passing through the Incised Meanders was surprisingly easy.

Their route/philosophy of travel was described by Ray as "puro en el rio"—meaning, they never climbed above river level. "What we did during that trip was sort of redefine the whole concept of canyoneering," Ray says. "Before that, canyoneering was described by some people as a combination of hiking, climbing, and rafting. We defined it as a combination of hiking, bouldering, rappelling, and swimming. I kind of think the whole notion of using a raft is cheating, like riding a horse."

Ray and his team members embarked on their Rio Urique trip toting 80-pound packs, in which they carried rock-climbing gear, wetsuits, and flotation devices for their packs. "Whenever the canyon would box up, we would swim our packs through," Ray says. "It proved to be a very workable system."

To say the least. In the intervening years, Ray, with various other expedition compadres, has descended the entire Sinforosa, as well as most of Batopilas Canyon. His 1993 Batopilas Canyon descent was halted by a waterfall/chasm/cliff/certain death kind of place. But, upon reflection, Ray and several other crazy New Mexicans decided that they could, indeed, pass through the spot that had stopped them dead in their tracks in 1993. So, as this book was going to press, they were down in Batopilas Canyon attempting to do just that. Meaning, Ray may very well be toast by the time you read these words, but, hey, that's the way it works out sometimes.

Ray understands that there may be people out there who doubt the authenticity of his exploratory claims, such being the nature of the egotistical world of exploration. "We have very strong documentation," he says. "We photographed ourselves at every major side canyon. Every team member kept detailed notes and journals during all of the trips. If anyone ever challenges us, we can prove that we did everything we said we did."

In addition to exploring parts of Copper Canyon Country that few gringos have ever seen, Ray feels he has played a big part in establishing canyoneering as a bonafide sport. "I've even talked to REI about manufacturing a line of canyoneering equipment," Ray says. "It is a wonderful sport, and I think it's going to get more popular."

Ray is also working hard on a documentary film about Copper Canyon Country, in which he was kind enough to interview Jay Scott and me, regarding our descent of Tararecua Canyon (see Chapter 5). Based on the Tararecua trip, I know

how difficult it must have been for Ray and his partners to pull
off the incredible canyoneering feats they have pulled off,
because the rivers and canyons they have descended are of a
whole different magnitude than Tararecua. My hat is off to
Russell and his various team members for not only doing what
they have done, but for doing it with a degree of dignity and
humility that is not often found in the world of exploration,
and certainly not in the world of canyoneering.

I also think they're crazy as hell, but that's a whole different story.

Anyhow, when my wife heard that I planned to venture
into Sinforosa country, she went ahead and doubled my life
insurance policy and began making plans for her post-M. John
life. She was as worried as I have ever seen her, and, when you
consider some of the bone-headed trips I've taken in my life,
that's saying a mouthful.

Why, then, did I feel compelled to visit the area if it was so
potentially dangerous? The answer in simple: the Sinforosa is
the wildest part of Copper Canyon Country. Few are the gringos who have ever visited it. It also offers the best chance for
wildlife viewing in this part of Mexico. I have heard the Sinforosa boasts populations of mountain lions, bobcats, coyotes,
wolves, and maybe even grizzlies. (Grizzlies were native to
this area, but are now considered extinct in Mexico. I talked
with one professor a few years back, though, who assured me
he had uncovered evidence that grizzlies still dwell in the Sinforosa. He would not, of course, divulge the exact nature of
that evidence, nor would he tell me where he found it.)

Before leaving on my Sinforosa journey, I talked at length
with Russell, who had been to Guachochi several times. He
told me to head straight to the Hotel Molina, the owner of
which was an amateur cartographer. Maybe, Russell speculated, I could dial into the drug situation while sitting in the
comfort of the hotel's restaurant rather than dialing into it out
on the trail while staring down the muzzle of a rifle pointed at
me by someone named Scarface Jose. Sounded like a good
enough plan to me.

We arrived at the hotel, which is a very nice place, by
the way, just in time to eat lunch and fall in love with the

waitress. She told us that, yes indeed, the owner, who was not around at the moment, had put together a map of the area, and she would be only too happy to lay a copy on us. It ended up that the map was a hand-drawn affair, but it boasted enough in the way of information that we thought we stood at least a 10-percent chance of finding the Sinforosa.

There were several mean-looking hombres hanging out in the restaurant as we ate, and they spent the entire meal giving me the hairy eyeball, I assume because I had the unmitigated gall to bring a Tarahumara in with me. I sorely wanted to ask about the Sinforosa's mortal danger quotient, but they didn't look like they really wanted to chew the fat with me, so I, for once, decided to leave well enough alone.

After having talked with Russell, I had already decided to descend into the canyon from the Cumbres de Sinforosa. According to Russell, the other alternative, to descend from Cumbres de Huerachi, would be a more civilized hike, with a small village, Huerachi, at the bottom of the canyon. Russell had camped in Huerachi before and found it very hospitable. I was more in the mood for a purely wilderness hike, so we opted for Cumbres de Sinforosa, which was about an hour's drive south of town. And a wild drive it was. We arrived in Guachochi during the third day of what ended up being an unprecedented six-and-a-half straight days of rain. The road out of Guachochi, which didn't seem like it would be an interstate highway under the best of circumstances, was nothing more than endless, red-clay mud connected by a series of long, deep, and mucky, lake-sized, mud "puddles." I spent the entire drive in low-range granny gear. It wasn't long before I began to wish that I had, somewhere along the line, purchased some of the kinds of religious items most vehicles in Mexico display in abundance on their dashboards. It ended up that we never really came close to getting stuck, but it was tense every inch of the way.

The drive from Guachochi, though trying, was beautiful. And every inch of the way, we followed the most intricate system of rock walls I have ever seen. Every part of Copper Canyon Country boasts its fair share of rock walls, but nowhere has the craft of wall-building reached the height

achieved between Guachochi and Cumbres de Sinforosa. Not
only did these walls go on for kilometers and kilometers on
both sides of the road, but they were flawlessly built, using no
mortar whatsoever. We got out of the Jeep to check these
things out. They were as solid as any wall could be. A lot of
rock walls are rickety. I've even had a few come out from
under me while climbing over them with a pack on my back.
But, these walls were in a league of their own. You could climb
on them, sit on them, probably even drive a Jeep over them,
and they wouldn't even flinch.

After 30 grueling minutes, we passed through the nice little
hamlet of Cieneguita (not to be confused with the Cieneguita
near Munérachi). From there, we could see, off in the distance,
a canyon rim. And it looked like a mighty big one. Half an hour
later, we pulled up in front of a little store at Cumbres de Sinforosa. We had heard in Guachochi that there was a store here,
but we were quite surprised by how new and nice it was. It was
a veritable department store, with a wide array of fresh and
canned food, clothing, and household items. We asked the
owner what a nice facility such as his was doing out here near
the end of the world. He said he serviced an extremely large
area, and—what could he say?—business was good.

We asked where the trailhead was, and then, sort of sheepishly, we casually wheedled our conversational way around to
the local drug cultivation situation. He said things were
squeaky clean and quiet up and down the Sinforosa, because,
basically, the army had spent the better part of a year killing
and/or arresting everyone thereabouts who so much as ever
even once thought about planting a dope plant.

In one way, this information was relieving. In another way,
it was anything but. Either way, we drove the last kilometer
from the store to the trailhead. When we got there, there was
a Mexican family laying out a picnic. We pulled up behind
them, shot the breeze for a few minutes, then ambled over to
the close-at-hand overlook. Now, you've got to understand
that one of my least favorite words in the English language is
"breathtaking." Damn, I get tired of that word. Yet, there is no
other way to describe my reaction to first laying eyes on the
Sinforosa Canyon system. I literally could not breathe. It was

like every molecule of air had been sucked out of me by way
of some sort of reverse artificial resuscitation. Instantly, every
other visual experience I had ever had in Copper Canyon
Country was relegated to the psychic trash heap. Everything
else suddenly seemed like small taters.

Then, I turned my head about 20 degrees and was stunned
to observe that the canyon I had been ogling over was "only"
a side canyon, Arroyo Guachochi. The main canyon was about
15 kilometers off in the distance, beckoning us to come on
down for an extended look-see.

Sahuaripa and I met eyes. We didn't need to speak. It was
one of the most awesomely beautiful places either of us had
ever seen, and we were dumbstruck, awestuck, and speech-
less, a situation that doesn't often happen to me. At the same
time, the Sinforosa was one seriously deep mutha. We knew
we were in for an arduous hike.

The trail into the canyon started a few hundred meters
from the overlook, near a small Tarahumara house. We drove
over, and Sahuaripa asked the man of the house if we could
park Worf in his yard for a few days. It was a labored conversation because, somewhere between Creel and Guachochi, we
had passed a Tarahumara sub-dialect border, and Sahuaripa
said it was tough to understand his tribal compatriots in these
parts. On the drive down from Creel, we had tuned in Radio
Free Tarahumara, which broadcasts out of Guachochi,
because I don't think Sahuaripa likes my taste in cassettes.
(He has never warmed up to Depeche Mode or the Utah
Saints.) After a while, I asked Sahuaripa what the DJ was babbling on about. Sahuaripa said he had no earthly idea; he
couldn't understand a word the man was saying. And he still
preferred the station over Depeche Mode and the Utah Saints.

The Tarahumara man said it would be fine and dandy for us
to leave the Jeep in his yard. He pointed us to the trail down
into the canyon and told us about a small cave about an hour
away where we could camp that night. No sooner had we
cinched our packs but the rains returned. We were soaked
through within minutes.

Since this was going to be such a ball-buster of a hike, I had
pared my gear down to only the most basic essentials. I didn't

even carry a sleeping bag, only a light bivvy sack and a tent. I nixed carrying a stove, figuring that we would cook over a fire.

By the time we found the cave, which was less a cavern than it was a slight rock overhang, it was deluging. It was a couple of hours before dark, and we just hunkered down. There was no place big enough to pitch the tent, and, whenever the wind kicked up, we got a taste of precipitation.

Towards dinnertime, Sahuaripa mentioned something about boiling up some water for a cup of coffee. I said that would be fine with me, but we would have to gather wood and start a fire, because the stove was back in Creel. He looked at me as incredulously as one person can look at another without walking over and smacking them.

He asked, through clenched teeth, "What do you mean the stove is back in Creel?" I responded that since I was camping with a self-proclaimed master firemaker, I didn't think we needed the goldanged stove, and, besides, I said, I was looking to save weight.

Which made him even more pissed off. It would have been one thing, he said, if I had simply forgotten the damned thing, but, now he learns that I *intentionally* left it behind in order to save a few measly pounds on our backs. He said in no uncertain terms that one, the Almighty couldn't build a fire after three consecutive days of rain and two, next time my weenie self deemed an MSR Whisperlite Internationale stove and a liter of fuel "too heavy," let him know, and he would be only too happy to carry it himself.

We didn't talk much the rest of the night. Dinner consisted of several candy bars each, washed down with some nice, cool, highly refreshing water. Sahuaripa crashed out in a huff. I felt like dog dung.

It rained all night. By dawn, it was raining as hard as I have ever seen it rain in Tarahumara-land. We decided to wait the rain out. We sat there all morning. Then we sat there all afternoon. Then we enjoyed a nice evening of sitting there. All day, it stopped raining for only a few minutes. As the sun set, we enjoyed another tantalizing meal of candy bars and, yes, water. It rained all night and, once again, when we awoke, it was, you guessed it, raining. We decided then and there to punt our Sinforosa expedition. Not only did the idea of hiking in a monsoon not titillate us, but, at the same time, we started worrying about whether or not we would be able to drive out. The mud was bad enough driving in. It could only be far worse now.

Once our decision to dunk the hike was made, we sprinted up the hill. It was hard hiking, as the trail was slick as snot on a brass doorknob. We realized then that the descent to the Rio Verde would have been treacherous because of all the mud and slippery rocks.

After laying some canned food on the Tarahumara family in whose yard we had parked Worf, we drove back to the store, where we snacked a little. The drive back to Guachochi was intellectually captivating. Several times, I looked out my window only to see the mud-covered back of Worf making its way ahead of the front of Worf. Once again, granny gear got a workout. This marked the first time I had taken Worf south of the border. After having driven a Toyota four-wheel-drive pick-up for years, I had decided to make a leap of faith and buy an American-made vehicle. That leap ended up being well worth it. Worf performed wonderfully and, as much as I loved my Toyota, there is no comparison between the torque of a Toyota and that of a Jeep Wrangler with a 4.2-liter, 6-cylinder motor.

We went straight back to the Hotel Molina for breakfast, where, I am happy to report, that same waitress was on duty. We looked and smelled like hell, and she commented on that fact, which endeared her to me even more. I asked if she would like to go hiking in the deep canyons with me sometime, a seemingly forward enough question that Sahuaripa almost choked on his chorizo. He didn't know whether to laugh or to sprint towards the door. She said something along the lines of how she would much rather eat mud, but thank you for the invite anyhow.

We decided to take the scenic route back to Cusarare. At Rocheachi, the road forks with the lefthand fork going to directly to Creel and the righthand fork going indirectly to Creel, via Norogachi. This is one astounding drive, the kind of four-wheel adventure that leaves you feeling more beatup than if you had hiked the entire distance. It's also a road I would love to mountain bike on. We stopped counting at fifty the number of times we had to drive across rivers or arroyos with water in them. At one point, during a river crossing in the middle of Norogachi, which is a fair-sized town near the headwaters of the Rio Urique, the water came halfway up the side of the Jeep.

I love exhilarating drives like that. We laughed our heads off the entire way, free and easy, with a tankful of gas and nothing but the endless dirt roads of the Sierra Madre ahead of us. It took five hours to reach Cusarare, and, by the time we got there, it was time for a cold beer or maybe ten. It was also time for some strange feelings to set in. I have gotten lost and taken the wrong trail and such more than a few times in Copper Canyon Country. But, never had I blown a trip off like we had just done. I told Sahuaripa that I really wished things had worked out, weather-wise. He said not to worry, that the Sinforosa would still be there when I next drove down to Tarahumara-land from the Colorado High Country. He patted me on the shoulder and said, essentially, "Pard, we still got a lot of hiking to do together. So, relax, and don't think in terms of success or failure in this context. Everything's an experience."

Then he took his leave, walking through the darkness towards his little house, which he shares with his wife and his five kids. And I drove back to Creel, which I had done so many times before.

Particulars

This is a tough one, because I never really made it into the canyon. The hike we wanted to take can be found on the 1:50,000 Cieneguita map, as well as the 1:250,000 Guachochi map.

The biggest problem here is access. It's easy enough to get to Guachochi from Creel, because there are daily buses in both directions. But, to get from Guachochi to either the Cumbres de Sinforosa or the Cumbres de Huerachi will be trickier. You can try hitching, but traffic will be sporadic at best. I would recommend trying to hire a taxi in Guachochi.

According to Russell Ray, there is a good burro trail all the way from Cumbres de Guerachi to the village of Guerachi, on the banks of the Rio Verde. There is definitely a nice trail all the way from Cumbres de Sinforosa to the Rio Verde, although I have only hiked on a small part of it.

There are several hotels in Guachochi, the nicest being the Molina. I recommend you stop in there to talk with the owner. He has a hand-drawn map that may prove of value. Also, the food there is good, and there's this one waitress. . . .

Anyhow, before you descend into the Sinforosa, please ask around about the drug situation. It is my understanding that the army has things well under control, but it can't hurt to ask for the most up-to-date skinny you can lay your ears on.

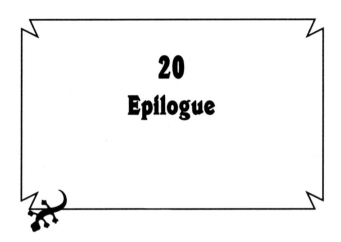

20
Epilogue

The week before my deadline for the first edition of this book, I interviewed a professional kayaking/rafting guide who plies his trade on the Arkansas River near where I used to live. This guy looked to be about fifty. He was a schoolteacher for twenty years and was spending his "retirement" working as a salaried river rat. An educated man, with enough years under his belt to have developed perspective.

The photographer who was with me asked this man if he had kayaked "all over the world." Fundamental enough question. The answer, surprisingly, was an emphatic "no." Not intoned in an unfriendly fashion, mind you. Stated just strongly enough that there was no doubt as to where this man was coming from. He went on to tell us that, in his opinion, Americans should not recreate themselves in the Third World, for reasons unexplained. Overlooking for a moment that there are plenty of places "all over the world" that are not Third World—Australia and Norway come to mind—where you could kayak, were you so disposed, I was, nonetheless, struck. Even though we didn't pursue the subject, the timing could not have been worse.

The very day before this conversation took place, I had essentially finished the first edition of this book with the exception of the Epilogue. At the same time that I was seriously pumped at the thought of having this project behind me, I was—and still am—very nervous about its potential negative implications for the Tarahumaras and their turf. The conversation with the kayaker did not help matters any, because, I suspect, his reasoning was based on the "fact" that "we" inevitably adversely impact the "primitive" cultures that oftentimes serve as ambience-enhancement units in the boon-dock locales we backpack through in the name of R & R.

It's not like this is something I have never mentally dealt with before. Walt Borneman, managing editor of Johnson Books, and I both believe that this book is primarily reactive, in the sense that tourism is already on the increase in Tarahumara-land. But it is not lost on us that these words will likely also prove to be proactive, insofar as they will encourage certain numbers of visitors, who otherwise might have never heard of Copper Canyon Country, to check the place out. As well, it may encourage visitors who otherwise might never have ven-tured farther than the Chihuahua-Pacific train to hoist their packs and head out into the backcountry.

Meaning, because of my work, the Tarahumara culture will come in contact with more outsiders than it would if I had just gone ahead and fallen off that cliff in Tararecua Canyon in 1986, my chips cashed in five years before beginning this book project.

Okay, so I am a pimp, of sorts. I take the money while Cop-per Canyon Country takes the physical impact. I can live with that. Because, as such, I can get away with admonishing visi-tors to use cultural condoms during all social intercourse with Tarahumara-land. And because I agree with Skip McWilliams that the Tarahumaras are already being raped by the Mexican timber industry. Therefore, the Tarahumara culture actually needs gringo backpackers to come tromping through its back-yard in ever-increasing numbers. Granted, that provides fairly good rationalization for one who may be searching pretty des-perately for just that. But it's good rationalization. And, it's rationalization necessitated by the axe, the chainsaw, and the pesos they provide.

Backpackers give the Tarahumara culture an economic alternative. The Tarahumara culture has entered the late twen-tieth century. It has entered the monied economy. There is no turning back the clock on either of those realities. And, even if there was, it would not be up to us to do the turning back. The

Tarahumaras are hunters and gatherers. They are enjoying the gathering potential of that which the twentieth-century, monied economy offers. They still seem to prefer their own culture, and their culture is strong enough to "ward off"—for lack of a better term—those aspects of outside cultures that they don't like. At the same time, of course, gringos armed with cash and trinkets are materialistically strong enough to overcome even the most determined resistance.

It seems inevitable. Once a place gets hot on the tourist circuit, it's only a matter of time before people start saying how "you should have been here ten years ago." I wish I knew for certain that Tarahumara-land will not suffer from its newfound popularity. Historic precedence indicates that it is already too late. You know, once the first American or European comes walking into camp, you might as well sell your cultural stock because, from then on, it's a bear market, whether you're dealing with missionaries, loggers, or . . . backpackers.

If there is a chance for a different scenario, Tarahumara-land is it. It has everything necessary to maintain its cultural integrity while, concurrently, allowing outsiders to share in its majesty. The Tarahumaras own their land communally. They have a rock-solid culture mostly resistant to and distrustful of external influences. They have independent-thinking individuals who, on the whole, prefer remaining true to themselves. Combine that with extreme minimum-impact visitations on our part and, for once, there may be no head-hanging twenty years down the road. Not for the gringos. And not for the Tarahumaras.

Amen and Miller time. . . .

Annotated Bibliography

Abbey, Edward. *Abbey's Road.* New York: Dalton, 1979. One chapter on Copper Canyon Country. Not very good.

Artaud, Antonin. *The Peyote Dance.* New York: Farrar, Strauss and Giroux, 1976. English translation of "Les Tarahumaras." Last half was written from the author's digs in a French psycho-ward. Very weird.

Bennett, Wendell, and Zingg, Robert. *The Tarahumara, an Indian Tribe of Northern Mexico.* Glorieta, New Mexico: Rio Grande Press. A scientific study of the Tarahumaras and Tarahumara-land.

Bradt, Hilary, and Rochowiecki, Rob. *Backpacking in Mexico and Central America,* Cambridge, Massachusetts: Bradt Enterprises, 1982. (95 Harvey Street, Cambridge, Massachusetts 02140). Contains but one chapter about Copper Canyon Country—actually guest-written by A. R. Alexandrocvich—but, it's a good chapter. Nice book for getting an overview about hiking in Latin America.

Boudrea, Eugene. *Move over, Don Porfirio: Tales from the Sierra Madre.* Sebastopol, California: Pleasant Hills Press.

Boudrea, Eugene. *Trails of the Sierra Madre.* Capra/Scrimshaw, 1973.

Carlson, George. *A Tarahumara Portfolio.* Reno, Nevada: University of Nevada Press, 1983.

Cassel, Jonathon F. *Tarahumara Indians.* San Antonio, Texas: Naylor Corp., 1969.

Dunne, Peter Masten. *Early Jesuit Missions in Tarahumara.* Berkeley, California: University of California Press, 1948.

Fisher, Richard. *National Parks of Northwest Mexico.* 3rd Ed. Tucson, Arizona: Sunracer Publications, 1988. (P. O. Box 40092, Tucson, Arizona 85717). The author, a professional guide/backcountry photographer, provides us with good art and sensitive observations.

Fontana, Bernard. *Material World of the Tarahumara.* Tucson, Arizona: Arizona State Museum, 1979. Great overview of Tara arts and crafts.

Fontana, Bernard. *Tarahumara: Where Night Is the Day of the Moon.* Flagtaff, Arizona: Northland Press, 1979. Ethnological observations augmented by good photography.

Fontana, Bernard; Burns, Barney; and Faubert, Edmond. *The Other Southwest.* Phoeniz, Arizona: Heard Museum, 1977.

Forgey, William, M.D. *Wilderness Medicine,* Merrillville, Indiana: ICS Books, Inc., 1987. (One Tower Plaza, Merrillville, Indiana

46410) The best book I have ever seen to prepare backcountry users for that which we all hope never happens—a wilderness medical problem.

Franz, Carl. *The People's Guide to Mexico.* Santa Fe, New Mexico: John Muir Publications. (P. O. Box 613, Santa Fe, New Mexico 87504) Simply the best book ever penned about general travel in Mexico. As a matter of fact, one of the best travel books period. Doesn't deal with Tarahumara-land, but deals with everything else about the country. A great read even if you never venture south of the border.

Ilg, Steve. *The Outdoor Athlete.* Evergreen, Colorado: Cordillera Press, Inc., 1987. Everything the backpacker needs to know about preparing physically. Contains sport-specific exercise regimens.

Kennedy, John. *Tarahumara of the Sierra Madre: Beer, Ecology and Social Organization.* Arlington Heights, Illinois: AHM Publishing Corporation, 1978.

Kennedy, John. "Bonds of Laughter Among the Tarahumara Indians: A Rethinking of Joking Relationship Theory," in *The Social Anthropology of Latin America—Essays in Honor of Ralph Leon Beals.* Los Angeles: Latin America Center, University of California, 1970.

Kennedy, John, and Lopez, Raul. *Semana Santa in the Sierra Tarahumara: Comparative Study in Three Communities.* Los Angeles: Museum of Cultural History, University of California, 1981.

Lumholtz, Carl. *Unknown Mexico: Explorations in the Sierra Tarahumara and Other Regions, 1890-1898.* Glorieta, New Mexico: Rio Grande Press. Considered the bible of Tarahumara-land.

Roca, Paul. *Spanish Jesuit Churches in Mexico's Tarahumara.* Tucson, Arizona: Univeristy of Arizona Press, 1979.

Schultheis, Rob. *The Hidden West.* Berkeley, California: North Point Press, 1983. Again, but one chapter. Interesting observations by the author of *Bone Games.*

Sheridan, Thomas E., and Naylor, Thomas H. *Raramuri—a Tarahumara Chronicle, 1607-1791.* Flagstaff, Arizona: Northland Press, 1979.

Index

About the Author

M. John Fayhee is a contributing editor to *Backpacker* and a veteran outdoor writer who has written for *Sports Illustrated, Outside, Sierra, Islands, Adventure Travel, Summit,* and *Canoe.* Fayhee lives with his wife, Gay Gangel-Fayhee, in Summit County, Colorado, where he works as an editor/writer for the *Summit Daily News.*

Fayhee is also the author of *Along the Colorado Trail.* His next book, *Up at Altitude: A Celebration of Life in the High Country,* will be published by Johnson Books in the fall of 1994. He is currently working on a book about his experiences in the world of martial arts.

For more information on

Copper Canyon Lodges

*Riverside Lodge in Batopilas
and Sierra Lodge in Creel*

1-800-776-3942 or 1-810-340-7230

(U.S. number)